# Reducing Poverty and Sustaining the Environment

## The Politics of Local Engagement

# Reducing Poverty and Sustaining the Environment

## The Politics of Local Engagement

Edited by
Stephen Bass, Hannah Reid,
David Satterthwaite and Paul Steele

Earthscan Publications Limited
London • Sterling, VA

First published by Earthscan in the UK and USA in 2005

ISBN-13: 978-1-844071-16-6 paperback
ISBN-10: 1-84407-116-2 paperback
ISBN-13: 978-1-844071-15-9 hardback
ISBN-10: 1-84407-115-4 hardback

Typesetting by TW Typesetting, Plymouth, Devon
Printed and bound in the UK by Bath Press
Cover design by Anthony Waters

For a full list of publications please contact:

Earthscan
8–12 Camden High Street
London, NW1 0JH, UK
Tel: +44 (0)20 7387 8558
Fax: +44 (0)20 7387 8998
Email: earthinfo@earthscan.co.uk
Web: **www.earthscan.co.uk**

22883 Quicksilver Drive, Sterling, VA 20166-2012, USA

Earthscan is an imprint of James & James (Science Publishers) Ltd and publishes in association with the International Institute for Environment and Development

A catalogue record for this book is available from the British Library

Library of Congress Cataloging-in-Publication Data

Reducing poverty and sustaining the environment : the politics of local engagement / Steve Bass [et al.], editors. p. cm.
Includes bibliographical references.
ISBN 1-84407-116-2 – ISBN 1-84407-115-4
1. Poverty – Developing countries – Prevention – Case studies. 2. Environmental management – Political aspects – Developing countries – Case studies. 3. Poverty – Environmental aspects – Developing countries – Case studies. 4. Local government – Developing countries – Case studies. 5. Developing countries – Environmental conditions – Case studies. 6. Environmental justice – Developing countries – Case studies. I. Bass, Stephen, 1958–

HC59.72.P6R43 2005
339.4'6'091724 – dc22

2005003305

The research that led to this publication was funded by the Department for International Development (DFID). However, the views expressed do not necessarily reflect that of official UK Government policy.

# Contents

# List of Tables, Diagrams and Boxes

## TABLES

## DIAGRAMS

# BOXES

# List of Photographs

# Acknowledgements

The editors are particularly grateful to Melissa Leach (Institute of Development Studies) and Frances Seymour (World Resources Institute) for their constructive review of early drafts of this manuscript and suggestions for improvements. Jon Anderson (Natural Resource Policy Advisor at the US Agency for International Development) also provided helpful comments. We are also grateful to all the chapter authors for their patience and help in responding to queries, and their support with reviewing chapters.

We are also grateful to the UK Department for International Development (DFID) which funded the research on which many of the chapters are based and provided support for putting together this volume. However, the views expressed do not necessarily reflect that of official UK Government policy.

Thanks are also due to Bill Antrobus of Deer Park Productions and staff at Earthscan for converting our messy manuscript into this final product.

*Stephen Bass*
*Hannah Reid*
*David Satterthwaite*
*Paul Steele*

# About the Authors and Editors

## CHAPTERS 1 and 12

**Stephen Bass** is a Senior Fellow at IIED, having previously been Chief Environment Adviser at the UK Government's Department for International Development. He has focused on participatory environmental and natural resource policy, principally in Western Asia, the Caribbean and southern Africa, as well as at the international level. He has published several books on sustainable development and forestry. *steve.bass@iied.org*

**Dr Hannah Reid** is a Research Associate at the IIED, where she has worked with the human settlements, biodiversity and livelihoods, and climate change programmes. Prior to this she spent three years in South Africa, obtaining her PhD in biodiversity management. She has worked with a variety of government agencies, non-governmental organizations (NGOs), donors and community organizations on a wide range of environment and development-related issues in the Philippines, Bangladesh, Australia, Zimbabwe and Zambia. *hannah.reid@iied.org*

**Dr David Satterthwaite** is a Senior Fellow at the IIED and also on the teaching staff of the London School of Economics and of University College London. He has been editor of the international journal *Environment and Urbanization* since its inception in 1989. He has written or edited various books published by Earthscan, London, including *Squatter Citizen* (1989 with Jorge E. Hardoy), *The Earthscan Reader on Sustainable Cities* (1999), *Environmental Problems in an Urbanizing World* (with Jorge E. Hardoy and Diana Mitlin, 2001) and *Empowering Squatter Citizen: Local Government, Civil Society and Urban Poverty Reduction* (with Diana Mitlin, 2004). In 2004, he was

made an honorary professor at the University of Hull and also awarded the Volvo Environment Prize.
*david.satterthwaite@iied.org*

**Paul Steele** is an environmental economist working on the politics of pro-poor environmental change. While at DFID, he worked in Africa and Asia on the integration of environmental issues within poverty reduction strategies and fiscal policy. He is now based in Sri Lanka and has worked with the World Bank, DFID, the United Nations Development Programme (UNDP), the World Conservation Union (IUCN) and the World Resources Institute (WRI) on the politics of environmental change, particularly in Asia.
*steele@sltnet.lk*

# Chapter 2

**Maheen Zehra** is an independent consultant who was previously associated with the IUCN. She steered the process of the mid-term review of Pakistan's National Conservation Strategy as part of the National Strategy for Sustainable Development process and has worked extensively on poverty and environment issues in Pakistan.
*maheen@strat-ops.org*

# Chapter 3

**Luz Stella Velásquez Barrero** is an associate professor and researcher at the Institute of Environmental Studies (IDEA), National University of Colombia, Manizales. She was trained as an architect and has a PhD from the University Politecnica de Cataluña of Barcelona. She has been closely involved in developing the Local Agenda 21 in Manizales.
*bioluzve@hotmail.com*

# Chapter 4

**Dr John G. Taylor** is professor of politics and director of the Development Studies Programme at South Bank University, London. He has researched in, and published books, articles and research papers on,

sociological theories of development, social development and environmental issues, with particular reference to China, South-East Asia, Indonesia and East Timor. He has also provided training in participatory poverty assessment techniques to Chinese researchers working on World Bank Health Projects, to the Chinese State Council's Leading Group on Poverty Reduction, and to the Chinese Ministry of Finance. Most recently, he worked with UNDP as a senior development adviser to the government of East Timor on the design and implementation of the country's first National Development Plan.
*johngtaylor@hotmail.com*

# CHAPTER 5

**Godber Tumushabe** is an independent environmental law and trade policy analyst engaged in research on a broad range of environmental, trade and human rights issues in Eastern and Southern Africa. He is currently executive director of the Advocates Coalition for Development and Environment (ACODE), a Uganda-based independent public policy research and analysis think tank. He also teaches environmental law, international law and the science of law at Makerere University, Kampala. He is co-editor of *Governing the Environment: Political Change and Natural Resources Management in Eastern and Southern Africa* (ACTS, 1999)
*gtumushabe@acode-u.org; acode@acode-u.org*

**Claire Ireland** is an environment specialist with experience in Africa. Her background is in environmental policy and management for sustainable development. One of her focuses has been on the linkages between poverty and environment, particularly ensuring the integration of environmental issues in poverty reduction strategies. She has worked as a policy adviser in international and national NGOs, based both in the North and South, as a technical specialist within the UK's DFID and, most recently, as an environmental adviser for the government of Uganda for the Plan for Modernization of Agriculture (2001–2003). She is now working as an environment and development consultant at the IDL group.
*claire.ireland@theidlgroup.com*

# CHAPTER 6

**Hassan Bdliya** is a natural resources management consultant currently leading DFID's Joint Enhancement of Wetlands and Livelihoods Project in northern Nigeria. Previously, he worked for the IUCN on wetlands conservation projects and for many years was with the Nigerian Federal Ministry of Environment.
*hansliya@hotmail.com*

**Jean-Paul Penrose** is the environment adviser for DFID's development programmes in West Africa and Iraq. Previously, he has worked for the IFC in Peru and for the UK's Environment Agency.
*jp-penrose@dfid.gov.uk*

**John Chettleborough** is Christian Aid's Nigeria programme manager. He has previously worked for DFID, the Canadian International Development Agency and Voluntary Service Overseas (CIDA) on environment programmes in Nigeria.
*chettleborough@dfid.gov.uk*

# CHAPTER 7

**Yves Renard** has been involved in natural resource management and sustainable development in the Caribbean over the past three decades. He has particular interest and experience in the facilitation of participatory policy and institutional development processes. He served as executive director of the Caribbean Natural Resources Institute (CANARI) between 1992 and 2001. He currently works as an independent consultant.
*yr@candw.lc*

# CHAPTER 8

**Phillipa Holden** is an ecologist whose research focus has been on rangeland management in savannah ecosystems. She has worked as a freelance consultant in Southern Africa, focusing on protected area planning, development and management, local community involvement and development, ecological land-use planning, ecotourism and best environmental practice.
*phillipa@hixnet.co.za*

**David Grossman** is an ecologist with experience in various aspects of ecological, social and economic factors that affect rangeland and wildlife management.
*dawg@mweb.co.za*

# CHAPTER 9

**Julie Thomas** is an environmental professional whose career has focused on engaging communities in environmental issues. Over the past ten years, she has supported African and UK NGOs, and local and national governments, in developing participatory planning processes. On the project in Tanzania from which Chapter 9 was developed, she worked to bring a community perspective to an essentially scientific intervention. Based in the UK, she currently works for the World Wide Fund for Nature (WWF) where her work addresses bringing a livelihoods perspective to WWF-UK's international work.
*jthomas@wwf.org.uk*

**Geoffrey King** is a freelance environmental planner with 23 years' development experience in Africa. His career has spanned the shift from technocratic 'blueprint' interventions, through to more people-based process approaches, to environmental management. An integrator at heart, his main contribution has often been to bring meaning to the whole from the disparate threads of individual efforts.
*kingg@dwaf.gov.za*

**Susan Kayetta** is a community engagement specialist with long experience in her native Tanzania. Her career has included work with Oxfam, SNV (Dutch volunteer aid) and several civil society organizations. She worked as a community engagement specialist on the SMUWC project, and later as its team leader during its last year. She currently works for Water Aid, based in Dar es Salaam.
*skayetta@yahoo.co.uk*

# CHAPTER 10

**Sheela Patel** is the founder/director of the Society for the Promotion of Area Resource Centres (SPARC), and **Sundar Burra** is an adviser to SPARC. SPARC is the NGO in the Indian alliance of SPARC, *Mahila Milan* and the National Slum Dwellers Federation.
Sheela Patel and Sundar Burra can be contacted at *sparc1@vsnl.com*

**Thomas Kerr** works with the Asian Coalition for Housing Rights in Bangkok.
*achr@loxinfo.co.th*

# CHAPTER 11

**Liliana Miranda Sara** trained as an architect and taught urban planning at university level in Peru. She is currently executive director of the Cities for Life Forum.
*lmiranda@ciudad.org.pe*; web page: *www.ciudad.org.pe*

**Julio Díaz Palacios** is a medical doctor who was elected mayor of Ilo for three consecutive periods from 1981–1989, and was also twice elected to Peru's Congress. He is the president of the advisory council of Cities for Life Forum and is currently developing consultancy activities as a specialist on urban environmental issues and democratic decentralization in Peru.
*jdiaz@ciudad.org.pe*

# Acronyms and Abbreviations

| | |
|---|---|
| ACODE | Advocates Coalition for Development and Environment (Uganda) |
| ACWF | All China Women's Federation |
| ADB | Asian Development Bank |
| AIDS | acquired immune deficiency syndrome |
| AKF | Aga Khan Foundation |
| AKRSP | Aga Khan Rural Support Programme |
| BCS | Baluchistan Conservation Strategy (Pakistan) |
| CAIR | Centros de Atención Integral al Reciclador (Centres for Integral Services for Recyclers, Colombia) |
| CANARI | Caribbean Natural Resources Institute |
| CBO | community-based organization |
| CIAD | Centre for Integrated Agricultural Development (China) |
| CSIR | Council for Scientific and Industrial Research (South Africa) |
| DANE | Colombian national statistics department |
| DFID | UK Department for International Development |
| EIA | environmental impact assessment |
| ENR | environment and natural resources |
| ENR-SWG | Environment and Natural Resources Sector Working Group (Uganda) |
| FAO | United Nations Food and Agriculture Organization |
| GEA-UR | Manizales Urban Environmental Studies Group (Colombia) |
| GEF | Global Environment Facility |
| ha | hectare |
| HIPC | highly indebted poor countries |
| HNW | Hadejia Nguru Wetlands (Nigeria) |
| ICLEI | International Council for Local Environmental Initiatives |
| IDEA | Institute of Environmental Studies (Colombia) |
| IFI | international financial institution |
| IIED | International Institute for Environment and Development |

| IMF | International Monetary Fund |
|---|---|
| IUCN | World Conservation Union |
| kg | kilogram |
| km | kilometre |
| LEAT | Lawyers Environmental Action Team (Tanzania) |
| m | metre |
| mg | milligram |
| mm | millimetre |
| MDG | Millennium Development Goal |
| MoU | memorandum of understanding |
| MP | member of parliament |
| NEAP | national environment action plan |
| NEMA | National Environment Management Authority (Kenya, Uganda) |
| NFDP | National Fadama Development Programme (Nigeria) |
| NGO | non-governmental organization |
| NPEP | National Poverty Eradication Plan (Kenya) |
| NPES | National Poverty Eradication Strategy (Tanzania) |
| NRSP | Natural Resources Systems Programme (DFID) |
| NSDF | National Slum Dwellers Federation (India) |
| OECD | Organisation for Economic Co-operation and Development |
| OECS | Organization of Eastern Caribbean States |
| OPP | Orangi Pilot Project (Karachi) |
| PEAP | Poverty Eradication Action Plan (Uganda) |
| PMA | Plan for Modernization of Agriculture (Uganda) |
| POT | land-use plan (Colombia) |
| PPA | participatory poverty assessment |
| PPA | power purchase agreement |
| PRS | poverty reduction strategy |
| PRSP | poverty reduction strategy papers |
| RBWO | Rufiji Basin Water Office (Tanzania) |
| RDP | Reconstruction and Development Programme (South Africa) |
| RSP | rural support programme (Pakistan) |
| SA | South Africa |
| SIDD | self-financing irrigation and drainage district (China) |
| SINA | National Environmental System (Colombia) |
| SMUWC | Sustainable Management of the Usangu Wetland and its Catchment (Tanzania) |
| SPARC | Society for the Promotion of Area Resource Centres (India) |

SWAP        sector-wide plan for the environment and natural resources sector (Uganda)
SWG         sector working group
TANESCO     national electricity company (Tanzania)
UK          United Kingdom
UNCED       United Nations Conference on Environment and Development
UNDP        United Nations Development Programme
UPPAP       Uganda Participatory Poverty Assessment Project
US          United States
USAID       United States Agency for International Development
VO          village organization (Pakistan)
VRA         villagers' representative assembly (China)
WDR         *World Development Report* (of the World Bank)
WFP         World Food Programme
WfW         Working for Water (South Africa)
WHO         World Health Organization
WO          women's organization (Pakistan)
WRI         World Resources Institute
WSC         water supply corporation (China)
WUA         water-user association (China)
WWF         World Wide Fund for Nature

# 1

# Introduction

*Stephen Bass, Hannah Reid, David Satterthwaite and Paul Steele*

## THE FOCUS OF THIS BOOK: THE DYNAMICS OF POLITICAL CHANGE ON POOR PEOPLE'S ENVIRONMENT

If poverty and environmental problems persist, it is, in large part because poor people and environmental concerns remain marginalized by – and from – sources of power. Poor people are unable to access resources, services and political processes; in effect, they are excluded from the institutions and benefits of wider society. Public environmental goods are appropriated to serve the interests of more powerful private individuals and companies, who keep environmental interest groups on the political margins. As C. S. Lewis pointed out, what we perceive as 'man's power over nature' turns out, invariably, to be the power of some people over others, with nature as its instrument.

Yet, in recent years, we have observed cases where poverty is being reduced at the same time as the environment is being managed more sustainably. Where this occurs, it is frequently because imbalances of power have begun to be corrected. On the surface, this might be attributed to the stormy tactics of an environmental campaigning group, or to the sheer financial power of an external development agency. Below the surface, however, there are multiple currents that contribute to the sea change. Together, they can turn the tide from one where stakeholders complain that 'there is no political will', to one where stakeholders realize that political will can be changed, for the better, by their own actions.

This book seeks to understand the dynamics of political change for achieving pro-poor environmental outcomes on the ground. The main themes addressed include the following:

- Broadening the definition of poverty beyond conventional income-based or consumption-based criteria highlights the importance of poverty-environment linkages. It reveals many environment-related entry points for poverty reduction, especially for strengthening poor people's livelihoods through greater access to natural resources and environmental services and for reducing environmental health risks.

- 'Good local governance' is central to improving environmental management and reducing poverty, as well as to their successful integration. A key part of this good governance is effective and representative local (village or community) organizations that are often distinct from formal government structures.
- It is difficult for 'external' groups – whether they are national governments, donor agencies or even large non-governmental organizations (NGOs) – to really understand and support pro-poor political and governance changes.
- Actions to address environmental problems can be effective entry points for political and governance changes.

An understanding of these themes is best gained from particular case studies. Although there is a considerable body of research on the links between poverty and environment, perhaps too little attention has been given to politics – although this is beginning to change. Over the last decade, discussions of natural resource degradation have shifted from a concern over resource availability to a concern over who controls resources (Forsyth et al, 1999). There has been a comparable shift in discussions of how to reduce poverty – away from the focus on changing outcomes (hunger, disease, inadequate income, etc.) to changing the underlying causes of these outcomes in each locality (inadequate asset bases, including access to land and other resources; poor people's lack of political voice; anti-poor, undemocratic and unaccountable governance; inadequate protection of civil and political rights; etc.; see Chambers, 1995). Indeed, since most poverty and environmental degradation has political underpinnings, so, too, will most effective poverty reduction initiatives and good environmental management. This book presents ten case studies that analyse these issues in very different contexts.

## THE CASE STUDIES: POLITICAL CHANGE IN AFRICA, ASIA AND LATIN AMERICA AND THE CARIBBEAN

Table 1.1 lists the case studies included in Chapters 2 to 11. Most of them centre on integrating 'pro-poor' aspects within environmental

**Table 1.1** *The case studies*

| The case studies | Region or nation | Main focus | Main actors |
|---|---|---|---|
| Chapter 2: 'Creating space for civil society in an impoverished environment in Pakistan' | Northern areas of Pakistan | Programme to support local participatory institutions develop and sustain local natural resources | Village organizations; support from Aga Khan Rural Support Programme |
| Chapter 3: 'The Bioplan: Decreasing poverty in Manizales through shared environmental management | Manizales, Colombia | Preparation and implementation of a city-wide environmental plan | Municipal government, local university and community organizations |
| Chapter 4: 'Environment-poverty linkages: Managing natural resources in China' | Various regions in China | Review of donor experience in establishing links between environmental improvements and poverty reduction | Village committees and assemblies, as well as donors |
| Chapter 5: 'The evolving roles of environmental management institutions in East Africa: From conservation to poverty reduction' | East Africa | Changes needed in environmental management institutions to make them more effective in combining poverty reduction and natural resource management | Institutions with responsibility for environmental management |
| Chapter 6: 'Stories on the environment and conflict from northern Nigeria' | Hadejia Nguru wetlands in northern Nigeria | How environmental change was primarily driven by external groups and investments, which impoverished many local groups and caused local conflicts | Farmers, pastoralists and those who fish, and their interactions with local government and external institutions |
| Chapter 7: 'The sea is our garden: Coastal resource management and local governance in the Caribbean' | Coastal Saint Lucia | 'Pro-poor' coastal resource management | Diverse resource users and local authorities |

3

Table 1.1 Continued

| The case studies | Region or nation | Main focus | Main actors |
|---|---|---|---|
| Chapter 8: '"Working for Water" in a democratic South Africa' | South Africa | Employment creation programme to clear invasive species for water management and provide benefits for low-income groups | Government agency and groups contracted to manage project |
| Chapter 9: 'People, perspectives, and reality: Usangu myths and other stories' | Usangu region in Tanzania | How diagnoses of what was wrong and what needed to be done were driven by politics, including interests external to the region | National and local governments, as well as various international agencies |
| Chapter 10: 'Community-designed, built and managed toilet blocks in Indian cities' | Mumbai, Pune and other cities in India | Improving provision for toilets and water in 'slums' | Community-based organizations formed by the urban poor, as well as municipal authorities |
| Chapter 11: 'Concertación (reaching agreement) and planning for sustainable development in Ilo, Peru' | Ilo, Peru | The methods and means by which elected urban authorities addressed environmental issues | Municipal government, neighbourhood organizations and local NGOs |

management (for example, the Working for Water programme in South Africa, the Bioplan in Colombia, coastal resource management in Saint Lucia, several projects in China, and reforms in the environmental management institutions of East Africa). Three focus on integrating better environmental management within interventions aimed at reducing poverty (the community toilets in Indian cities, the village organizations in northern Pakistan, and many of the municipally supported community initiatives in Ilo, Peru). Two studies reflect on the extent to which donor and government initiatives failed to support poverty reduction or better environmental management (Usangu in Tanzania and the Hadejia Nguru wetlands in northern Nigeria).

The case studies were selected to offer diversity in terms of the nation and the kind of settlement where they were implemented (e.g. large city, smaller urban centre, rural area and small island), the economy (predominantly agricultural, industrial and service economies), the nature of the intervention and the main actors or drivers (from international agency, to national agency, local government, local NGO or community-based organization). International agencies had a role in most case studies, although in some this role was very minor both in terms of funding and in designing the initiatives described.

The selection began with suggestions from the UK government's Department for International Development (DFID) of DFID-supported projects that had managed to bring both environment and poverty reduction in from the political margins. Their authors are principally DFID staff and consultants involved in these interventions (including academics and staff from NGOs). Further studies were proposed by IIED, principally to widen the range of experiences to urban areas and to Latin America, and to broaden the types of author. The latter is important since perception of political change can be as 'political' as the change itself. The resulting set of case studies offers views from a range of stakeholders – government officials, donors, academics and NGOs – based in the countries themselves and from high-income countries.

Even if single 'projects' or 'interventions' appeared to be the most important element in tackling poverty and environmental issues, the authors were encouraged to look behind and beyond them. They were challenged to situate political change in the broader social, political and economic context where it takes place and to look outside the artificial boundaries that donor institutions tend to create. It is to this broader context we now turn.

# THE CHANGING POLITICAL CONTEXT

Major political changes are underway in many of the case study countries. These changes include civil conflict and unrest – still ongoing in some countries (such as Peru, Colombia and Pakistan) and recently ended in others (Nigeria, South Africa and parts of East Africa). Conflict casts a long shadow over all aspects of the development process – and resource use and environmental policy are no exception. Many countries, at the national level, have experienced some moves towards greater democracy and accountability (e.g. South Africa, Tanzania, Nigeria and Peru) but some have moved away from these (Pakistan). This has had major implications for who is able to access public benefits, such as environmental services. However, the extent to which these national trends have led to pro-poor changes in different regions and localities is very country specific. Local-level government remains weak in most countries, but in others it has been gaining more power during recent years (e.g. Saint Lucia, Colombia and India). In many countries, the private sector has come to take a more active role in development and environmental management (e.g. East Africa and Saint Lucia), while in other countries, the state remains dominant (especially China). Civil society, represented by many types of organizations, is also becoming more active in many countries – improving poor people's own possibilities to organize themselves and represent their interests (e.g. India, Peru, East Africa and Colombia). In other countries, long-standing civic institutions – often based around faith groups, such as mosques and churches – have important roles. Finally, development agencies are very strong in some countries (e.g. in much of sub-Saharan Africa), but less influential in others, where they have had minor roles in some of the case studies (especially those in Peru and Colombia).

It is the power relationships between these different stakeholders that we focus on – and how the environment interacts with these power relationships (see Diagram 1.1). The relative importance of the different relationships depends upon the stakeholders involved and where they are situated. Thus, in many of the case studies, poor people's involvement with – and perceptions of – formal government are quite limited. For them, the informal institutions that shape their immediate reality seem much more relevant.

# MAPPING POWER RELATIONSHIPS: POLITICAL INFLUENCES AT FOUR LEVELS

The ten case studies each consider the extent to which particular development activities and/or institutional changes have contributed to pro-poor environmental outcomes. All demonstrate a basic point: local and national politics (and, in some cases, regional and global politics), investments, and patterns of tenure and control are major influences on environmental change and on the scale and depth of poverty.[1] Diagram 1.1 illustrates the different levels where politics influences the form that donor-funded interventions take, as well as their outcomes.

Level 1 features low-income groups, made up of households and individuals, who face the realities of poverty and environmental deprivation with which this book is concerned. The household and community politics at this level also require consideration.

In level 2, local governments and other local implementers interact with local political, economic and social interests of varying degrees of power and influence, as well as low-income groups.

National government is depicted in level 3, which, particularly during the last 10 to 15 years, has introduced political changes, such as different forms of decentralization and democracy. These changes have powerfully influenced local contexts within most low- and middle-income countries.

Level 4 depicts international actors – in this instance, donor agencies. For all donor agencies, politics partially determines which countries are supported, which sectors are prioritized and what development assistance instruments are used. In all bilateral agencies, politics inevitably affects the extent to which development assistance is insulated from commercial and foreign policy priorities. Changes in government orientation usually bring about changes in this balance. Such factors might be considered less influential for multilateral agencies; but these agencies depend primarily upon rich world governments for their funding base and are supervized by boards dominated by representatives of rich world governments. Thus, political influence is inevitable, even if it is often well hidden. There are many institutional constraints faced by all international agencies, related to their structure. The agencies were set up primarily to provide development assistance to national governments and find it difficult to deal with local institutions. They are also constrained by what their political supervisors perceive as 'efficient' aid delivery. This includes great pressure to keep down staff costs relative to total funding, and pressure to implement and demonstrate results quickly.

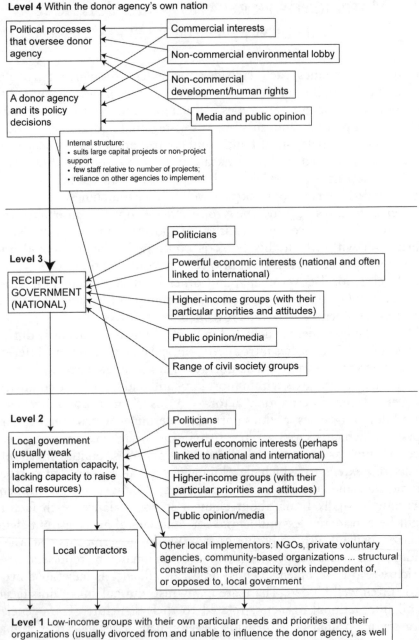

**Level 4** Within the donor agency's own nation

Political processes that oversee donor agency

Commercial interests

Non-commercial environmental lobby

Non-commercial development/human rights

A donor agency and its policy decisions

Media and public opinion

Internal structure:
• suits large capital projects or non-project support
• few staff relative to number of projects;
• reliance on other agencies to implement

**Level 3**

RECIPIENT GOVERNMENT (NATIONAL)

Politicians

Powerful economic interests (national and often linked to international)

Higher-income groups (with their particular priorities and attitudes)

Public opinion/media

Range of civil society groups

**Level 2**

Local government (usually weak implementation capacity, lacking capacity to raise local resources)

Politicians

Powerful economic interests (perhaps linked to national and international)

Higher-income groups (with their particular priorities and attitudes)

Public opinion/media

Local contractors

Other local implementors: NGOs, private voluntary agencies, community-based organizations ... structural constraints on their capacity work independent of, or opposed to, local government

**Level 1** Low-income groups with their own particular needs and priorities and their organizations (usually divorced from and unable to influence the donor agency, as well as the national government except occasionally through their local implementers)

*Source:* Satterthwaite, 2001

**Diagram 1.1** *The different interest groups at different levels that affect the form and flow of development assistance to projects*

This book is primarily about what happens on the ground regarding initiatives for poverty and environmental management, and the political influences that arise within the locality or region where an initiative is implemented. This means a focus, primarily, on levels 1 and 2 in Diagram 1.1, albeit with a particular interest in how what happens on the ground is influenced by national governments and international agencies.

## CLOSING THE GAP BETWEEN THE POOR AND THOSE WHO SEEK TO SUPPORT THEM

One important point, illustrated by Diagram 1.1, is the physical and institutional distance between the intended beneficiaries at level 1 and the international donors – as well as the many intermediaries who link the two. Take, for example, the local group-external donor relations that seem to be key to many of the studies in this book. Level 1 depicts particular groups who suffer deprivations. At the other end, there is the donor agency, which works within its own complex political economy and institutional structure, and which inevitably influences what can and cannot be supported and how and when support is provided. The link between the two is formed through information-gathering, consultative processes, and/or negotiations through which particular problems are identified that are considered deserving of external support, with interventions designed to address these. As the case studies make clear, this identification is not an easy process, in part because of deficient information – especially with regard to the exact nature of the deprivations and who suffers from them, and the ways in which these are rooted in complex local political economies and environmental contexts. The two ends are also linked by the institutions through which the funding is channelled. This is usually a national government agency, which, in turn, may be channelling the funding to a mixture of local government agencies, private enterprises and, occasionally, NGOs. These, too, have their own political economies and institutional structures.

Within the process of problem identification and ongoing disbursements, there are usually no formal political or institutional channels through which 'the intended beneficiaries' can directly influence 'the donors'. The intended beneficiaries (or those who are adversely affected by donor-funded interventions) cannot vote in the donor nations and do not have elected politicians in these nations to whom they can turn. There is also the large physical distance between them and the donor agencies (and the rich world governments that fund them), as well as language barriers. The intended beneficiaries may have no clear channels of communication to the staff within the agency that is funding the project.[2] Donor agencies' decisions and financial management practices are not necessarily transparent to local groups. For example, one doubts whether village committees in China know much about the operations or decision-making structures of the World Bank. In general, opportunities for the intended beneficiaries of donor-funded interventions to influence the design, implementation and management of these interventions will depend upon their own government. As several of the case studies make clear, the scope for donor-funded interventions to be pro-poor is much influenced by the extent to which national and local government structures, through which funding is channelled, *enable or require* them to be 'pro-poor'. In one sense, this is obvious. But recognizing this fact does not mean that there are easy ways for donors to address this, or even that the knowledge exists on how to do so.

Diagram 1.1 understates the complexities at each level and the influences that travel from level 1 upwards – for instance, the ways in which low-income groups can influence local governments and other local implementers, including through claim-making and resistance. It also understates the measures taken by many international donors to support a more equal and participatory engagement with citizens and community organizations.

This raises another issue that will become evident in each of the case studies: the difficulties facing any external agency (whether government, donor or NGO) with regard to really understanding the local context in which their investments will be made. Many projects struggle to ensure that their purpose and processes fit in well with complex local contexts. Most have to be designed with limited local economic, social and environmental data. External agencies or their local partners generally have to rely on whatever data exists about the locality; they rarely have the time or the funding to support new primary data collection and analysis. Yet, there are often very large deficiencies in basic demographic, economic, social, environmental and ecological data. And those who design the project often fail to draw on local knowledge, including the perspectives and priorities of groups who have limited incomes and asset bases, even when the project is justified on the basis of addressing these groups' 'needs'.[3] These deficiencies can be addressed in two ways:

1  sophisticated local data-gathering; or
2  support for local institutions that have local knowledge and accountability downwards (to level 1), and that are permitted the

scope to make decisions or change directions to suit local conditions and needs.

# WHAT DO WE MEAN BY POVERTY?

Over the last 15 years, our understanding of what constitutes poverty has changed considerably, even if this understanding has yet to be incorporated in the ways that most governments and international agencies define and measure it. Central to this changed understanding is a shift from poverty seen and measured as one or two outcomes (for instance, hunger or under-nutrition) to poverty seen and measured not only by outcomes, but by the factors that underpin such outcomes (e.g. lack of income, assets, civil and political rights, voice, and rule of law and services, including safety nets).

A significant part of this change has been to incorporate environmental and political aspects within the definition of poverty. Box 1.1 lists eight aspects that are now commonly considered to be part of 'poverty'. Clearly, there is considerable variation between the groups in the importance allocated to each of these aspects. Many aspects of poverty are strongly interconnected, and in many nations, large sections of the 'non-poor' population also suffer from elements of deprivation.

---

## Box 1. DIFFERENT ASPECTS OF POVERTY[4]

1. *Inadequate and often unstable income* (including inadequate consumption of necessities that need to be purchased, such as food, safe and sufficient drinking water and medicines). Inadequate income is often exacerbated by problems of indebtedness, with debt repayments significantly reducing the income available for necessities. For most rural and many urban households, food production for own consumption is an important cost-saving component that contributes to net income. Low-income groups may also be seriously affected by high and/or rising prices for necessities (e.g. food, water, rent, transport, access to toilets and school fees).

2. *Inadequate, unstable or risky asset base.* This includes a lack of material assets, such as ownership or the right to use productive land or draw resources from it; savings and stores; and non-material assets, including literacy and educational attainment. Most rural poverty has its roots in a lack of access to productive land (and the water needed for production). Relationships within and outside families are often an important part of an asset base, as these can provide money, goods or other important support in times of difficulty.

---

3   *Poor-quality and often insecure, hazardous and overcrowded housing.* In most urban and some rural contexts, housing can be a poor household's main monetary asset if individuals have, or can negotiate, ownership rights. A house is also a store for other goods (also assets) and may provide space for income-earning activities (household enterprises or renting out space). Overcrowding is generally more serious among the urban poor than the rural poor, although in terms of persons per room, many poor rural dwellers also face high levels of overcrowding. Poor households often suffer from insecure housing tenure, either because they rent a property or because they lack rights to the site that it occupies.

4   *Inadequate provision of 'public' infrastructure* (e.g. piped water, sanitation, drainage, roads and footpaths), which increases the disease and, often, the work burden. For many rural dwellers, provision of all-weather roads has considerable importance in increasing their access to markets and services.

5   *Inadequate provision of basic services*, such as day care, schools, vocational training, healthcare, emergency services, public transport, communications and law enforcement. For most poor urban dwellers, the issue is access, not proximity; for many poor rural dwellers, the main issue is their distance from services and the high cost of accessing them.

6   *Limited or no safety net* to mitigate risks – notably, to ensure that basic consumption can be maintained when income falls or crops fail, and to ensure access to housing, healthcare, schools and other necessities when these can no longer be paid for.

7   *Inadequate protection of poorer groups' rights through the operation of the law.* This includes laws, regulations and procedures regarding civil and political rights, occupational health and safety, pollution control, environmental health, protection from violence and other crimes, and protection from discrimination and exploitation. For large sections of the rural poor, the key issue is the protection or enhancement of their land rights or natural resource use rights.

8   *Poorer groups' lack of a voice and their powerlessness within political systems and bureaucratic structures*, leading to little or no possibility of receiving entitlements to goods and services; or of organizing themselves, making demands and getting a fair response; or of receiving support for and developing their own initiatives. In addition, they may have no means of ensuring accountability from aid agencies, NGOs, public agencies and private utilities, and of being able to participate in defining and implementing 'their' poverty-reduction programmes.

# THE IMPLICATIONS OF EXPANDED POVERTY DEFINITIONS FOR THE ENVIRONMENT AND POLITICS

If poverty is defined and measured solely on whether individuals or households have sufficient *food* or the *income* to obtain it, then their environmental deprivations and other links to environmental conditions are not immediately apparent. The political aspects highlighted by such narrow definitions of poverty tend to be confined to 'why the political system did not make provision for food or income for those who lack it'. If poverty definitions give wider consideration to *assets*, natural resource issues immediately become apparent because many poor people depend upon access to natural resources for some, most or all of their livelihoods. This (relatively modest) change – from poverty seen as inadequate consumption to poverty seen as inadequate asset bases to enable adequate consumption – has major implications for poverty and environment linkages. It highlights the importance of increasing access to (environmental and non-environmental) assets in reducing poverty, and how a lack of access to assets will underpin poverty.

If poverty definitions also give consideration to whether people have access to 'adequate' housing and basic infrastructure and services, this has major environmental significance since these are either the primary means by which environmental health risks are reduced (e.g. safe and sufficient water, as well as good sanitation and reduced physical hazards in the residential environment), or the primary means by which the health impacts of these risks is limited (e.g. healthcare, emergency services and knowledge of self-treatment through education). It is worth noting the strong links between poverty and environmental health risks (including incomes and assets lost because of resulting ill health, injury, premature death and the costs of treatment), which also imply strong links between poverty reduction and improved environmental health. Environmental health burdens are much larger – both in absolute terms and in relation to non-environmental health burdens – for people in low-income nations compared to those in high-income nations. There are comparable disparities in absolute and relative terms within the populations of low- and middle-income countries between poor groups and non-poor groups.

Thus, politics comes increasingly to the fore as our understanding of poverty expands to incorporate not only 'adequate food intake', but also 'adequate assets' (including access to land, 'adequate' housing, infrastructure and services). This is because political systems influence the distribution of assets within a society and determine who benefits from governments' housing policies and public investments in infrastructure and services.

Provisions for safety nets (aspect 6 in Box 1.1) are generally recognized as the responsibility of government and a legitimate concern for donor agencies. As several case studies illustrate, one important component of impoverishment is the erosion of poorer groups' access to 'open access' or common property resources that had previously been their main safety net. Aspects 7 and 8 concern the role that the twin pillars of government have in reducing poverty (or perpetuating or increasing it). Poverty reduction obviously depends upon progress towards the rule of law, independent of political considerations, that treats all citizens equally (including ensuring that all have the capacity to access it), and upon democratic systems in which poorer groups have a voice and influence.

Inadequate protection of poorer groups' rights through the operation of the law (aspect 7 in Box 1.1) has obvious environmental dimensions when considering whether poor groups obtain or maintain access to resources (including common property and open access resources). It also has environmental dimensions in relation to how well the law protects poor groups from environmental hazards, including those arising from government projects. Poorer groups' lack of a voice, and their powerlessness within political systems and bureaucratic structures (aspect 8), also have obvious environmental dimensions. By addressing this aspect of poverty, poor groups may be able to have their needs and priorities recognized, understood and responded to by political systems and bureaucratic structures within governments and international agencies.

An expanded definition of poverty – covering all eight aspects described in Box 1.1 – is particularly important for this book because it points to many ways of reducing poorer groups' vulnerability to stresses, hazards and shocks. One reason for the emphasis on assets in poverty definitions is because of their role in enabling low-income households to cope with stresses (e.g. increased prices for purchased necessities or reduced income), hazards (e.g. injury or illness of an income earner) or shocks (e.g. a flood). The lack of provision for healthcare and emergency services that is included in definitions of poverty is because these services greatly reduce people's vulnerability to the impacts of environmental health hazards. Safety nets are also central to reducing vulnerability, although these take many forms, including those organized and managed by poor groups themselves (e.g. community-based savings groups and reciprocal relations). There are obvious links between access to safety nets and a 'voice' through which demands can be made of political or bureaucratic systems.

This book aims to be clear about the distinction between environmental resources/assets and environmental hazards; otherwise, discussions about the links between poverty and the environment tend to become very confused. For instance, poverty is almost always associated with high levels of risk from multiple environmental health hazards (including diarrhoeal diseases, typhoid, intestinal parasites, malaria and dengue fever, as well as exposure to serious chemical and physical hazards at work). However, contrary to the assertions of many documents (and what might be termed the 'orthodox' view of poverty-environment relations), this is often not 'environmental degradation' in the sense of poverty being a major factor in damaging or reducing the natural resource base. Several of the case studies add to the evidence that poverty is rarely a major cause of environmental degradation. When considering the first two aspects of poverty in Box 1.1, the main environmental dimension is access to natural resources (e.g. land, water, forests or forest products, and fisheries). When considering aspects 3 to 5, the main environmental dimension is environmental health risks in the home and its surrounding locale (e.g. biological pathogens, chemical pollutants and physical hazards). Aspects 6 to 8 are concerned with the primary means by which poorer groups' access to natural resources is protected, the quality of the resources is maintained, and rights to freedom from environmental hazards (i.e. healthy living and working environments) are guaranteed.

Environmental changes that are not directly related to poor groups' own resource base can also affect their incomes or asset bases – for instance, the direct and indirect impacts of climate change and the availability and price of resource inputs into their livelihoods (including water and access to resources from areas that they do not own, such as open access and common property resources).

A concern for poverty and the environment thus means:

- a concern for how access to natural resources provides an adequate and environmentally sustainable income/asset base for those who are totally or partially dependent upon this;
- a concern for sustaining important environmental regulatory roles, especially those that provide protection from extreme weather events;
- a concern for how environmental hazards can be reduced.

## How political change can support pro-poor environmental outcomes

Virtually all measures to reduce poverty or to improve environmental management will conflict with the power base and interests of particular individuals, political interests, enterprises or institutions. Almost inevitably, those whose interests are threatened or poorly served will seek to prevent or subvert these measures and will often use the law or political or bureaucratic connections to do so. The case studies present various stark examples of this, including instances of corruption or practices that can be judged to be corrupt. In many of the studies, natural resources provide the livelihoods for most of the population, and political power is usually closely intertwined with wealth generated by the exploitation of natural resources. Key decisions regarding what resources are exploited, by whom and the form of that exploitation are political and tend to be made independently of a concern for poverty reduction or environmental management. And when environmental issues do receive political attention, it is not necessarily guaranteed that it is poor groups' environmental problems that will be highlighted. However, the case studies also include examples of processes where systems are developed to give more attention to the priorities of the poor, and to better natural resource management and environmental health.

If the evils of poverty and natural resource degradation are underpinned by political structures and processes, changing these processes is key to promoting pro-poor environmental outcomes. All of the case studies are, in part, stories about the processes through which governance systems are turned towards the needs and priorities of the poor and improved environmental management. In effect, the quality of 'governance' for the intervention and its surrounding context is the substrate for good environmental management and poverty reduction.

The term 'governance' rather than 'government' is used because our interest is not only in the performance of government institutions (political, bureaucratic or legislative), but also in the nature and quality of their relationships with civil society actors (including citizens, community organizations, private enterprises and local NGOs). In other words, we are concerned with how power and authority are actually exercised at all levels. Many international donors may be involved in supporting decentralization and democratization because these are recognized as being central to governance improvements that will enable better development and environmental management – but these are, inevitably, highly politicized issues.

Each time the World Bank publishes a new *World Development Report* (WDR), more developmental problems and gaps become evident. This results in the WDR proposing increasing numbers of 'requirements' for good governance (45 are listed in 1997, 78 in 1998, 106 in 2000, and 116 in 2002). Three types of dilemma thus arise. First, 'good governance' cannot be implemented in the abstract, but needs to be rooted in the realities of particular contexts in each of the four levels presented in Diagram 1.1. Second, many of these requirements cannot be acted on by government alone, but require decentralization to different actors and partnerships. Third, in order to implement 116 governance requirements in most low- and middle-income countries, the priorities, critical paths and feasibilities will have to be assessed. They should be tested against the problems that affect most people, particularly the poorest and least powerful groups. We need to identify 'what works' in tackling the environmental and poverty issues that matter most, as well as to identify what Grindle (2002) has called 'good enough governance'. Studies of how 'good enough' change actually occurs provide better insights into the conditions and dynamics of reform than studies of impediments to 'ideal' change. This is the approach taken in this book.

The task is important because, after decades of development assistance and over 30 years of discussion on sustainable development, a shamefully large proportion of the world's population is still poor, and trends in natural resource degradation and disruption to local and global environmental systems continue to be negative. This poor record reinforces the need for a better understanding of how development assistance can support both poverty reduction and better environmental management. Perhaps it is the failure to support measures that encourage 'good governance', or that control 'bad governance,' that best explains development assistance's patchy record.

Looking to the future, how can governments in poor countries and international agencies meet their own ambitious targets for environmental management and poverty reduction expressed in the Millennium Development Goals (MDGs)? It is not clear that they will be any more successful than they have been with previous international targets and commitments – unless they can change the economic and political underpinnings of environmental degradation and impoverishment. This is a challenge that is addressed in the final chapter of this book.

# ENDNOTES

1    There are obvious differences between rural and urban areas in the influence of land ownership patterns on poverty and on natural resource management. In rural areas, this is primarily about access to land or natural resources for livelihoods. In urban areas, it is primarily about access to land for housing; therefore, this is not a significant influence on natural resource management. However, access to land in most urban contexts is important from the perspective of livelihoods since low-income groups not only seek access to land for housing, but also a location with access to employment or other income-earning opportunities. The fact that so many

low-income settlements in cities are in locations that are dangerous or are located in precarious areas, such as on floodplains or unstable slopes, is because these are often the only sites on which low-income groups can settle in order to be close to income-earning opportunities.

2   Some projects have sought to address this through participatory engagement. During recent years, some international agencies have sought to make themselves more accountable to the 'intended beneficiaries' and to put more safeguards in place so that the projects they fund do not have anti-poor consequences.

3   See, for instance, the discussions of 'whose reality counts' and the politics of 'scientific knowledge' in Chambers (1995), Leach and Mearns (1996), Broch-Due and Schroeder (2000) and Stott and Sullivan (2000).

4   Drawn from Mitlin and Satterthwaite (2004), as well as from other people's work, especially Amis (1995), Baulch (1996), Chambers (1995) and Moser et al (1993).

# REFERENCES

Amis, P. (1995), 'Making sense of urban poverty', *Environment and Urbanization*, vol.7, no.1, April, pp145–157

Baulch, B. (1996), 'The new poverty agenda: A disputed consensus', *IDS Bulletin*, vol. 27, no. 1, pp1–10

Broch-Due, V. and Schroeder, R. A. (eds) (2000) *Producing Nature and Poverty in Africa*, Nordic African Institute, Uppsala

Chambers, R. (1995) 'Poverty and livelihoods; whose reality counts?', *Environment and Urbanization*, vol.7, no.1, April, pp173–204

Forsyth, T. and Leach. M. with Scoones, I. (1999) *Poverty and Environment: Priorities for Research and Policy – An Overview Study*, Institute of Development Studies, Brighton

Grindle, M. S. (2002) *Good Enough Governance: Poverty Reduction And Reform In Developing Countries*, Kennedy School of Government, Harvard University, Harvard; Paper prepared for the World bank Poverty Reduction Group

Leach, M. and Mearns, R. (1996) 'Environmental change and policy; challenging received wisdom in Africa', in M. Leach and R. Mearns (eds) *The Lie of the Land*, The International African Institute in association with James Currey and Heinemann, Oxford, pp1–33

Mitlin, D. and Satterthwaite, D. (eds) (2004) *Empowering Squatter Citizen: Local Government, Civil Society and Urban Poverty Reduction*, Earthscan Publications, London

Moser, C. O. N. (1996) *Confronting Crisis: A Summary of Household Responses to Poverty and Vulnerability in Four Poor Urban Communities*, Environmentally Sustainable Development Studies and Monographs Series No. 7, The World Bank, Washington, D.C.

Moser, C. O. N., Herbert, A. J. and Makonnen, R. E. (1993) *Urban Poverty in the Context of Structural Adjustment; Recent Evidence and Policy Responses*, TWU Discussion Paper DP #14, Urban Development Division, World Bank, Washington, D.C.

Satterthwaite, D. (2001) 'Reducing urban poverty: Constraints on the effectiveness of aid agencies and development banks and some suggestions for change', *Environment and Urbanization*, vol. 13, no.1, pp137–157

Stott, P. and Sullivan, S. (2000) *Political Ecology: Science, Myth and Power*, Oxford University Press, Oxford

Wratten, E. (1995) 'Conceptualizing urban poverty', *Environment and Urbanization*, vol.7, no.1, April, pp11–36

# 2

# Creating Space for Civil Society in an Impoverished Environment in Pakistan

*Maheen Zehra*

---

This case study explores a rural development initiative in the remote, resource-poor Northern Areas of Pakistan. The Aga Khan Rural Support Programme (AKRSP) not only changed the socio-economic and political face of the Northern Areas, it also helped to inspire national environmental and natural resource policy processes to work for poverty alleviation.

## FROM EARLY INNOVATIONS IN BANGLADESH...

In order to understand AKRSP, we must present the story of change in a small district by the name of Comilla in east Pakistan (present-day Bangladesh). These events, from the late 1950s, form an important point of origin for AKRSP. They brought together two individuals to whom much of the credit for AKRSP's achievements must be attributed – the late Akhter Hameed Khan and his disciple Shoaib Sultan Khan.

The association of these two development leaders began in 1959 when Shoaib Sultan Khan was an assistant commissioner of Comilla. This district was selected by Akhter Hameed Khan, then director of the Pakistan Academy of Rural Development, to orient and train the new professional class of rural development specialists. Between 1959 and 1969, Akhter Hameed Khan proved through his work in Comilla that poverty arises not out of a lack of resources, but from persistent disempowerment. What poor people need – and can make good use of – is empowerment in the form of some technical knowledge, perhaps some catalytic financial support, but most of all, institutions that give them the right to decide on all of the issues that affect their lives.

In 1969, when Shoaib Sultan Khan revisited Comilla, the district's socio-political dynamic had radically changed. He summarized his observations in these words:

> I could not believe the changes brought about by Khan Sahib's approach to development in the area ... I did not come across a single paddy field, which was not scientifically planted. The *thana* (police station) training and development centres, as he had visualized, have become the real symbols of development as against *thana* building, which for centuries had been the symbol of law and order. The condition of the poor people had changed beyond recognition. Traces of poverty were nowhere visible and even today, 30 years after Khan Sahib's departure, Comilla district has a per capita income of US$600 compared to the national per capita of US$220 for Bangladesh.

When the Aga Khan Foundation (AKF) began to seek ways of initiating development interventions in Pakistan's Northern Areas, particularly for the Muslim Ismaili community, it was not surprising that it was interested in the work of Akhter Hameed Khan and Robert Chambers, as well as in other innovative rural development approaches. Akhter Hameed Khan's Comilla project was finally selected as a model and, in 1981, AKF contacted Akhter Hameed Khan to seek his leadership in establishing AKRSP. At that time, Akhter Hameed Khan was busy dealing with the teething problems of the Orangi Pilot Project (OPP) – an initiative employing Comilla principles in an impoverished urban setting in the slums of Karachi. Akhter Hameed Khan approached Shoaib Sultan Khan to take on the role, but stayed personally connected as he was keen to see further implementation of the approaches being tested in Comilla. In 1982, Shoaib Sultan Khan formally took up the post of AKRSP's general manager

## ... TO FACING HUGE CHALLENGES IN ONE OF THE POOREST PARTS OF PAKISTAN

In order to understand the enormous range of environmental and poverty challenges that were to be faced by AKRSP, several aspects of the geographical, political, administrative and natural resource setting, as well as the economic profile, of the Northern Areas need explaining.

21

The Northern Areas lie where three important mountain ranges of central Asia meet – namely, the Himalayas, the Karakorums and the Hindukush. Within a 100km radius of Gilgit, the main regional city, there are more than two dozen peaks ranging from 5500m to 8000m. The harsh and remote high mountain valleys are among the most demanding settings for human survival, and present huge challenges for social and economic development.

The Northern Areas have long been militarily sensitive – lying between India, China, Russia and Afghanistan. They cover an area of 43,760 square kilometres. In 1981, the population was estimated at 574,000. In addition, Chitral to the west, which has been traditionally associated with the Northern Areas and which is included in AKRSP's work, is home to around 900,000 additional people. The Northern Areas are home to eight major ethnic groups: the Baltees, Shins, Yashkuns, Mughals, Kashmiris, Pathans, Ladakis and Turks, who speak dialects of Balti, Shina, Brushaski, Khawar, Wakhi, Turki, Tibetan, Pushto, Urdu and Persian. Despite a very small population, the Northern Areas also present a very diverse sectarian picture with the presence of four Muslim sects: Shia, Sunni, Ismailis and Nurbakshis. This sectarian profile plays a significant role in the socio-political dynamics of the area.

The political and administrative system in the Northern Areas was a combination of the pre-partition *numberdari* system, introduced by the British, with the traditional *jirga* system. This arrangement ensured fiscal compliance and a basic rule of law – but it also respected the independence and autonomy of the various local communities. It was, essentially, a compromise arising from the inability of the British to enforce law and order directly in the remote valleys of the Northern Areas. Resistance to direct administrative control was prevalent and this had disadvantages – for example, it precluded many investments in economic and social infrastructure (roads, irrigation channels, schools, medical facilities, etc.). The *Mir*, a local notable, was entrusted with levying and collecting *maaliya* (taxes on water usage and agricultural produce). The local *jirga*, a collection of respected elders, maintained law and order in the community, adjudicating on criminal offences and disputes relating to agricultural property and grazing rights. There has, traditionally, been an informal hierarchy of command which is inter-generational, ethnic based and, therefore, socially acceptable. There has been strong acceptance of such authority, which is premised on accountability and accessibility. The dominant ethnic group tradition-ally assumed leadership roles, consistent with their pre-eminent social status, which was acquired on the basis of either the services rendered to the British Raj or their close relationship with religious hierarchy. On the other hand, the external forces of modernization have been strong and potentially divisive. These have lent increasing urgency to the need to develop and strengthen mechanisms which allow the wider community to retain control over common resources.

The evolution of politics, economics and governance has created new dynamics, as well as dissonances, in the Northern Areas. In 1974, Prime Minister Bhutto's socialist government dissolved the *numberdari* system and abolished *maaliya*. In its place, it introduced an ostensibly more proactive system of local government, charged with carrying out development work for the local communities. This represented one aspect of the process of integrating the Northern Areas within the country as a whole (i.e. into the national administrative framework).

At present, the Northern Areas has a legislative council, headed by a federally appointed chief executive and consisting of 24 locally elected members who elect a deputy chief executive. The whole region is under federal administration and is run by a commissioner in Gilgit, who is directly under the control of the Ministry of Kashmir Affairs and Northern Areas, Government of Pakistan. However, the Northern Areas remain politically different from the rest of Pakistan. The people of the Northern Areas do not elect members to Pakistan's national assembly, thus creating a sense of isolation. Attempts by various governments to bring the region under the constitutional cover of Pakistan have not met with success. The major reason cited by government functionaries for this failure has been the area's close proximity to the disputed regions of Jammu and Kashmir.

The people of the Northern Areas may not be voters, but they are also not directly taxed by the government of Pakistan. Rather, they receive a number of subsidies. In spite of these, the local economy is based on subsistence farming and grazing, with limited productivity principally due to climatic constraints, but also constrained by limited soil and water – much of the area is a 'mountain desert'. Physical infrastructure is inadequate, and the wage labour industry is underdeveloped, limiting off-farm employment opportunities. Most employment opportunities are provided by the tourism industry. After the construction of the Karakorum Highway linking Pakistan and China, market towns emerged along the highway, especially between Gilgit and the border. The economy is only diversifying close to the highway, where a shift is taking place from production of staple subsistence crops to market-oriented cash crops such as potatoes, apples and cherries. Trade also occurs with China, mostly in cheap consumer items. Overall, the economy of the region is weak, with 37 per cent of the population living under the poverty line (Government of Pakistan, 2003). The most impoverished communities are those that are located in high-altitude glacier valleys. Some of these communities have nomadic livelihood patterns.

Local people have traditionally enjoyed usufruct rights for grazing animals in pastures, as well as for collection of fuelwood and some timber for construction needs. The communities historically regulated the use of these natural resources through unwritten but mutually agreed laws, which the *Mirs* would enforce. There were far fewer local traditions for conservation of wildlife, which was hunted both by local people as well as outsiders. After the abolishment of *Mirdom*, the environment was degraded at a rapid rate. The root cause of this was the loss of tenure that local people had over their natural resources. The government took ownership of most of the forests and all of the wildlife without the capacity to plan, regulate, monitor or account for these resources. Consequently, the local population continued to deplete the environment. The extent of degradation of forests, pastures and wildlife has been correlated highly with the degree of government control – and also, increasingly, with pressure from outsiders. Recent research by the World Conservation Union (IUCN) and AKRSP concluded that natural forests and wildlife under complete government control are the most degraded resources (Virk et al, 2003). Wildlife suffered due to over-hunting and loss of habitat through overgrazing and deforestation. In comparison, the pastures, which are not regulated by government, are in good condition as a result of continued community control. There is a strong incentive for sustainable management of this resource because it is essential for local people's subsistence.

# AKRSP's APPROACH: 'SOCIAL ORGANIZATION'
## TACKLES POVERTY AND NATURAL RESOURCE DEGRADATION

With this changing and challenging scenario, Shoaib Sultan Khan's AKRSP set out to improve the overall quality of life of the people of the Northern Areas.

When he began work in 1982, the socio-political scenario of the Northern Areas was quite chaotic. The abolishment of the *Mirdoms*' traditional governance structures 12 years earlier had created a vacuum at the grassroots level. There was no common cause for the communities to rally around except religious leadership, which was divided on a sectarian basis, or the Pakistan People's Party. Initially the space left by the *Mirs* was not occupied effectively by the Pakistan government, AKRSP helped to fill the political vacuum. This was quite deliberate as, according to Shoaib Sultan Khan, powerful institutions have to be democratized in order to provide local communities with the opportunity to participate in decision-making. In order to put this principle into action, the first consideration was which community to begin with. After a careful anthropological and geographical analysis, the Gojal community in Hunza was selected. Gojal is an Ismaili community, which – in comparison to other sectarian groups – was much more open to outsiders, especially a group representing the Aga Khan.

AKRSP's first objective in the 'field' was to help form local participatory institutions, filling the 'power vacuum' at least at local levels. Its approach was to encourage village communities to develop their own socio-economic institutions so that they would be able to work with government, elected bodies and other development agencies – the latter groups being seen as 'service deliverers' and not those that set the local agenda. In addition to tackling the lack of community organization, the initial focus of the programme addressed the critical constraints of limited environmental assets, limited financial assets and, often, a non-existent physical infrastructure. It also tackled extensive gender problems, such as access to education, mother and child health, isolation from decision-making at the community level, and complete absence from the political arena.

The first challenge for AKRSP was to develop leadership mechanisms at the grassroots level in order to provide a shared vision for the development of village lands, skills and institutions. Building on local traditions of self-help and cooperation, the AKRSP established village organizations (VOs). Uniquely, they involved the heads of every household in the village. VOs were initially men's enterprises; but within three years, separate women's organizations (WOs) also became active stakeholders in socio-economic development. These VOs and WOs, which were based on basic principles of participation that were familiar from previous traditions, became successful grassroots institutions, and came to initiate many activities leading to economic development – initially through working together on 'productive physical infrastructure'. The basic strategy was to approach the communities without a pre-conceived package of intervention, since the initial thrust of the programme was to organize rural people to harness their own potential for undertaking projects which they wanted to implement and were capable of sustaining. The productive physical infrastructure was selected on criteria that included equity, productivity

Source: S. Bass

**Figure 2.1** *Every household is represented in a village organization, which meets to agree development plans and arrangements with service organizations*

and sustainability – and was seen as an investment towards improving the VO. Organizations established through this approach met both the expectations of AKRSP and the aspirations of villagers, rallying people around a common cause (i.e. increased productivity and a better quality of life). During recent years, second infrastructure investments have been sponsored, including larger schemes by clusters of VOs. An obligatory members' savings programme was instituted for each VO or WO, through which the community can work together and develop collateral so that loans can be raised – partly so that they can go on to make good use of the productive physical infrastructure. Training of villagers has been an important element of the programme, with 'village specialists' being supported to become, for example, livestock health specialists or forestry specialists. These individuals help the community to demand the right kinds of support from government and non-government service providers. The savings and credit services are now in the process of being devolved to a new micro-finance bank.

Since the major livelihood of local communities was based on agro-pastoral activities, the productive physical infrastructure tended to be followed by support for improving agriculture, livestock, and forest productivity and credit services, mainly for agricultural inputs. AKRSP

Source: S. Bass

**Figure 2.2** *Womens organizations are now widespread, improving power for women in the household, and bringing about new enterprises that enable women to benefit from local environmental wealth*

initially focused on agriculture, horticulture and livestock. In 1985, when participatory village surveys revealed a lack of firewood to cook and heat homes, the IUCN and AKRSP set out to conduct detailed research on the current and future needs for fuelwood in the Northern Areas. This led to a joint forestry project, initially tackling the problem of a lack of fuelwood by building on best local forestry practices. It is interesting how subsequent surveys were to reveal new shortages of wood: for timber – when incomes began to rise, people wanted to build houses; for fodder – when irrigation opened up, crops began to be planted and people wanted to stall-feed livestock in order to protect the crops; and, latterly, for landscape reasons – with the full opening of the Karakorum Highway, tourism mushroomed and villagers observed how well-wooded 'mountain oasis' villages were favoured.

Environmental conservation was not originally an explicit part of the objectives of AKRSP. However, from the beginning, natural resources were recognized as a key capital asset. The sustainable use approach became, through consultation with villagers and development experts alike, a defining objective of AKRSP early in its life.

By the end of 2001, AKRSP had organized 3940 VOs and WOs comprising 147,381 members (including 49,841 women) and covering

27

88 per cent of the rural households in the Northern Areas and Chitral. These VOs and WOs evolved into 309 clusters/local development organizations, which fostered linkages with 2000 other organizations. A good example of one prominent local development organization is the Karimabad Area Development Organization. This is now a large independent enterprise run on commercial lines, similar to the Bangladesh Rural Advancement Committee (BRAC), with its income used for various development projects.

However, this clustering of organizations did not happen all over the Northern Areas, which may be attributed primarily to the sectarian diversity of the region. Access to AKRSP, in practice, if not in principle, was restricted to certain communities of the Northern Areas. AKRSP has never been able to overcome the perception that it is an instrument of the Ismaili sect, despite a policy decision taken by AKRSP to allocate 73 per cent of resources to non-Ismaili communities. Throughout its existence, AKRSP has faced fierce opposition from some of the sectarian groups, especially in the region of Diamer district, which is adjacent to Kohistan. This has been particularly problematic in the wake of the Islamization of Pakistan during General Ziaul Haq's regime and the upheaval in Afghanistan.

In spite of this, AKRSP has made huge achievements in involving local communities in the rural development of the Northern Areas. If the key institution has been the VO or WO, the village saving and productive physical infrastructure schemes have helped to keep the organizations vital. Through them, villagers identify collective goals and contribute to achieving them.

Conventional thinking on the subject of what AKRSP calls 'social organization' is beginning to change. At the outset, the replicability of the AKRSP model was questioned on the grounds that it would only work if communities were ethnically homogeneous, and if assets were distributed in a relatively egalitarian fashion. This view has been debunked following successful replication of the AKRSP model in Chitral, the North-West Frontier Province and in the Punjab. More recent views question the need for prior formation of VOs, especially in the light of a growing tendency to see them as an end rather than as a means (the target of increasing 'numbers of VOs' can be a diversion from the aims of rural development). Akhtar Hameed Khan argues that it may not be necessary to create a formal community organization prior to an activity. The community could converge around activities, offering contributions. For example, in the case of community schools, the community members could provide a teacher and a room, and then form an organization to assist and monitor their children's schooling.

The organization could be formal or informal and its composition would change as some children graduated from the school and others entered.

Another provocative thesis proposed by Dani (1988) and Omar Ashgar through his work in SUNGI is that most regions do have indigenous organizations, and building on these could lead to much more sustainable grassroots organizations, as opposed to building new organizations from scratch. Omar discovered in his fieldwork that various AKRSP village organizations eventually split and assumed new compositions that coincided with *mones*: traditional social organizations that pre-dated the AKRSP interventions. The SUNGI Development Foundation, the PATAN Development Organization and Oxfam have also adopted this philosophy of social organization by strengthening, where possible and feasible, existing community-based organizations that have evolved indigenously, rather than creating new ones. Perhaps AKRSP made too hasty an assumption that the deposition of the *Mirs* had removed the old institutional framework – because some elements of it clearly remained in place.

## IMPROVING GOVERNANCE: AKRSP AS A COMPLEMENT TO GOVERNMENT, NOT A SUBSTITUTE

A major challenge (which could also be seen as an opportunity) was the fact that the administrative structures created by the federal government were weak, both financially and in terms of their capability to support socio-economic development in a vast and difficult terrain such as the Northern Areas. This weakness ensured AKRSP's overwhelming presence in rural parts of the Northern Areas, a predominance that made it all too easy to forget that it can never become a viable alternative to government, with the latter's far broader responsibilities. However, the AKRSP has effectively replaced government in rural development, providing many of the services usually supplied by government agencies. In contrast, in urban areas such as Gilgit and Skardu, in development issues such as large infrastructure projects, and in policy-making, the AKRSP's influence is more modest. Nevertheless, AKRSP has played a key role in building the capacity of the public sector. Government staff of newly founded federal structures in the Northern Areas, such as the Planning and Development Department, benefited immensely from the presence of AKRSP – either through indirect exposure to AKRSP through their own local communities, or directly as a result of working together. Staff from the forestry, fisheries and wildlife department were trained either through AKRSP's training sessions or through deputation to various AKRSP programmes.

In this regard, the role played by donor agencies cannot be neglected. After observing the initial success of AKRSP, the donor community was attracted to the Northern Areas, where Shoaib Sultan Khan was successfully addressing problems by converting the potential that people had into solutions. This led to considerable dialogue between donors and the Kashmir Affairs and Northern Areas Affairs Division on several capacity-building and infrastructure development proposals, with the condition that community involvement would be overseen by AKRSP. This donor push resulted in significant development initiatives, such as the Northern Areas Education Project (sponsored by the World Bank and the UK Department for International Development, or DFID) and the Northern Areas Health Project, both implemented with AKRSP as a partner.

## STRENGTHENING CIVIL SOCIETY THROUGH INTERACTIONS

One significant (though less well documented) area of AKRSP's impact has been in the political system of the Northern Areas. Members of the legislative council, who are still elected on the basis of religious or political party affiliation, now come primarily from amongst the leaders of the VOs or local development organizations. Over the years, the political understanding and expectations of the general public have also tremendously improved – development competence and/or performance are now major criteria for winning votes in an election.

From the people's perspective, AKRSP is the most competent development agent in the Northern Areas. This is, indeed, recognized, although not explicitly admitted, by the government, which recently called on AKRSP to help establish *dehi* councils (rural councils) as a first step towards introducing the current plan for devolution of power in the Northern Areas. However, in some sections of local administration, the impression that AKRSP is trying to replace the government's service delivery mechanisms is still prevalent.

Capacity for leadership in the Northern Areas has also improved remarkably. There was a time during the late 1980s and early 1990s when people from other parts of Pakistan led all AKRSP programmes. Today, local staff members run all major AKRSP programmes. However, there now is a danger of closing doors to diversity.

The organized civil society movement in the Northern Areas also owes its emergence and recognition to AKRSP. The community-based organizations and formalized VOs created by AKRSP have legal identities that facilitate business and other transactions. They are thus independent non-governmental organizations (NGOs) able to interact directly with local and federal government, as well as with donors. In some areas where people could not access AKRSP's services and programmes, due to community differences, indigenous grassroots organizations emerged as an alternative, where one or two individuals worked for or observed AKRSP and, hence, founded their own community-based NGOs. The Naunehal Foundation, operating in the Nagar Valley (a Shiite community) is one such example, as is the Karakorums Area Development Organization. Both of these organizations enjoy donor confidence and community support, largely as a consequence of their informal association with AKRSP. This was one approach adopted by AKRSP to resolve the sectarian problem – creating a model and allowing, or encouraging, other groups to 'copy' it without full association with AKRSP.

The private sector – which was almost non-existent in the Northern Areas prior to 1982 – was promoted by the enterprise development programme of AKRSP. There are several enterprises, such as Hunza Carpets and dry fruit merchants, that have gained good access to national and international markets.

Thus, the process of village-level organizational development, once initiated by AKRSP, gradually began to turn into one of institutional transformation on a much wider scale. More diverse institutions were created in order to meet basic human needs.

## MATURING INSTITUTIONS GET TO GRIPS WITH ENVIRONMENTAL ISSUES AND INFLUENCE POLICY

From 1986, AKRSP staff began to manage the environment 'beyond the irrigation channel', and forest protection committees were established by some VOs (e.g. in Nagar) to deal with natural forests. AKRSP's donors had been encouraging its various natural resource programmes to improve coherence between each other, especially on the issue of environmental sustainability. The growing link between AKRSP and the federal National Conservation Strategy – formed at professional seminars where environment and development leaders explored the principles of, and opportunities for, sustainable development – meant that

AKRSP could no longer ignore its environmental responsibilities. IUCN and AKRSP fielded a reconnaissance study in early 1991 to examine the feasibility of a community-based natural resource management project. This led to a project entitled Conservation of Biodiversity with Rural Community Development, which was based on the social infrastructure of VOs and WOs, and was funded by the Global Environment Facility (GEF).

This pilot project led to a full Mountain Areas Conservancy Project, jointly implemented by IUCN and the World Wide Fund for Nature (WWF) with the support of AKRSP. The basic principle was the same as that held by AKRSP: conservation activities are unlikely to be sustainable over the long term unless local communities are actively involved. The new approach involved ecological landscape management at large spatial scales. Covering four areas totalling 16,300 square kilometres, the project had three major goals:

1 Empower, organize and enhance the capacity of local communities to conserve biodiversity.
2 Enhance the value of biodiversity to local people.
3 Create a policy, legislative and financial framework conducive to community-based conservation.

As a result of policy advocacy by the project, the federal and provincial governments agreed that 80 per cent of all hunting licence fees collected would be turned over to the local conservation fund. This major achievement was made possible by high-level lobbying by the AKF and IUCN. Some of this money is used for ongoing conservation activities, such as anti-poaching surveillance and population surveys, while some is used for more general local development activities, such as school construction. All decisions are made at the local level. In 2001, a trophy hunt brought US$20,000 to three communities in Baltistan. The community decided to use a portion of this money to provide the capital for an insurance fund to compensate shepherds for losses sustained from snow leopard predation.

At present, the government of the Northern Areas and IUCN are preparing the Northern Areas Strategy for Sustainable Development, with major conceptual contributions from AKRSP, which is on the strategy steering committee. The strategy was initially conceived of as a sub-strategy for conservation, under the Sarhad Provincial Conservation Strategy. The latter was primarily a document consisting of local environment reports, strategic policy frameworks on environmental issues, and lists of potential programmes and projects. The process in the Northern Areas began in 1999, under the Northern Areas Administration, with technical support from the IUCN. Again, it appeared that the focus was going to be on conservation, on developing a document, and with inputs and leadership provided to the administration solely by the IUCN. However, in 2000, the mid-term review of Pakistan's National Conservation Strategy (complemented by the international process undertaken by the Organisation for Economic Co-operation and Development's Development Assistance Committee to provide guidelines for sustainable development strategies) brought about a paradigm shift. There was a strong realization, both by government and by the IUCN (with a push from AKRSP), that rather than an exclusive focus on environmental protection, the broader issues of social, economic and ecological well-being needed to be addressed – conservation with an increased focus on poverty alleviation, and a more people-centred and demand-driven approach towards sustainable development. There was also a shift of emphasis from prototype solutions to processes and mechanisms for achieving sustainable development – from vast but 'dead' documents to 'live' systems that keep sustainable development on the agenda and deal with priorities and change. At this point, association with AKRSP offered the IUCN 'social' credibility and gave the IUCN the confidence to be able to shift its own – and government's – thinking from 'environment' to sustainable development. Therefore, the aim (and title) of the strategy shifted from 'conservation' to 'sustainable development'.

The approach of the Northern Areas Strategy for Sustainable Development was based on consultations with stakeholders, which included the public and private sector, NGOs, opinion leaders and common citizens. The public consultation process was held throughout the Northern Areas and was extremely well attended. The chances of success of the Northern Areas Strategy for Sustainable Development, compared to the Sarhad Provincial Conservation Strategy and the Baluchistan Conservation Strategy (BCS), are anticipated to be very high on the basis of its principles:

- Respect and adapt the principles of sustainable development to the particular circumstances of the Northern Areas.
- Respond to district-level and *tehsil*-level needs and aspirations as reflected in the ongoing work on social organization and the village organizations.
- Acknowledge and strengthen the existing, ongoing and expanding complementary relationships with civil society organizations.

33

- Respect the Pakistan National Conservation Strategy and Pakistan's commitments to the implementation of various multilateral environmental agreements.
- Propose an achievable, incremental and realistic programme for the Northern Areas, including a comprehensive and integrated approach towards meeting development and environmental conservation objectives.

# REVISITING SOME ASSUMPTIONS ABOUT POVERTY AND THE ENVIRONMENT

It is hazardous to make generalized statements regarding the relationship between poor people and the environment. AKRSP's work is no exception, as the Northern Areas present a very diverse context. However, AKRSP has been able to produce some evidence to challenge common perceptions, as discussed below. Tentative lessons from AKRSP's experience are also outlined.

## Perception: 'Poverty necessarily leads to environmental degradation'

A common perception exists that poor people degrade the environment more than the better off. However, in the case of AKRSP, much evidence suggests that the opposite is the case. Comparatively wealthier farmers with larger landholdings played a prominent role in large-scale land clearing, overuse of agricultural chemicals and pesticides, or over-extraction of groundwater. Similarly, pastoralists with large herds were more likely to overgraze resources than those with few livestock. On the other hand, the large numbers of poor people are often concentrated and highly visible in degraded environments, or are forced by richer farmers onto marginal lands that often have lower environmental capabilities. This issue was addressed by AKRSP, which empowered local communities through raising awareness about communal pasture management and development of local institutions, such as forest protection committees. Political pressure from local elites was immense; but they had to bow to popular demand from strong local institutions supported by AKRSP. Indeed, in most cases local elites have now joined these committees on an equal footing – thus tackling the root causes of environmental degradation and improving equity.

## Perception: 'Poor people are too poor to invest in the environment'

The ability to invest in the environment is site specific and depends upon local labour and non-labour input costs, and the types of technology needed for environmental care. AKRSP's experience shows that when the incentives are right, even poor people can mobilize enormous resources, particularly labour. The vast majority of productive physical infrastructures (voted by villagers themselves) were irrigation channels enabling harsh 'mountain deserts' to be turned into skilfully terraced 'oases'. The creation of these systems represents enormous investments of individuals' labour. Similarly, the forestry sector in the Northern Areas disproved that cost could be a constraint to tree plantation, with millions of trees being raised, planted and managed by villagers themselves. AKRSP helped people of the Northern Areas to overcome the high transaction costs associated with gaining access to cheaper services.

## Perception: 'Poor people lack the technical knowledge for resource management'

While poor people may not always be immediately aware of the effects of gradual (and sometimes imperceptible) environmental degradation, they are often blamed for things that are not their fault. AKRSP showed that poor people have an enormous store of 'indigenous technical knowledge' (e.g. of medicinal plants, water harvesting structures, game trails, non-timber forest products, seed selection and silviculture) and helped to remove barriers to its use. However, AKRSP also established that poor groups (and especially women) often lose out as a result of policies and processes that privatize resources and reduce complex bundles of rights into a single unitary right. In order to address one aspect of this issue, one member organization of the Aga Khan Development Network initiated a graduate scholarship programme through which merit-based scholarships were awarded to young men and women for higher studies in various Pakistan universities. The programme was initially only for the Hunza region, but was later made accessible to all regions of the Northern Areas. The programme was a huge success and resulted in an enormous improvement of local capacity for technical jobs, not only in the public sector but also within AKRSP.

## Perception: 'Despite many constraints, government can best look after environmental resources and the distribution of public benefits in the long term'

It is now clear that, where there is inefficient irrigation and indiscriminate logging in the Northern Areas, this is more often due to the actions of the government, rather than to communities. It is true that, in the past, awarding resource care to the poor sometimes led to environmental degradation – poor people felt that their rights to the resource might be revoked and thus overused these rights in the short term. AKRSP, on the contrary, showed that improving poor people's access to and control over the environment provided a powerful incentive for them to protect the environment rather than to destroy it – for example, through village-level conservation committees with regard to protecting forests and wildlife. This was apparent in some of the most impoverished areas (e.g. in Chapursan).

The IUCN/AKRSP pilot project for the conservation of biodiversity was initiated simultaneously in the Northern Areas and the North-West Frontier Province. Its appraisal mission noted a significant difference in the success of the project due to the people-centred approach adopted in the Northern Areas where the population of ibex increased by 40 to 45 per cent, with gains from trophy hunting going directly to the community.

Some critics of AKRSP express concern that the explicit linkage between natural resource management programmes and poverty reduction objectives has become weaker during the last four or five years. A recent evaluation of AKRSP by the World Bank (Ridley and Nelson, 2002) noted that there has been insufficient focus on technologies for the poorer households, and for those at high altitudes. Nevertheless, there are some impressive gains in terms of outputs and income. The evaluation noted that 'over the only period for which good income data are available, per capita farm incomes increased 2.7 times, from 1991 to 1997. An improved variety of wheat and maize, [and] growth in fruits, vegetables and livestock, have significantly contributed to increased farm income. The improvement was particularly impressive in forestry' (Ridley and Nelson, 2002). It noted that AKRSP's Dry Fruit Project has the potential to benefit a large number of people and to bring about a revolution in the cash economy. The project has not only identified the raw material, but perfected its processing through indigenous equipment costing 25,000 rupees (against 6 million rupees for imported equivalents). Above all, it has helped local people to access international markets.

Source: S. Bass

**Figure 2.3** *Village organizations have been working to transform harsh mountain deserts into productive oases with horticulture and tree plantations. Village organizations invest in irrigation from glacier melt-waters, attracting commercial, public and foundation support*

## INFLUENCING NATIONAL POLICY ON RURAL DEVELOPMENT: THE IMPORTANCE OF LEADERSHIP

AKRSP has been a major development catalyst at the local level (principally the village). It has helped to strengthen politics and government at the district and Northern Areas level through support to

37

VO and WO leadership, raising public expectations of competence from their leaders, and developing the capacities of VOs and government staff together. AKRSP has now been asked to help the government organize rural councils as a basis for the devolution of power. However, it has not been able to overcome several sectarian divisions, or the suspicions of some government officials. Alliances with environmental organizations, notably the IUCN, were able to forge environmental and sustainable development initiatives and strategies. At the national policy level, environmental groups were able to highlight AKRSP's approach as a model for sustainable development in resource-poor areas. Shoaib Sultan Khan was a key influence in both establishing other rural support programmes and in influencing the national conservation strategy. Through several high-level interactions, he helped government to start 'thinking and acting like a non-governmental organization'.

During the middle to late 1980s, Shoaib Sultan Khan convinced Sartaj Aziz, who headed the National Commission on Agriculture (and later became federal minister for agriculture), along with Chowdhry Anwar Aziz, who was minister for local government and rural development, to set up the National Rural Support Programme. In 1987, Arbab Jehangir, chief minister of the North-West Frontier Province, invited Shoaib Sultan Khan to start the Sarhad Rural Support Programme. In 1993, the prime minister of Pakistan, Nawaz Sharif, was strongly impressed by the international recognition of Shoaib Sultan Khan when he learned that the Philippines government had honoured him with the Magsaysay Award. This resulted in the donation of 500 million rupees to the National Rural Support Programme. During late 1990s, when Sartaj Aziz became the finance minister, Shoaib Sultan Khan's interaction with him resulted in the establishment of the Pakistan Poverty Alleviation Fund. In 1997, he influenced Shahbaz Sharif, chief minister of Punjab, to commit 500 million rupees for the Punjab Rural Support Programme. A key factor behind these successes of Shoaib Sultan Khan with policy-makers was his civil service background and international connections, as well as his credibility with donors and other key NGOs.

However, with respect to its influence on national policy, as an institution, AKRSP has not taken a proactive approach, and has been particularly elusive regarding sharing lessons. This has only recently started with the initiation of the Rural Support Programmes Network, of which AKRSP is a member. Most of the lessons have reached the policy level either through Shoaib Sultan Khan or through donor-driven evaluations of AKRSP. It is astonishing to note that a successful programme such as the AKRSP does not even have a website of its own.

Very few of its documents are available through the AKF website, and most of the field research is still only available in AKRSP's Gilgit office. This hampers dissemination of AKRSP's various successes.

If it has not been proactive in influencing policy, the evidence suggests that AKRSP has served as an iconic example for national policy-making for poverty alleviation and rural development, although this has not been well documented.

*First, the model has been widely replicated for rural development.* There are at least eight rural support projects throughout Pakistan that, to some extent, owe their basic approach and often key staff to AKRSP, as well as support by policy-makers who came to appreciate AKRSP. These projects had established some 20,000 community organizations by 2000, about five times the number of AKRSP organizations. They are now active in nearly 80 (out of a total of 109) administrative districts. AKRSP's experience and skills have been employed in the National Rural Support Programme, the Chitral Agricultural Development Project, the Sarhad Rural Support Corporation, the Ghazi Barotha Taraqiati Idara, the South Asia Poverty Alleviation Programme, the Punjab Rural Support Programme, and the activities of other Aga Khan organizations.

Overseas, together with similar AKF rural programmes in India, Kenya, Mozambique and Tajikistan, AKRSP's ideas have spread far and influenced the design of rural development in nearly every continent. None of the programmes mentioned offer comprehensive analyses that attempt any attribution to AKRSP. An evaluation of the National Rural Support Programme, conducted in 1998, is largely positive in its assessment, but not quantitative (UNOPS/IFAD 1998). To the extent that all such schemes are successful, some part of their success may be attributable to the model pioneered by AKRSP.

The core principle behind these rural development programmes with a link to AKRSP – and back to Comilla – is that *organization of the poor* is the best means of alleviating poverty. In all of these programmes, broad-based homogenous membership was extended to all members, and decision-making occurred on the basis of consensus by each member, who came to realize that common economic and political interests are best served by working together. Supporting agencies, such as government and other development agencies, may provide technical and financial assistance, but should not infringe upon the sovereignty of the community organization. In other words, community participation ensured development for and by the people.

*Second, national environmental policy has changed,* largely through the interaction of AKRSP and the IUCN, and a new, participatory environmental policy process offers opportunities for AKRSP leaders to improve others' awareness of AKRSP's principles. The late 1980s were formative years for the National Conservation Strategy, the prime environmental planning framework for Pakistan. By that time, the concept of community empowerment in rural and urban areas had picked up momentum due to the success of the Orangi Pilot Project and AKRSP, and community participation was identified as the '11th' principle for National Conservation Strategy implementation. During one of the meetings of the strategy steering committee, Shoaib Sultan Khan made a detailed presentation on AKRSP. This was a turning point for both the strategy formulation process and the approaches that were being identified for tackling its various programme areas. Community participation now became the *first* principle and an ex-staff economist from AKRSP prepared a detailed paper on how this principle could be implemented, drawing practical lessons from AKRSP programmes. The consultative process undertaken by the National Conservation Strategy heavily replicated AKRSP's approaches, and all 14 core areas identified institutional development at the community level as a key approach for successful implementation of the 68 programmes that were identified under these core areas.

*Third, some influence of AKRSP can be seen in the Pakistan Poverty Reduction Strategy.* There are three national programmes that comprise a substantial part of the Pakistan Poverty Reduction Strategy. These are less closely modelled on the AKRSP, but draw on its basic concepts. The first is Khushhali Bank, which has been established as a public-private joint venture with initial capital of 1.7 billion rupees provided by 16 commercial banks. Its broad-based ownership structure is a reflection of its social awareness and support for poverty alleviation, largely modelled on AKRSP's micro-finance schemes and founded by Shoaib Sultan Khan. The second is the Khushhal Pakistan Programme, which is primarily designed as a social intervention aimed at generating economic activity through public works in the country. A sum of approximately 9 billion rupees has been released under the Khushhal Pakistan Programme (the Poverty Alleviation Programme). Schemes under the programme have been identified and selected at the district level through active community participation. The third is the Pakistan Poverty Alleviation Fund, funded by the World Bank and supported by the government of Pakistan, with the purpose of enhancing the availability of resources and services to the poor. Shoaib Sultan Khan himself conceptualized this programme and actively pursued policy-makers to bring the idea to fruition.

# CONCLUSIONS

The evidence of AKRSP's success shows that sustainable development can emerge even where there is poverty, poor environmental assets, high environmental hazards, sectarian divisions and weak government. A vision that is clear and compelling to all, strong leadership, good social organization and local institutional strengthening are key, as is government providing the space for change.

The main ingredients for success, in AKRSP's case, appear to be the following:

- *Social organization is crucial, otherwise the huge social and environmental challenges cannot be met.* Collective action is required; but the transaction costs will be excessive unless organization is good. Any community organization should be based on equitable principles (in this case, secular principles since every household is a member of the VO).
- *Through collective action, problems could be resolved.* The vast majority of people in the Northern Areas were poor (but not destitute or incapable), all faced environmental hazards, and all lived in a remote region. Inequity, which is difficult to fight, was less prevalent. In addition, a government vacuum made change possible. The influence of the Pakistan government in the remote Northern Areas was very weak, and AKRSP was the only outside body with any degree of authority.
- *Problems were visualized as having 'potential'* – for example, the 'livelihoods' approach (focusing on what people have and their potential) was more productive than a 'deprivations' approach. As in Comilla, AKRSP appreciated that there could be no substitute for community assessments of poverty and the state of the environment. AKRSP pioneered the use of participatory appraisals in Pakistan, enabling the (common) problem and potentials to be defined in local terms. 'Fur-and-feather' conservation was never the priority of AKRSP, and the natural resource management programme keenly focused on sustainable use (without explicitly using the term) – which led to an inclusive approach to the environment, encompassing improvements in the quality of life.
- *Transferring power from an influential few to the marginalized majority is possible only through effective leadership development.* Initially, the visionary leadership of Shoaib Sultan Khan inspired the idea of AKRSP and helped to raise both funds and community

interest. Later, investing in leadership at the village level (e.g. VO chairmen and village specialists) was critical for local vision and delivery. Investment in leadership has changed the political climate: communities now expect leadership and good performance from their political representatives, and many of these representatives are often people trained through AKRSP.

- *Clarity and consistency of goals and procedures helps all players to contribute.* Villagers understood the simple 'deal' on offer by AKRSP, while the government could understand the development vision. The rules of the game were not changed (even though AKRSP was frequently encouraged by individual donors' infatuation with novelty to change).

- *Donors focused on learning and providing support to catalyse broader activities.* Donors supported the vision and values of AKRSP, but were not able to interfere much. They were resigned to learning rather than leading. This unusual degree of international respect and interest was paramount in encouraging government to take the initiative seriously.

- *Environmental resources and infrastructure mattered to the poor.* When in a position to agree on priorities because social organization had been achieved, most villages consistently chose infrastructure and natural resource activities.

- *The economics have to be right.* If communities are to invest in their own environmental and developmental improvement, they need financial power. Joint VO savings, even at a very low level per household, enabled this to occur. Communities need to acquire business power through enterprise development based on sustainable natural resource management.

- *Communities will reinvent traditional common property norms.* When faced with the need to balance public and private interests, approaches such as establishing forest protection committees were spontaneously adopted.

- *Local institutional capacity-building is essential in order to realize sustainable development in the local context.* AKRSP started first with VOs and WOs, and then moved to clusters and watersheds in order to achieve ends that required transactions at higher levels. Such successes made it clear to government that national and provincial sustainable development strategies alone were inadequate – they needed to be articulated locally. Pakistan's current devolution process may have come about through international pressure to democratize; but AKRSP's VO approach (now being considered as a model for rural councils) may finally give rise to participatory democracy at the local level.

- *Sectarian divisions can only partly be overcome.* Sustainable outcomes arose by encouraging, for example, two VOs in one village, or 'indigenous' community-based organizations in others, to emerge with their own name, and with only loose associations with AKRSP. But such divisions cannot be fully overcome.

- *Sustainable development policy only takes off when there are concrete examples.* For example, when the National Conservation Strategy Committee learned of AKRSP, its rather conceptual discussions turned to the real local case of AKRSP. But AKRSP's policy interventions were 'invited' more than they were 'volunteered' – donors encouraged policy-makers to seek AKRSP out. In turn, the National Conservation Strategy concept changed in order to balance its ecosystem perspective with a community-first perspective. News of AKRSP spread to other policy arenas (notably, rural development); as a result, AKRSP was 'copied' by the government-organized national Rural Support Programme.

- *It is difficult to make progress on all policy fronts – alliances are needed.* IUCN-Pakistan was the environmental ally, seeing in AKRSP a real opportunity to test the emerging international paradigm of community environmental management. AKRSP saw in the IUCN a way of handling communities' need for environmental regimes, as well as a good adviser to help handle donors' environmental concerns.

- *Finally, integrating poverty reduction with environmental management takes time.* Good results began to be seen after ten years. But the real story has taken 20 years to develop.

## REFERENCES

Dani, A. A. (1988) *Peripheral Societies in a Nation State: A Comparative Analysis of Mediating Structures in Incorporation Processes and Development*, Ph.D. thesis, University of Pennsylvania, Pennsylvania

Government of Pakistan (2003) *Economic Survey 2001–2002*, Government of Pakistan Finance Division, Islamabad

Ridley, S. and Nelson, M. (2002) *The Next Ascent – An Evaluation of the Aga Khan Rural Support Program*, Pakistan, World Bank, Washington, D.C.

UNOPS/IFAD (1998) *National Rural Support Program – Program Evaluation Report*, UNOPS/IFAD

Virk, A. T., Sheikh, K. M. and Marwat, A. H. (2003). *NASSD Background Paper: Biodiversity*, IUCN, Pakistan, and Northern Areas Progamme, Gilgit

# 3

# The Bioplan: Decreasing Poverty in Manizales, Colombia, through Shared Environmental Management

*Luz Stella Velásquez Barrero*

## INTRODUCTION

Manizales is well known for pioneering the development of a broad-based Local Agenda 21 that involved many groups in its definition, implementation and monitoring from 1993–1998, and this chapter includes some details of its political underpinnings. However, as with other Colombian cities, during recent years, it has had to face the economic, social and territorial problems associated with the growth in urban and rural poverty, much of it linked to armed conflict. As a result of this conflict, the coffee-growing region where Manizales is located has received many in-migrants displaced from their homes by violence. This has accelerated the processes of unplanned urban growth, the invasion of public space, the deforestation of areas that have high ecological value and the destruction of the city's protective green belt. Many new settlements have developed illegally on unstable hillsides, creating high risks of localized landslides.

In order to improve the living standard of the poorest people and to mitigate the effects of the cultural and family disintegration experienced by people displaced by violence, the municipal government, universities, businesses, non-governmental organizations (NGOs) and community organizations have gathered economic, institutional, technical and community resources to develop the Local Environmental Action Plan, or Bioplan.[1] This chapter summarizes the experience with shared management for the development of various Bioplan programmes and projects: productive bio-communes, community bio-enterprises, urban eco-parks, community agri-nurseries and the Bank for Micro-credit.

## BACKGROUND

In high-income countries, the development of Local Agenda 21 programmes and projects depends to a great extent upon obtaining changes in patterns of consumption and waste generation among the population, promoting clean production and protecting areas with particular ecological importance. However, in lower-income nations, municipalities must give priority to local agendas that create solutions for reducing poverty because of the proportion of people facing problems stemming from unplanned urbanization; the invasion of public space; the very poor-quality housing in which many live with serious consequences for their health; a lack of green areas and recreational facilities; the loss of urban landscapes with particular cultural or aesthetic importance; the deterioration of the architectural heritage in central areas; and, finally, unemployment, violence and insecurity for the public at large.

Three-quarters of Colombia's population live in urban areas. The environmental effects of economic instability, social inequality and urban and rural violence are felt in most major cities. At present, there is a rapid growth of marginal populations in intermediate cities as a result of the armed conflict. According to the Permanent Committee for the Defence of Human Rights in Colombia (Comité Permanente para la Defensa de los Derechos Humanos), displacement in Colombia has affected more than 2.5 million persons during the past eight years; in 2002, the displaced population reached 523,000. As a result of armed conflict, the coffee region's ecological area, including Manizales, Armenia, Pereira, Cartago, Ibagué and smaller rural-urban[2] centres with about 4 million inhabitants, has become a region for receiving displaced persons, particularly from Chocó, Cauca and Nariño departments.

Colombian cities take in many migrants without being able to offer them appropriate conditions for meeting basic needs or even sufficient space for achieving any kind of environmental quality. The existence of undeveloped land having high ecological value and low market value, and the search for more profit by urban land 'developers' have led to the creation of settlement patterns and service networks that are increasingly difficult to operate and maintain, with higher infrastructure and user costs. Changes in land use generally affect the local environment adversely. Extending the city into ecological and natural preservation areas and high-value agricultural land has created disorderly growth and, in and around Manizales, the risk of landslides on deforested hillsides. Most marginal neighbourhoods around cities lie in areas with identifiable environmental problems: land, air and water pollution, soil erosion and overcrowding. These factors go hand in hand with the growing demand by local communities for infrastructure and services, especially for the collection and disposal of solid and liquid wastes from residential areas. These areas have become critical because they do not offer people any chance of improving their living standard.

## THE CONTEXT: URBAN AND RURAL POVERTY IN COLOMBIA AND MANIZALES

In Manizales, as in other intermediate-sized cities in Colombia, the rate of environmental and social deterioration has increased during the past five years. Between 1998 and 2002, the Colombian population living in poverty grew by 29 per cent and in 2003, 47 per cent of the population were below the poverty line (about 20 million people). Income inequality (the GINI coefficient) now stands at 0.57; the wealthiest 10 per cent of the population receive 77 times more income than the poorest 10 per cent. Average per capita income is dropping rapidly. Colombia's ranking in the Human Development Index has dropped significantly: in 1996 the country was at 49th place; in 1998 it dropped to 53rd place; and now it is at 68th place.

In Manizales, in 2002, 15.6 per cent of the population (53,264 inhabitants) were below the poverty line with 3 per cent (10,243 inhabitants) in extreme poverty.[3] Nationally, 13 per cent of the population are unemployed, with 28.3 per cent under-employed. A significant number of cities have unemployment rates of nearly 20 per cent; for Manizales, the rate is now 19.4 per cent, with 33.1 per cent under-employed. Within Colombia, urban poverty has grown significantly as a result of violence and the large internal population displacements. The coffee region has received 5 per cent of the displaced population (Bogotá received 23 per cent, the next two largest cities, 16 per cent), and between October 2000 and March 2003, Manizales-Pereira and Armenia received 38,643 persons. According to data of the Social Solidarity Network (Red de Solidaridad Social), Manizales received 1224 families (4579 persons) during that period.

There is also an alarming increase in violent deaths in Colombia: over 40,000 violent deaths were recorded in 2003 with a rapid rise in the number of young persons killed, especially males. The armed conflict was responsible for 6000 violent deaths in 2002. The paramilitary forces are believed to be the principal agents of displacement, followed by the guerrillas, the military forces and the urban militias.

One of the greatest environmental problems Colombian cities now face is the informal or illegal settlements. The poor who lack the resources to buy into the official market for land for housing settle spontaneously or purchase land from illegal developers.[4] Much of this land is in environmental preservation areas such as tropical forests, Andean forests, wetlands, riversides and steep slopes. Many sites are at risk from landslides (as can be seen in Manizales, Medellín and Pereira) or from periodic floods (as in Bogotá, Montería and most of the Atlantic coast). Equally, the settlements developed by the poorest displaced persons temporarily or permanently increase the vulnerability of these ecologically valuable areas that are unsuitable for building urban infrastructure. These areas lose their environmental value and become areas at high risk of landslides or floods. Even though in Colombia the municipal land-use plans (POTS) include environmental considerations in the definition of urban boundaries and zoning and growth limits for appropriate house building, public service provision and safety for human habitation, the conflicts generated by the pressure of developers and builders, along with conditions in the land market, have limited the application of the law. In Manizales, for example, there are inconsistencies between the proposed boundary for the area deemed suitable for development and the boundary marking out areas of physical risk and areas for conservation. There has been much unsuitable development during the past three years, so more areas are at risk of landslides. At present 1880 houses need to be relocated, affecting 7896 persons; 5000 houses also need to be rebuilt.

In Colombia, the coverage of public services and the infrastructure that these require have improved substantially during the past decade, according to the *Living Standard Survey* (*Encuesta sobre Calidad de Vida*) done by DANE (the national statistics department). Coverage in urban areas now reaches 94 per cent for electricity, 89 per cent for water, 71 per cent for sewage and 93 per cent for waste collection and street cleaning. Despite this, according to the Ministry of Health's Environmental Directorate, in Colombia during 2000, one out of ten inhabitants fell ill because of problems associated with the quality of water and one out of every two inhabitants was at risk of falling ill because of poor water. Among the 800 water treatment plants in Colombia, only 10 per cent meet international drinking water standards. In addition, 85 per cent of municipalities dispose of wastewater into surface watercourses. The consequences for the environment and human health are increasingly serious. In Manizales, public services coverage for domestic water, street lighting, solid waste collection and telephones is 98 per cent and is judged to be excellent. However, the sewage infrastructure has problems because of the city's mountainous topography, especially serving individuals living on slopes at risk of landslides and erosion.

Another urban problem that deserves particular attention in Colombia is the management of solid waste. At present, 94 per cent of urban solid wastes are collected; in Manizales, solid waste collection covers 100 per cent of the city. The quantity of waste has increased considerably during recent years: in 2000, production was 0.7 kilograms per inhabitant. Organic residues represent 54 per cent of the total. The recycling plant manages to process only 80 per cent of solid waste.

In Colombia, 47 per cent of solid waste is treated with systems controlled directly by municipalities. Most systems are open landfills, though there are some recovery plants and recycling plants. Landfill sites are generally located on municipal land. Close to these sites, illegal settlements develop to house people whose livelihood is based on recovering and selling materials separated from the waste. These settlements are of very poor quality, and the communities and the work that the inhabitants undertake create serious health problems. These include respiratory and skin diseases and intestinal parasites, as well as the risks created by infestations of rats, cockroaches and mosquitoes as these are major transmitters of the diseases that affect the population settling near the landfill.

The application of the environmental standards of Law 99 led to the first recycling plants being built. This has occurred mostly in large and intermediate cities. Manizales was a pioneer in setting up a recycling plant and its plant recycles mainly plastics, paper, glass, card and scrap iron. The management of organic waste continues to be a problem for the landfill's life cycle, despite research into converting organic waste to organic fertilizer (*Bioabono*) and building a small plant for this purpose. In Manizales, waste processing and recovery is undertaken by formal cooperatives who work as enterprises. This is the most striking facet of solid waste management in Colombia because positive social, economic and cultural experiences have made it possible to plan for marginal communities to participate in projects for waste management businesses.

# SUMMARY OF ENVIRONMENTAL POLICIES IN MANIZALES

The municipality of Manizales lies in the tropical zone, to the west of the Andes, Colombia's central mountain range. Rural areas account for 397.1 square kilometres of the municipality's territory; in 1997, these areas had a population of 57,057 inhabitants concentrated in seven administrative entities known as *corregimientos*. The urban area covers 42.9 square kilometres, with a population in 1997 of 358,194 inhabitants concentrated in 11 administrative entities called *comunas*. From the beginning of the 20th century, coffee production underpinned the development of the city and coffee is the municipality's main agricultural product. During the 1920s, Manizales was actually Colombia's second most important city economically and politically (after Bogotá, the capital), and many public investments were made. The city's importance within Colombia declined during the end of the 1930s when coffee prices fell on the international market, and transport and communications links between Bogotá and other cities improved. However, this historic importance helps to explain why two universities of national rank were established in Manizales. Today, the city has eight universities with some 25,000 students.

The urban area of Manizales lies in the very moist forest of the mountains and its topography of steep slopes, high rainfall (2200mm per annum) and 78 per cent humidity restrict urban expansion up the hillsides. It could be argued that Manizales has already surpassed the natural limits to its expansion and must seek alternative ways of managing growth – for instance, through increasing density in selected areas and through reusing existing buildings and lots. For this reason, proposals to define and allocate land use are inevitably linked to restrictions on development on the hillsides. The city has also suffered from various disasters, including earthquakes and landslides, and this helped to develop an official attitude and policy towards risk reduction.

Municipal autonomy has been important for Manizales and the outcome of the process of decentralization that has been taking place in Colombia since the mid 1980s has been very positive in increasing the roles of municipal authorities in social and economic development. The development of environmental policy in Manizales between 1990 and the present can be summarized in various stages (see Table 3.1).

In order to better understand how the Bioplan actually developed and the influence of politics, it is important to include a description of its development, along with outlines of the administrations of the last four

**Table 3.1** *Background and context of environmental policy and the Bioplan in Manizales*

| Year | Policy/programme | Colombia | Manizales | Project and participants |
|---|---|---|---|---|
| 1990 | National Network for Disaster Prevention and Relief | Technical and methodological debate about the city-environment relation, and disasters; creation of local committees for disaster prevention in Colombian municipalities | Process of shared research between the municipality and the universities to better understand the reality about disasters and their relation to Manizales's environmental impacts | Map of natural and human-induced risks in urban Manizales and definition of protected green areas, such as urban eco-parks, undertaken by local government, universities and disaster-prevention institutions |
| 1992 | Our own agenda: Colombia at the United Nations Earth Summit in Rio | A principal point of reference for drafting environmental management plans in Colombian cities; also for defining the principles of Colombian environmental policy | Promotion and creation of the Municipal Environmental Committee and the Manizales Urban Environmental Studies Group (GEA-UR) | Environmental agenda of Manizales Local government, universities, and local and community environmental committees |
| 1993 | National Programme for Urban Environmental Research | Drafting a conceptual and methodological model for writing urban environmental profiles | The profile in Manizales becomes the principal instrument for promoting research and management in the municipality | Municipal Environmental Policy Biomanizales: undertaken by local government, universities and community commitees |
| | Ministry of the Environment formed in Colombia | Definition of urban environmental policies, coordinated with SINA (National Environmental System – Law 99, 1993) | Beginning of programmes and projects coordinating local, regional and national institutional plans to comply with Law 99 | Local government, universities, regional development agencies (Corporación Regional Ambiental) |
| 1994 | National Programme for Urban Environmental Studies | Theoretical model for Sustainable Cities in Colombia: Bio-cities | Development of the basis for a management and research programme to draft the basic concept and methodology for the Bio-cities proposal | Proposal for environmental policy for the Manizales Municipal Development Plan: Bio-Manizales; developed by Urban Environmental Studies Group |

| Year | Initiative | Objectives | Results | Actors/Participants |
|---|---|---|---|---|
| 1995 | Development and decentralization plans for Manizales: the environmental dimension | Advances in formulating theoretical and methodological proposals to take on urban environmental problems; Support for local planning and citizen participation | Policies, programmes and projects for Bio-Manizales and the Olivares Bio-commune's environmental agenda are integrated | Manizales Calidad Siglo XXI Development Plan; Environmental policy for Manizales; involvement of local government, municipal council, territorial planning council, universities, business associations (Gremios), NGOs, Olivares Bio-commune community associations |
| | Corona Foundation Prize for architectural project to Olivares project in Manizales | Sustainable development proposal in sectors affected by urban poverty | Urban revitalization project, integrating projects and programmes for physical infrastructure, and social and environmental policy | Urban revitalization of Olivares Bio-commune; Municipal government, National University of Colombia, Corona Foundation |
| 1996 | Urban Environmental Policy for Colombia: Best Cities and Towns | Working for the priorities in local environmental management; model for sustainable cities | Local environmental action plan; Priority for developing programmes and projects in bio-tourism, bio-transport, recreational environmental education in eco-parks, and integral management of residues and recycling | Bio-Manizales Local Environmental Action Plan; Environmental agendas for communes (neighbourhoods); Involvement of local government, municipal council, territorial planning council, international cooperation agencies, private sector, industry associations (Gremios), merchants, NGOs, community enterprises, Olivares Bio-commune community associations |
| 1997 | Law for Territorial Order (Ordenamiento Territorial), Law 388/97 | Integration of the environmental dimension as the organizing axis for territorial order plans; Proposal for defining environmental regions or eco-regions | Environmental proposals on use of land, green protective areas and recreational public spaces; reserves for agricultural production; natural reserves; urban architectural heritage; and citizen participation in environmental concerns | Urban and urban-rural Bio-Manizales: Territorial Order Plan Involvement of local government, municipal council, territorial planning council, international cooperation agencies, private sector, industry association, universities, business associations (Gremios), merchants, NGOs, community businesses, community associations, coffee associations |

Table 3.1 Continued

| Year | Policy/programme | Colombia | Manizales | Project and participants |
|---|---|---|---|---|
| 1998–1999 | Urban management for sustainable cities in Latin America | Proposals for improving local urban management and defining instruments for permanent evaluation of policies and programmes of municipal development plans | Building urban sustainability indicators for the municipality | Design of the Information System for Sustainable Development involving Economic Commission for Latin America, national university, local universities |
| 2000–2003 | Environmental policy in the National Development Plan: A Change for Building Peace | Constructing a development model so that sustainable economic development and the search for peace are the plan's guiding principles | A shared process of research, management and evaluation for the Bio-Manizales plan aimed at decreasing urban and rural inequality and poverty | Manizales Ciudad Viva (Manizales: A Living City) development plan; Bio-Manizales development plan; local environmental action plans for sustainable development for neighbourhoods (comunas) and rural neighbourhoods (corregimientos); inter-university cooperation agreement for sustainable development of the Bio-Manizales plan; setting up the Observatories System for Sustainable Development in Manizales; consolidation of the community bio-enterprises<br><br>Multiple local, national and international actors, and emphasis on community participation |

,mayors. These show significant variations between these administrations in complying with and developing Bioplan programmes. During each period there was a different emphasis regarding projects and programmes.

The administration of Victoria E. Osorio (1990–1992) was significant for the social welfare of the poorest groups. There were social and environmental improvements, especially in disaster prevention and assistance. Policies, projects and programmes to improve housing and public space, and physical security for such spaces, were also important during this period. People living in high-risk hillside locations were resettled in other areas of the city. These projects were developed in association with the engineering and architecture schools at Universidad Nacional and the school for social work at Universidad de Caldas. In the San Cayetano, El Paraíso and Yarumales neighbourhoods, 2320 homes were built for very marginal inhabitants. At the end of the administration there were 63 per cent fewer houses located in high-risk areas. In areas with high physical vulnerability and unstable ground conditions, the municipality purchased land to hold as green protected areas. A smaller number of landslides occurred and more areas were reforested. Important urban ecosystems also entered a recovery phase. This was the beginning of effective environmental policies in the city's planning. Green protected areas were turned into eco-parks, with educational programmes and recreation.

In 1990 the Municipal Environmental Committee was established, in which the universities and the organizations with responsibility for preventing disasters were included. This committee was limited to academic and technical matters and thus did not ensure the participation of the municipal government and the public. Despite this, the committee was the main promoter of conservation for the steep hill areas and reserves. It proposed that these should be made into protected green areas and eco-parks to serve three purposes: to prevent disasters; to protect areas with valuable ecological functions; and to increase the amount of open space within the city. The committee was dissolved as a result of political and administrative changes; but, as noted earlier, between 1990 and 1992, many low-income households were relocated from the sites at high risk from landslides, the number of dwellings located in high-risk zones was reduced and a total of 360 ha had been reforested as protected green areas.

Eco-parks combine provision for recreation, environmental education and conservation, while also keeping buildings off of sites that are prone to landslides or other hazards. During this period, 168 ha of protected green areas were incorporated within the municipality, corresponding to

9 per cent of its total area. In addition, the municipality established a new city boundary which included environmental conservation as an alternative means of disaster prevention and provided tax incentives for the owners of these areas. For the owners of dwellings in high-risk areas, there were land-exchange schemes so that they could resettle on safer sites, with the high-risk areas recovered for use as forest. Also during this period, the Office for Preventing and Dealing with Disasters was created within the municipality, and a policy was formulated to integrate the themes of the city's physical vulnerability and its physical suitability for urban expansion.

Under Mayor Germán Cardona (June 1992 to December 1994), there was a significant period of economic growth. Fiscal restraint led to a 64 per cent real increase in the municipality's income and a 139 per cent increase in capital investment. Investment in 1994 reached 59.9 per cent of the budget; in addition, public-private companies were set up for water, green site management, road infrastructure and transport.

During 1992 to 1993, the Colombian government defined urban environmental policies connected to an inter-institutional process under the leadership of the Ministry of the Environment (Ministerio del Medio Ambiente). Law 99 of 1993 (Article 65) became the legal basis for joint work between local authorities, researchers and officials of the National Environmental System (SINA). As a result, programmes and projects were developed, coordinating national, regional and local efforts to comply with Local Agenda 21.

In 1994, the Manizales Urban Environmental Studies Group (GEA-UR) created the basis for a research programme with concepts and a methodology for creating BIOCITIES sponsored by COLCIENCIAS, and the group drafted the environmental profile for Manizales as a case study. This research led to the theory and methodology needed for tackling urban environmental problems in Manizales, supporting local planning and encouraging citizen participation. This pilot project included community organizations; as a result, the environmental management proposal for Biocomuna Olivares (one of Manizales's poorest districts) was drafted.[5]

In 1995, the development plan 'Manizales 21st-century Quality' ('Plan de Desarrollo Manizales Calidad Siglo XXI') brought together the Biomanizales policies, programmes and projects with the Olivares environmental agenda. During this year, the Fundación Corona awarded its prize for architectural research to the Biocomuna Olivares project, which was part of the Manizales urban regeneration programme. The Manizales development plan's environmental policies then became a benchmark for urban environmental planning in many

Colombian cities. Even so, the plan met with opposition in the city council because it restricted the 'developers'. The mayor and the universities worked hard to overcome such opposition and to achieve broad agreement among all parties.

The years 1993 to 1995 were a significant period in Manizales with regard to economic growth and to the municipality's fiscal performance and the growth of its revenues and capital investments in real terms. The process of administrative and fiscal decentralization within Colombia at that time also obliged municipalities to transform public enterprises into mixed ownership entities which took over the administration of parks and green areas (Re-greening Manizales), the management of the water supply (Waters of Manizales – Pure Water), the management of solid wastes (Green City) and the sanitation services (Sanitation Enterprise of Manizales).

This was also an important period in the consolidation of environmental management in Manizales because of the municipality's support for the university's initiative to develop the urban environmental profile of Manizales. The profile provided the technical basis for management and allowed the formation of an inter-institutional work team to carry out the research. Programmes and projects of importance to community environmental education were formulated and the first community environmental committees were set up. These were followed by the first community environmental agenda, with environmental priorities for Manizales.

For the first time, Manizales had a budget explicitly allocated to environmental policy in which a large part of the municipality's financial surplus was invested. The budget equalled 21 per cent of the total municipal investment budget, of which 15 per cent went to environmental education programmes, community training and tax incentives for those protecting areas of ecological importance to the city, while the remaining 6 per cent was used to purchase land for use in environmental protection and conservation. However, unusually heavy rain resulted in landslides in areas that had not previously been considered high risk. At least 226 families lost their houses and lives were lost. As a result, the municipality had to spend much of the budget it had set aside for environmental policy on dealing with this emergency, on constructing new infrastructure works and on preparing land upon which the displaced population was to be resettled.

Under Mayor Mauricio Arias (1995–1998), the Bioplan became part of the sustainable development concept with the integration of economic, social, environmental and disaster-prevention/land-use management dimensions. During this period, the municipality took on the

Biomanizales project. The municipality and the universities worked together to solve the problems of Manizales, and this became a framework for broader cooperation and participation, which later survived changes in administrations.

In 1996 the municipal environmental agenda and the local environmental action plan were drafted to meet the needs of the municipality and its local environmental area. The agenda for 1997 to 2000 included bio-tourism, bio-transport, environmental recreational education in eco-parks, and integral management of waste and recycling. By this point, the process was operating well, with growing institutional and public participation. However, funds for environmental policies decreased significantly and this hampered ongoing research and management. Because of this, a follow-up system was instituted for Bioplan programmes and projects. With the support of the Latin American Social and Economic Commission, the Monitoring and Evaluation Project for Sustainable Development in Manizales came into being.[6]

In 1997, Bioplan became part of the Manizales Land-use Plan, with specific environmental proposals regarding the urban boundary; land use; protective green areas and public spaces for recreation; reserves for agricultural production and food security; natural reserves; and conservation for architectural heritage, with emphasis on regenerating the historic city centre. At the time, there were difficulties with including the universities and the commune's environmental committees in the plan's drafting process because of the exclusionary attitude of the private consultants whom the municipal government had hired to draft the document. However, after the Territorial Council of the National Planning Department (Consejo Territorial de Planeación) – in which civil society is represented – rejected the proposed plan, the consultants were obliged to engage in a process of participation and agreement. One of the most striking facets of this process was the impromptu programme for training in environmental issues offered to the consultants by community associations and local universities. During 1998 and 1999, universities and community associations continued with programmes and projects, without the support of the municipal government. Bioplan had been included in the development plan, but no funds were allocated to it.

During this period, 1995–1998, a start was made to develop urban sustainability indicators for the municipality, and the universities organized environmental training and education for the continuation of Bioplan. International relations were also important: St Nazaire became a sister city; in addition, many agreements on urban, environmental, education and health issues were signed. These included environmental management with Curitiba; urban management with Chile, Argentina, Brazil, Peru, and Trinidad and Tobago; the Caribbean cities Gemitis Project for disaster prevention; and the strategic urban development centre for Iberian America. Biomanizales, as laid out in Bioplan (1997–2000) Local Agenda 21, was integrated within international cooperation through the Latin American Network of Urban Environmental Studies and the International Council for Local Environmental Initiatives (ICLEI). Bioplan also began presenting performance indicators.

Under Mayor Jorge Rojas (1998–2000), Bioplan continued as an integral part of municipal environmental policy. But only 4.7 per cent of the municipal budget was allocated to it and only 2.3 per cent was spent. There was less investment in infrastructure for disaster prevention and assistance, and in the environmental education required for managing the municipality's green protected areas and eco-parks. Technical decisions on territorial planning and management became the preserve of local officials. The local planning authority's technocratic outlook made legal compliance the main issue, to the detriment of the previous emphasis on participation in planning processes. The community was thus disconcerted and felt distanced from government institutions; there was conflict, isolation and a split between civil society and local government.

In 1999, there was a political crisis in the municipality. Legal and political investigations led to a recall of the mayor, when it was proven that he used part of the municipality's financial resources in his private business affairs. During this time, all investment programmes and projects were suspended. But the political crisis did not halt the development of Bioplan's programmes and projects; they proceeded under the leadership of community associations in bio-communes and with the coordination and permanent support that the universities provided.

Germán Cardona was re-elected in 2000. During his administration, the Bioplan became the principal tool of the municipality's environmental policy, with the private sector beginning to participate in the management, and with an agreement between the local authorities and the city's eight universities to create an integrated management structure. Concrete projects were begun, including eco-parks, public space and the redevelopment of the historic centre. In Biocomuna Olivares, the physical infrastructure for public services was developed further, in association with different community associations and environmental services companies. One of the period's main achievements was the initiation of the sustainable development observatories.

Thus, between 2000 and 2003, Bioplan again became a real part of the Municipal Development Plan, with programmes, projects and a budget. Economic, social and environmental meta-indicators for Bioplan and the sustainable development observatories were set up in each comuna. In addition, permanent training for community leaders, communal action committees (*acción comunal*), local administrative committees (*juntas administradoras locales*) and ecological groups commenced; in turn, these leaders organized 'education days' in the observatories in their communes and neighbourhoods. Despite the fact that during this period there was investment in infrastructure and recreation, the indicators for inequality and poverty worsened significantly, and it became essential that more decisive encouragement should be provided to community enterprises if rural and urban poverty was to be reduced in Manizales.

Today, Bioplan is developing a planning model that integrates research, management and evaluation, coordinated with community participation. Research centres are developing detailed environmental profiles for different territorial units, the communes and rural neighbourhoods. The profiles have made it possible to identify the main active factors in the local urban dynamic and to characterize the essential features of its complexity. Identifying problems and potentials makes it possible to define actions and set priorities, seeking solutions that take into account the particular local situations, under the leadership of the universities. Management of programmes and projects is shared between the municipality, institutions, NGOs and community organizations, although the actual organization of each case depends upon what is most suitable. Evaluation involves an ongoing process of gaining knowledge through using indicators related to the environment, economy, society and Bioplan programme investment and management; this is done through observatories and with university and citizen participation (see Diagram 3.1).

## THE BIOPLAN IN ACTION

In order to provide a concrete framework for the actions of Bioplan Local Agenda 21, action plans were implemented in the 11 urban communes and 7 rural neighbourhoods that make up Manizales. The action plans sought to decrease poverty in the city and to reduce the social and territorial segregation of people who were displaced by violence. Because many people in Manizales are now vulnerable and poor, the general purposes of the Bioplan were defined as follows:

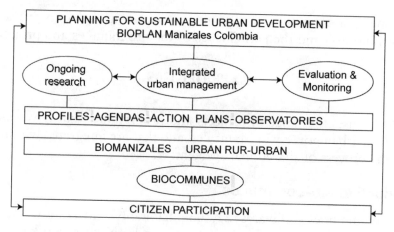

**Diagram 3.1** *The Bioplan*

- *Healthy environment versus pollution*: renovate urban infrastructure in marginal or peripheral areas and recuperate public services networks, transportation systems and systems for the integrated management of solid waste and recycling.
- *Safe environment versus natural risks*: decrease people's vulnerability to all types of disasters in marginal areas. Improve the quality and safety of houses, public spaces and recreational facilities. Use building techniques appropriate to the topography and optimize urban design.
- *Environmental regeneration of the marginal central area versus urban renovation and relocation*: recuperate degraded areas and preserve the urban and architectural heritage in the city centre without displacing the marginal population. Maintain the inhabitants' identity and sense of belonging in their environment.
- *Territorial interaction versus social and spatial segregation*: promote equality in municipal investment in land in order to benefit the poorest population. Incorporate priority actions for environmental management in marginal areas. Coordinate community efforts to make good use of the potential for environmental action in the communes where the poorest people live.
- *Information for all versus selective information*: promote social awareness through education, information and knowledge about local conditions for all citizens. Encourage participation by environmental and community organizations, as well as by NGOs, in observatories in communes and neighbourhoods.
- *Participatory planning versus technocratic planning*: promote community participation by leaders, commune inhabitants and institu-

tional representatives in planning processes in order to guarantee consultation and the permanence of the programmes and projects.

# EXPERIENCES

Table 3.2 lists the range of projects and programmes that have sought to reduce urban poverty in Manizales, and that are integrated within the ongoing process of shared management.

## Productive bio-communes

Two communities – Olivares (21,203 inhabitants) and Tesorito (32,720 inhabitants) – are developing programmes and projects to work together to solve common problems (e.g. the increase in poverty from rising unemployment; reception of people displaced by violence; deteriorating infrastructure and public spaces; increased risk of landslides; and pollution of rivers). As a priority, they are developing strategies for integrating displaced persons socially and economically. Based on the strategy of Biocomuna Olivares, they have created productive bio-communes, studied the area's environmental potential to create local environmental action plans and set up the following projects: *bosque popular* (popular wood/small forest) and Olivares eco-parks, sustainable development observatories, water parks and community nurseries.

## Community bio-enterprises

The coffee region's Recyclers' Association has provided 'third-way' business advice (i.e. socio-entrepreneurial) to many community organizations in managing and treating solid waste; recycling and processing solid waste is strongly supported by the work of community associations and cooperative groups organized as enterprises. In Manizales, Bio-servicos and Ciudad Verde (Green City) are cooperatives that provide environmental services. At present, 326 families work in these cooperatives, which undertake recycling, and these are the co-owners of the recycling plants. In Colombia, government experience with solid waste management by building solid waste treatment plants has been unsuccessful. For example, in the city of Villamaría, Caldas, technical problems in the plant led to it being shut down; in Montenegro, Quindío, higher than anticipated maintenance costs made the plan uneconomical. In Manizales, the recycling plant had to be temporarily closed because it was unprofitable; reopening required the joint efforts of the municipality, the Chamber of Commerce and the Regional

Table 3.2 The Bioplan in action; decreasing poverty in Manizales, 1995–2003

| Project | Goal | Number and mode of employment | Participants and leaders | Support mode |
|---|---|---|---|---|
| Productive bio-communes | Integrate economic, environmental and social sustainability to create jobs and decrease poverty<br>Green infrastructure built | Diverse | Universities, municipality, environmental authority, IDEA-Manizales, community associations of Olivares and Tesorito bio-communes | Community, technical, administrative, political, associative through business and trade organizations (gremial, empresarial)<br>Educational, economic, infrastructure, governmental |
| Community bio-enterprises | Consolidate community enterprises with associative labour to provide environmental services<br>Integrated management of residues and recycling | 140 associates; 86 temporary staff; 7 technical assistants | Municipal waste collection company (Empresa Municipal de Aseo – EMAS), municipality, Eje Cafetero (Coffee Region) Regional Recyclers' Association, Institute for Environmental Studies (Instituto de Estudios Ambientales – IDEA), Fundación Social, Bioservicios Ciudad Verde | Community, technical and economic through business and trade associations |
| Urban eco-parks | Convert reserves and the 'urban jungle' into green protective areas<br>Recreational environmental education<br>Food security<br>Job creation | 15 environmental educators; 42 guides for bio-tourism; 25 maintenance persons; 3 technicians; 4 administrative persons | Foundations, NGOs, universities, Fundación Luker, IDEA, Confamiliares, Comité de Cafeteros | Community, technical, economic, business, educational, infrastructure, governmental |
| Community agricultural nurseries | Jobs for women-headed households<br>Food security | 89 women head of households; 3 environmental educators | Municipal environment authorities, Olivares Bio-commune environmental committee, IDEA, ICLEI, ZERI, Agrovivero Territorio Verde de Paz, Universidad de Manizales | Community, educational, economic, infrastructure, governmental |

61

## Table 3.2 Continued

| Project | Goal | Number and mode of employment | Participants and leaders | Support mode |
|---|---|---|---|---|
| Neighbourhood bio-markets | Producing, promoting and marketing agricultural products on a small scale<br>Food security<br>Promoting healthy consumption | Small farmers and merchants; salespersons; 92 families | Community environmental committees, growers' co-operatives, IDEA, Universidad de Manizales, Municipal co-operative development authorities, co-ops | Community, economic, governmental |
| Car washes | Temporary jobs for displaced persons<br>Decrease impact of carwashes | 180 temporary jobs | Social Solidarity Network, IDEA, Universidad de Caldas, Universidad Luis Amigó, municipality, municipal community development authorities | Educational, governmental |
| Sustainable development observatories | Production of the municipality's economic, social and environmental information<br>Permanent evaluation of the municipal development plan<br>Climate monitoring<br>Citizen participation<br>Diverse | Universities, support institutions supplying information, local administrative boards, communal action boards, community leaders, regional environmental authority, Ministry of the Environment, IDEA, municipality | | Community, technical, scientific, administrative, political, associative, trade and industry related, educational, economic, infrastructure, governmental |
| Micro-credit Bank CREER | Support through credit for community bio-enterprises<br>Promotion of family bio-enterprises | 3 direct jobs | Universities, municipality, Infimanizales, IDEA, Universidad Autónoma | Governmental, business, educational |

Recyclers' Association, part of the national association. ANR is now recycling only 15 per cent of waste. Even so, in business and community terms, this is one of Manizales's most important social and environmental investments. Recuperating the plant required efforts by the public and private sectors, by academics in the community organization sector and by a number of international environmental organizations. The plant now serves as an adviser for other mayors and municipalities, helping to establish recyclers' associations, coordinating a programme to promote source separation for wastes and working in public education. Because the dimension of solidarity is present in such organizations, members have access to health, education and housing benefits. In Centros de Atención Integral al Reciclador (Centres for Integral Services for Recyclers, or CAIR), the organization has funds for education, solidarity (i.e. emergencies) and rotating working capital. These enterprises are examples of environmental service providers that also offer good working conditions for recyclers; this improves their social and economic status and ends the social exclusion that they would suffer if they were informal waste-pickers on landfill dumps.

The greatest operational difficulties for Bioservicios and Ciudad Verde centre on competition for paper, plastic and glass with traditional waste merchants who purchase directly from non-associated recyclers, at lower prices. With the support of the social solidarity network (Red de Solidaridad Social), these people are being encouraged to join the various regional enterprises; this also diversifies the association's services. A database is in place for recycling sites for every product, making it possible to create targeted marketing strategies. Recyclers for paper, card, glass and plastic also gain bargaining power if they work together.

## Urban eco-parks and protective/productive forests

In 1989, in an effort to protect the physical vulnerability of Manizales's steep hillsides, most slopes within the city were converted into protected green areas. They have ecological value because of their diverse native flora and fauna, thus harbouring biological diversity; they also contribute to the cityscape. But local government fell into conflicts when it tried to preserve these areas because they are constantly being invaded by low-income groups; today their use for habitation or cultivation is restricted.

In 1995, the Manizales Development Plan made these slopes part of the urban environmental plan. Difficulties in defining exactly what uses were allowed, and where, stemmed from a lack of precision in defining

*Source:* Jorge Hernán Arango

**Figure 3.1** *Olivares bio-commune: Production of edible fungi, medicinal plants and compost*

property lines, as well as restrictions on extending any service networks to these areas. Paradoxically, between 1995 and 1996, more native forests and planted trees were destroyed in the city, the urban landscape deteriorated further and building and development considered inappropriate in terms of the topographical and ecological implications were constructed. In 1996, these areas became part of Bioplan as specially managed green areas with recreational potential, and were coordinated with the tourism and recreational environmental education programmes in eco-parks. In order to guarantee sustainability, Bioplan devised projects for alternate uses that had social and economic value, as opposed to merely placing restrictions to promote their conservation. A development plan for rural Manizales was also drafted, which included similar rural areas for special management.

In 1997, Law 388 required municipalities to include environmental considerations in their territorial development plans. This included working to manage and conserve any areas of environmental interest in the municipality, or those shared with neighbouring units. These considerations are, of course, a key basis for sustainable development in

*Source:* Jorge Hernán Arango

**Figure 3.2** *The recycling plant, Manizales*

cities and the countryside. Conceived as urban eco-parks, rural micro-basins, protective green areas and tropical forest relicts, they are the remaining strategic ecosystem and are important for preserving biodiversity. Because they are distributed in a balanced way and have great value as landscape, these areas of environmental interest are integral parts of Manizales's green protective/productive structure.

The areas were included in the city's development plan in 1989 and in just a decade, their total area increased by 56 per cent (or 6399 ha). Although Manizales is in possession of this important environmental potential, managing it is proving difficult. Because of this, it is important to promote alternative economic and social uses for sustainable development. Conflicts affecting these areas proceed mainly from incompatible use, ecosystem fragility, pressure from housing and cultivation, and the lack of continuity in environmental education programmes. Improving and regenerating these areas depends upon understanding the biological dimensions and controlling human activities. This is why we have proposed and created alternative programmes allowing public use and private gain in line with conservation and taking into account the temporary and permanent dwellers of Manizales.

## Observatories for sustainable development

In Colombia, there are practical difficulties involved in coordinating local government, other local institutions and citizens to work together under the idea of integrated management, as required by sustainable development. We also know that the technical experts who write plans have not been successful in 'bringing in' the community in a truly active way. Thus, municipalities require information and monitoring systems that citizens can readily understand, and these must be essential components of sustainable development, locally. If citizens can participate in processing the information and in assessing the results, they will be encouraged to participate in programmes and projects to improve the quality of their street, neighbourhood, commune, city or municipality.

How can a citizen participate? He or she can become part of the planning process for local agendas stemming from Agenda 21 and local environmental plans, and can participate in the work of the observatories. These are the principal instruments for participation. The observatories established in Manizales demonstrate that shared management and citizen participation are possible. The observatories are part of the monitoring system that was proposed to support local urban management. Using a considerable range of environmental, social and economic indicators (see Velásquez, 1998, for more details), citizens can continuously evaluate the performance of all activities laid out in the Manizales's development plan, and they can participate in follow-up and work in the programmes and projects.

In practice, setting up the observatories has been the joint effort of the local authorities, universities, business groups, institutions, NGOs and community organizations. They have provided information and technical and economic support to many projects in Manizales. One of the greatest contributions to this process has been the transmission of scientific and technical information, produced by universities and research centres, about the city to the wider population. This has occurred through the media in forms that are readily understood. The municipal sustainable development 'traffic signals' meet this need. A great range of data is collected on social conditions, the economy and the environment, and these form the basis for monitoring conditions and trends. Most are available for each of the territorial units for the city (the 11 *comunas*) and for the wider municipality. Based on this data, ten composite indicators have been developed (see Table 3.3). For each of these, scores have been derived which fall into one of three categories:

1  red, which indicates the existence of problems;
2  yellow, which gives a warning of possible problems;
3  green, which indicates good quality.

As Table 3.3 indicates, this allows a visual representation of where environmental problems are concentrated in terms of each sector and area within the city.

In order to improve management skills for the observatories, universities offer a number of training programmes for community and trade associations, as well as for institutions.

## The CREER (micro-credit) programme

This programme was created in Manizales in response to growing levels of poverty, including rising unemployment and under-employment. Other factors were the high interest rates charged by commercial banks and the onerous loan conditions from private borrowing. CREER finances the initiatives of citizens and of certain inter-institutional projects which require this level of funding. This is an alliance between the public and private sectors to provide resources in the technical, financial consulting and business education areas to people who have small-scale enterprises that are of no interest to high street banks and who, in any case, are unable to meet the normal conditions for loans. Certainly, the cornerstone of a banking system is trust. One could argue, however, that the traditional banking system was built on the basis of mutual mistrust. But micro-credit helps each person to reach his or her maximum potential.

Loans in the traditional banking system are based on guarantees and the backing of a joint debtor. For their part, building societies charge high interest rates for delays in payment. By contrast, the basic idea for CREER is to have faith in the user's human potential as he or she struggles to develop the small family business, micro-business or cooperative (*economía solidaria*). Thus, CREER attaches far more importance to strengthening human capital compared to financial capital.

The task of motivating people depends upon solidarity and social cohesion; it is based on economic sustainability and methodological rigour that ensure the efficiency and duration of projects. This is not a subsidy programme but a business development project to decrease informal employment and support family businesses and associative community businesses, providing a legal framework for people's economic activities. Business advice is offered, providing methodologies at workplaces.

**Table 3.3** *Environmental traffic lights: How each comuna scored for composite indicator of environmental quality*

| Composite indicators | The different comunas into which Manizales is divided | | | | | | | | | | |
|---|---|---|---|---|---|---|---|---|---|---|---|
| | 1 | 2 | 3 | 4 | 5 | 6 | 7 | 8 | 9 | 10 | 11 |
| Social well-being (including indicators of health, education, social security and income) | G | R | Y | Y | R | Y | Y | G | Y | Y | Y |
| Quality and accessibility of public services (based on provision for piped water, sanitation, electricity, gas, public telephones) | G | Y | G | G | Y | G | G | G | G | Y | G |
| Housing quality (based on quality of construction, density and provision of community services) | G | R | Y | G | Y | Y | Y | G | Y | Y | Y |
| Healthy environment (based on air and water quality and extent of noise and pollution) | G | Y | G | G | Y | Y | Y | G | G | Y | G |
| Possibility of enjoying public space (based on, among other things, access to parks and ecological reserves) | G | R | R | Y | R | Y | G | G | Y | Y | Y |
| Aesthetic and symbolic value of landscape (related to richness and variety of natural and built environment) | G | R | Y | Y | Y | Y | Y | Y | Y | Y | Y |
| Physical security of the area (based on level of risk from earthquakes, eruptions, landslides and floods) | Y | R | Y | Y | R | Y | Y | Y | Y | Y | Y |
| Citizen security (based on frequency of assaults, murders, traffic accidents and vandalism of public space) | Y | R | Y | Y | Y | Y | Y | Y | Y | Y | Y |
| Quality and efficiency of transport | G | Y | Y | Y | Y | Y | Y | Y | Y | Y | Y |
| Citizen participation in environmental issues (related to extent of participation in different projects and programmes) | R | G | Y | G | G | Y | G | G | Y | Y | R |
| Summary | Y | R | Y | Y | Y | Y | Y | Y | Y | Y | Y |
| *Score | 4912 | 2900 | 4241 | 5035 | 4095 | 4781 | 4834 | 5433 | 4348 | 4177 | 4290 |

*Notes:* R: red, which indicates problems; Y: yellow, which gives a warning of possible problems; G: green, which indicates good quality.

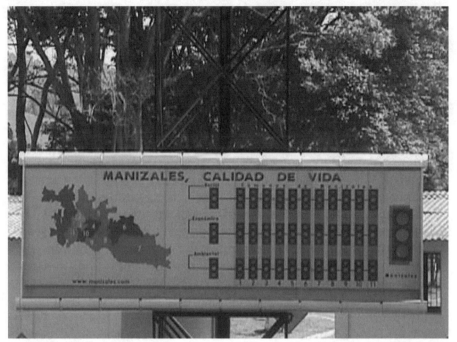

Source: Luz Stella Velàsquez

**Figure 3.3** *The notice board in the popular Forest El Prado showing the 'traffic light' indicators of environmental quality*

Credit can be provided to an individual or a group on a personal basis (*garantía individual solidaria*) for working capital or for agreed asset purchases, or to a legally constituted entity (*garantía asociativa solidaria*) for an agreed activity. This programme is intended to develop the principal business values of trust and solidarity and to develop coordination in the production chain among economic sub-sectors. The programme benefits small producers, artisans, craftsmen and women, as well as traders and service providers.

The United Nations Development Programme (UNDP) and private and public actors are jointly responsible for CREER. In Manizales, Infimanizales, the university (for training) and private entities[7] have joined the project. The Bank for Micro-credit came into being in February 2002 and loaned approximately UK£200,000 in its first year. By 2004, it is expected to have processed 4300 micro-credits and to have generated 8640 new jobs.

# CONCLUSIONS

- The environmental problems associated with poverty require alternatives – for example, a process of shared management and adopting sustainable practices (as a new culture with high value), in a partnership that includes government, academia, business and the community, with a view to reducing the urban and rural-urban poverty now affecting Colombian cities.

- The National Environmental System (SINA), created in 1993, has managed to integrate various legal, political and administrative mechanisms and instruments in order to institutionalize management and promote environmental participation in Colombia. Today, there are many experiences in Colombia that have gone beyond traditional planning practices under the concept of shared management by sustainable development where, in both cities and rural areas, the poorest segments of the population are hard pressed to find opportunities for improving their living standard in the immediate future.

- Manizales's Bioplan has managed to bring together local government, universities, institutions, NGOs and citizens in the shared environmental management of programmes and projects, generating alternatives that can improve the living standard of the lowest-income people. This population group has increased during the past three years as a consequence of internal migration in the coffee-growing region because coffee is experiencing an economic crisis and because there are more displaced persons in rural areas and small towns as a result of the various types of violence.

- Bioplan has managed to consolidate its cooperative ventures, which have improved the livelihoods of the poorest groups by providing the right direction for social policy and investment. The city's efforts to improve living standards for these groups must be recognized.

- In Manizales, increased migration to fragile ecosystems and the continual movement of persons displaced by violence have brought great pressure to bear on public resources and services; there is now a greater number of marginal persons. Environmental degradation affects the poor directly, with poor public hygiene, and physical and mental hardship. A qualitative improvement in local government has translated into greater political awareness of the environmental problems associated with poverty in the city, with priority given to building physical infrastructure and teaching small-scale entrepreneurship to people living in marginal settlements.

- Bioplan has implemented programmes for local capacity-building in planning and management, geared to improving the quality of the environment. Citizen participation in agreeing Bioplan has now progressed to permanent training in communities and community-based organizations, with the support of local government, institutions, the private sector and the universities, to identify environmental problems and the opportunities to overcome them.

## ENDNOTES

1  Bioplan is the local environmental action plan of Manizales Municipality, part of Agenda 21. Bioplan is made up of 11 communal environmental agendas (communes are the political and administrative units of the municipality's urban area) and seven village environmental agendas (villages are small human settlements in the rural area).

2  Rural-urban areas are transitional areas, part rural and part urban, which share social, economic and cultural conditions. They are strategic planning zones in the coffee-growing region.

3  Observatorio para el Desarrollo Sostenible del Municipio de Manizales (May 2003).

4  '*Urbanizadores piratas*' is the term used in Colombia for individuals who illegally sell plots of land that do not meet the requirements for development or are not suitable for building – and there is no guarantee that any infrastructure will be provided (i.e. roads, piped water, sewers or electricity lines). '*Pirate*' areas include those at risk of flooding or landslide. These illegal developments are evident in large cities where surveillance of, and control over, planning processes is more difficult. Informal settlements are those where titles for plots are not in order, the city's building code has not been properly applied and different forms of urban segregation exist.

5  For more details, see Velásquez (1999).

6  For more details, see Velásquez (1998).

7  For instance, DESCAFECOL, PROGEL, SUPER de Alimentos, RIDUCO and PASSICOL.

## REFERENCES

ANR (Asociación Nacional de Recicladores) (2001) *Documento para el Concurso Premio Nacional de Paz*

Asociación Regional de Recicladores del Eje Cafetero (2002) *Bioservicios y Ciudad Verde*, Manizales

Consejo Nacional de Planeación (1999) *La Casa de la Diversidad. Una sociedad plural interpela el plan Cambio par Construir la paz*, Tercer Mundo Editores, Bogotá

Departamento Nacional de Planeación Presidencia de la República. Plan Nacional de Desarrollo 1994–1998, El Salto Social, tomos 1 y 2

Departamento Nacional de Planeación Presidencia de la República. Plan Nacional de Desarrollo 1998–2002, Cambio para construir la paz, tomos 1 y 2

El Reciclador Organo informativo de la Asociación Nacional de Recicladores, Edición, Asociación para la Defensa del Reciclador

IDEA Universidad Nacional de Colombia Sede Manizales, Municipio de Manizales *Plan Sectorial Ambiental del Biomanizales. Bioplan 1999–2000*

IDEA Universidad Nacional de Colombia. Perfil Ambiental Urbano del Municipio de Manizales (2000) *Inédito*

Leyva, P. (ed) (1998) *El Medio Ambiente en Colombia*, IDEAM, Bogotá

Ministerio de Medio Ambiente-IDEA Universidad Nacional de Colombia (1997) 'Lineamientos para la Política Ambiental Urbana de Colombia', Santafé de Bogotá D.C., Bogotá

Programa CREER (2003) 'Una Opción Integral para el Desarrollo Sostenible y Empresarial', Infimanizales, Manizales

Velásquez, L. S. (1998) 'Agenda 21: A form of joint environmental management in Manizales, Colombia', *Environment and Urbanization*, vol.10, no.2, pp9–36, www.ingentaselect.com/09562478/v10n2/

Velásquez, L. S. (1999) 'The local environmental action plan for Olivares bio-comuna in Manizales', *Environment and Urbanization*, vol.11, no.2, pp41–50, www.ingentaselect.com/09562478/v11n2/

Velásquez, L. S. (2000) *Estrategias e Instrumentos de Gestión Urbana para el Desarrollo Sostenible en América Latina y el Caribe. Observatorios para el Desarrollo Sostenible del Municipio de Manizales, Colombia*, IDEA, CEPAL, Naciones Unidas, Municipio de Manizales, Manizales

# 4

# Environment-Poverty Linkages: Managing Natural Resources in China

*John G. Taylor*

## INTRODUCTION

During recent years there has been a growing interest amongst policy-makers, development practitioners and researchers in investigating the links between environmental conditions and poverty.[1] In many developing countries, it has become increasingly apparent that, in both urban and rural sectors, the living conditions of the poor are environmentally constrained. Recognizing that many poor communities are adept at using environmental resources in sustainable ways, donors are increasingly assessing how they can work with poor communities as agents of environmental regeneration in ways that also alleviate their poverty.

With this aim in mind, we investigated a number of environmental projects implemented in China during recent years, examining the extent to which they have improved the environment and reduced poverty.

The issue of linkages between environmental improvement and poverty reduction is particularly relevant for contemporary China, where the poor are more likely to reside in resource-constrained, western, upland areas, with poverty rates higher amongst children, the elderly and minority populations.[2] Appropriate policies for many of the remaining 106 million living below the poverty line must increasingly focus upon reducing the incidence of environmentally related, or environmentally conditioned, poverty.[3] In developing these policies, however, an additional, crucial issue is also being raised. In many projects implemented recently in China, there has been an increasing use of participatory approaches in both donor and government projects. In a major policy shift, the Chinese State Council has recommended that policies for poverty reduction focus on the development of participatory processes in village development planning. This shift is part of a growing trend in Chinese society, in which post-1978 reforms are increasingly requiring a greater decentralization of decision-making for effective policy implementation in a range of areas, and particularly service delivery. This decentralization is being accompanied by a growth of civil society organizations and the emergence of more open governance at the village level. In our assessment, we also examine this trend and its relevance for project implementation.

# RESEARCH

In our research, we selected 20 World Bank projects implemented during the 1990s, or currently in the process of implementation. These varied from environmentally focused interventions[4] with limited poverty alleviating outcomes, to multi-sectoral approaches that attempt to link and integrate poverty reduction with environmental improvements. From these, four World Bank projects were chosen for more detailed field research. These were:

1 *The Yangtze Basin Water Resources Project*, implemented in the central Chinese provinces of Hubei and Hunan, from 1995 to 2000. The project aimed to improve irrigation and drainage systems, and to promote flood control and hydro-power generation. These measures were accompanied by policies for reforestation, livestock and soil improvement. During implementation, the project targeted some poor counties, in addition to piloting the introduction of water-user associations.

2 *The Second Loess Plateau Project*, implemented in the central-western provinces of Shanxi, Shaanxi and Gansu, from 1999 to 2004. The project aims to improve sustainable use of land and water resources through an integrated small watershed management approach. Poverty reduction is being addressed through terracing, small dam construction, irrigation and forestation, enabling agricultural diversification and increases in productivity.

3 *The South-West Poverty Reduction Project*, implemented in the southern provinces of Yunnan, Guangxi, and Guizhou provinces, from 1995 to 2000. The project contained components covering a broad range of areas, from infrastructure provision to micro-credit

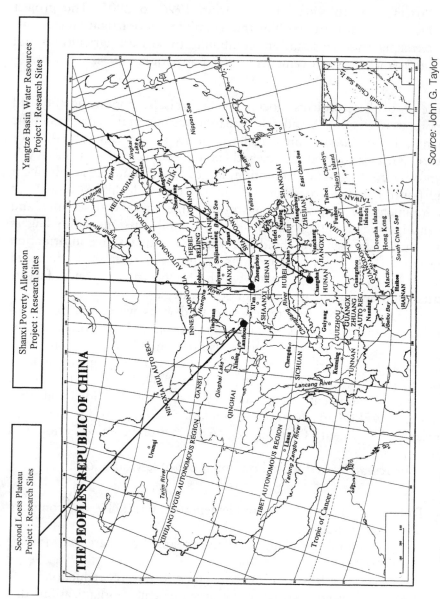

Diagram 4.1 *Project research site locations: Gansu, Hunan and Hubei provinces*

Source: John G. Taylor

and education, with environmental improvements focusing on terracing, improvements in irrigation and water supply.

4 *The Shanxi Poverty Alleviation Project*, implemented in Shanxi Province, north-central China, from 1996 to 2001. The project introduced measures such as the rehabilitation of irrigation systems, terracing and afforestation, combining these with agricultural and infrastructure improvements targeted at poor counties.

For each of these projects, documents, appraisals, monitoring and field reports were examined, and field research was undertaken on sites in the Shanxi, Loess Plateau and Yangtze projects (see Diagram 4.1 for locations). This enabled the researchers[5] to examine issues such as levels of project coverage and promotion, targeting, stakeholder involvement and poverty impact, together with more detailed local assessments of environmental and poverty constraints. Interviews with county and township officials were combined with group discussions with villagers and detailed farmer household interviews. The qualitative information generated from these investigations enabled the research to focus in greater detail on the extent to which specific environmental factors actually influenced villagers' livelihood strategies.

Findings from the desk review and field visits were then examined further, comparing these World Bank projects with other donor programmes and projects that have also tried to address environmental poverty linkages during recent years – designed and implemented by donors such as the Asian Development Bank (ADB), the United Nations Development Programme (UNDP), the World Food Programme (WFP) and the Ford Foundation. Comparisons were also drawn with recent Chinese regional environmental development programmes.

In our research, we focused on a number of key questions:

- To what extent has project implementation resulted in environmental improvements?
- Have these improvements been accompanied by increases in living standards?
- Has project implementation contributed to poverty reduction?
- Have the projects assisted in the development of organizations that enable further environmental improvements and poverty reduction?
- How could the projects be improved to facilitate policy linkages between environmental improvements and poverty reduction?

*Source:* John G. Taylor

**Figure 4.1** *Village in Jing Ning County, Southern Gansu Province, with watershed rehabilitated in the Loess Plateau Project (2001)*

## Environmental outcomes

In the areas in which they have been implemented, each of these projects has brought substantial environmental benefits. Take, for example, the case of an extremely poor village, Xingxing in Linduzhai Township, Longhui County, Hunan Province, assessed during our field research for the Yangtze project. Discussions with households provided a listing of the main features of the village's poverty at the start of the Yangtze project in 1995. Lack of water resources was cited as the main problem, with recurrent drought seriously affecting crops. Irrigation systems were inadequate, village pumps were in constant use, and families spent many hours queuing for water. Water conflicts were a regular occurrence. In an average year, 20 to 30 per cent of farming households lacked adequate grain supplies. Comparing this 1995 situation with the situation in 2001, we found that irrigation systems provided adequate water supply, households had their own taps, there were no grain shortages, cropping had been diversified, and fishponds were developed. Household expenditure had been reduced, particularly expenditure on water.

Similarly, the watershed rehabilitations undertaken in the Loess Plateau project have resulted in improved ecological conditions, with increased crop yields and diversification. These changes have enabled further improvements in crucial areas such as water storage and horticulture. The environmental interventions undertaken in the South-West and Shanxi projects have also resulted in substantial watershed and irrigation improvements, feeding into increases in crop yields and expansion of livestock-raising and horticulture.[6]

## Living standards

To what extent have these improvements in environmental conditions affected improvements in living standards? We attempted to answer this question by comparing projects with non-project villages, focusing both on increases in incomes and changes in indicators assessing quality of life. The results were mixed but, overall, the outcomes have been beneficial. For example, in our assessment of the Loess Plateau project, we compared project with non-project villages in three counties. In each case, project village households had, on average, seen their incomes doubled since 1999, but there had been smaller increases in household incomes in non-project villages.[7] Of the 20 households interviewed in the project areas, each attributed increases in their income to the impact of the Loess project. In the Shanxi project, per capita incomes increased from 620 yuan in 1995 to 1377 yuan in 1999 in the irrigation component, and from 468 to 699 yuan in the watershed rehabilitation component (US$1 is equivalent to 12.89 yuan, August 2003). Contrastingly, in the Shanxi project area, incomes in non-project villages declined to 354 yuan in 1999, even though they had been slightly higher than project village incomes in 1995. Similarly, in the two villages in which we conducted fieldwork in Hunan, for the Yangtze project, average per capita incomes increased from 718 to 1400 yuan from 1995 to 2000.

These increases in incomes appear, in some cases, to have fed through into overall improvements in quality of life. In the 20 interviews undertaken for the Loess Plateau project in the three project villages in Gansu counties, without exception, all villagers cited improvements in health and education as important results of the project. School fees had now become affordable. Although non-attendance at middle school was reported regularly by household members in non-project villages in Sanhe County, Jing Ning, southern Gansu, it was encountered only rarely in interviews in the neighbouring project villages of Xixiang County. Similarly, families in non-project households interviewed in another research area, Ningxian County, could not afford to send their sons to middle school, whereas this was not the case in project

*Source:* John G. Taylor

**Figure 4.2** *Eroded river valley in Jing Ning County, Southern Gansu Province (2001)*

households. Comparing project with non-project areas in the Shanxi project, we found significant improvements in nutritional levels between 1995 and 2000, accompanying project implementation. On the other hand, in the South-West project, despite its interventions being accompanied by components to facilitate improvements in health and education, differences between project and non-project villages were not marked.[8]

## Poverty reduction

Perhaps the most important issue for the projects is the extent to which their interventions have resulted in reductions in poverty levels. It is possible to make some assessment of this, where the projects have been implemented in poor counties. These were relatively few in the Yangtze project, but more numerous in the other projects.[9] However, quantitative assessment was made difficult by the fact that monitoring did not cover poverty levels, except in the irrigation component of the Shanxi project and the South-West project. In the former, it was estimated that

*Source:* John G. Taylor

**Figure 4.3** *Mother, children and grandmother in poor village, Yunnan Province, in area covered by the South-West Poverty Reduction Project (2000)*

the number of households living below the poverty line fell from 14.84 per cent to 8.9 per cent of the population during 1995–1999.[10] In the latter, numbers living in poverty have been reduced from 31.5 per cent to 18 per cent in project villages, compared with a fall from 21 per cent to 12 per cent in non-project villages during 1995–1999.[11] Improvements in the quality of life in the Loess project Gansu villages, noted earlier, were all recorded in poor villages, so it is reasonable to assume that the project had a positive effect on levels of poverty in these areas, despite the lack of data.

Although based on limited data and participatory assessments in relatively small areas, our research would appear to indicate that there is some basis for concluding that the environmental projects examined have contributed to improvements in household livelihoods and to reductions in levels of poverty. Definitive conclusions await more detailed research; but it would already seem that environmental interventions in the Chinese context can do much to improve income levels and the quality of life in poor areas.

## Enabling poverty reduction

From our research, it also appears that these projects can contribute to poverty reduction in a less direct way – by creating enabling organizations that facilitate poverty reduction. This can be illustrated by reference to the creation of organizations for the management and use of water in the Yangtze project.

Water-user associations (WUAs) and water supply corporations (WSCs)[12] were introduced into the project in order to deal with the problems facing water resources in China's rural sector: fragmentation of management amongst different administrative units; water wastage; inadequate supply; prices too low to cover water costs; increasing conflicts between water users; insecurity due to lack of water rights; revenue from water charges diverted to unrelated local government institutions; and poor maintenance of irrigation systems.

In most of the areas within the Yangtze project, the introduction of WSCs and WUAs appears to have resulted in marked improvements, notably in reducing wastage, improving canal maintenance and (thus far) in reducing water costs.[13] Environmentally, they have contributed to reduced flooding and soil conservation.

Designed largely to improve efficiency, however, they have also had other results, important for developing an improved framework for poverty reduction:

- First, the creation of WSCs and WUAs has been important in ensuring a regular, guaranteed supply of water to farmers, who then allocate water equitably through the associations. This contributes to both improved productivity and security, reinforced by the introduction of legal rights to water.
- Second, the operation of the WUAs is important in building capacity for increased farmer participation in decision-making. WUAs are democratic organizations, with elected executives responsible for implementing farmers' choices in the use and distribution of water. During visits to water-user associations in the Linduzhai irrigation component of the Yangtze project, farmers described in detail their involvement in the short-listing of local candidates on the basis of their expertise, and their organization of the ballot for chair and executive committee members.

Such improvements in security and participation are important bases for policies that address poverty; but, from our observations, WUAs have also contributed in more direct ways to poverty reduction. For example, we came across several cases of water-user executives consulting their members on deferral of water payments for poor households. These related particularly to households in which elderly people had no family support, single parent families, and households from which migrants had not been able to return remittances. In resource-constrained poor areas, time formerly devoted to waiting for water, collecting water and digging wells was now put to more productive use. In Xingxing village, Hunan Province, for example, all farmers interviewed cited newly available labour time as the main reason for increases in productivity and diversification. Additionally, women now had more time available since they no longer had to perform their traditional role of guarding irrigation channels during periods when they estimated that water would be released from villages upstream. Guarding was no longer necessary since households now had no need to fight for water, given the responsibility of the WUA to deliver agreed shares of water on a regular basis. Indebtedness previously incurred during drought periods had largely disappeared, and the absence of drought had led to substantial increases in agricultural productivity and diversification. An improved sense of security had led to increased (mostly male) migration from poor villages, resulting in increased incomes and, in some areas, more participation by women in water-user associations.[14]

Clearly, these results, based on an assessment of a relatively small area, cannot provide a strong basis for generalization. However, they do indicate that the promotion of organizations on the basis of an environmental need, such as water-user associations in the interests of efficient water use, appear to have contributed to reducing, in limited ways, some of the adverse effects of poverty by facilitating the development of enabling frameworks for poverty reduction. A similar trend was observed in the Shanxi project, where existing organizations became empowered through the impact of the project, notably in the area of gender.

The status and authority of local branches of the All China Women's Federation (ACWF) was enhanced through the increased importance of livestock breeding, made possible by increased incomes accompanying watershed rehabilitation. Building on their traditional roles in this area, women extended their involvement – training colleagues and increasing their control over the use of funds generated from pig rearing. Gradually, they gained predominance in this area of expertise, and resultant increases in their incomes gave them both more say in household finances and a greater degree of participation in village affairs, through lobbying the village committee, as a group.

Other examples from the projects include improved possibilities for developing forestry management by village communities in newly created areas of small watersheds, and the increasing influence of farmer groups on village affairs, resulting from the extension of areas such as fish pond development and horticulture, both made possible by environmental improvements.

This trend, creating possibilities for increasing participation by farming households in village affairs, also has to be related to recent changes in civil society and, particularly, to changes in village politics, to which we return later.

# IMPROVING ENVIRONMENT-POVERTY PROJECTS

This section continues to focus on the improvements in environmental conditions, living standards and poverty reduction tentatively observed in the projects examined, asking a further question: could such projects link environmental outcomes and poverty reduction more efficiently?

On the basis of our research, a number of areas can be highlighted as a guide to improving project implementation. We noted these in our initial review, prior to project selection. We then examined them in more detail in our field research, since it appeared that improving policies in these areas might increase the effectiveness of environmentally based projects in reducing poverty. Finally, we examined projects that seemed, currently, to be addressing these themes more directly than the World Bank projects examined initially.

## Monitoring

In the current Chinese context, monitoring of most environment-poverty projects still focuses largely on combining surveys of issues such as water and soil quality with measurements of increased grain yields, areas of slope land conversion and extent of agricultural diversification. These are then placed alongside surveys of household production, cultivation and income. If the latter show an increase during (and in the immediate aftermath of) the project, it is assumed that living standards have improved. Within this system, the ability of environmentally based projects in promoting environmental improvements to reduce poverty cannot be established adequately. Additionally, there are limits to the extent to which poverty and its impact upon households can be fully understood within this monitoring framework because it does not

*Source:* John G. Taylor

**Figure 4.4** *Grandmother and child, poor village, Ning Ling County, Northeast Yunnan (2000)*

address salient features of poverty, such as vulnerability and inequalities in access to household resources and consumption.

If monitoring of projects that link environmental improvements with poverty is to measure achievements in addressing these links, it must deal with several areas more adequately.

First, attempts should be made to measure vulnerability, using data on household assets (physical, human and social capital) in combination with data on formal safety nets, the functioning of markets and the range of activities that households pursue to manage risk. This data could then be combined with general panel surveys, monitoring the same households over time. Such processes would enable researchers to

**Figure 4.5** *Old man, outside his house, waiting for his family, Ning Ling County, Northeast Yunnan (2000)*

see how households deal with shock. However, a key role in monitoring should also be played by social assessments, since these are the only means through which we can understand features that are crucial in poverty areas, such as the role and functioning of informal safety nets, the impact of particular life cycle events on poverty, the operation of social networks and local strategies for minimizing risk. Such assessments could also ascertain the extent to which project components are addressing aspects of vulnerability.

Second, consideration needs to be given to the ways in which indicators are devised not just for monitoring environmentally based poverty, but – just as importantly – to understand more adequately the links between poverty and the environment. In some areas, this is fairly straightforward. For example, indicators of water-related illnesses can be measured alongside levels of access to safe water or, more specifically, quantity of water used per capita and available hours of water supply. To assess the extent to which water-related illnesses disproportionately affect the poor, access to safe water can be disaggregated into wealth quintiles; these are then compared with the prevalence of these illnesses amongst, for example, the richest and poorest 20 per cent of the population, and so on. However, in other areas, devising indicators is much more difficult. In all of the projects examined, phenomena such as deforestation, loss in soil fertility and water scarcity have contributed to poverty. Yet, how can indicators be devised that can assess the extent to which these phenomena have contributed to poverty levels? Measuring the changing extent to which poor households depend upon natural resources, for example, could entail developing indicators for the time spent by household members in collecting water and firewood, distances walked by women and children to collect wood for fuel, and the percentage of household income derived from forest products. Environmental problems influencing this indicator would be, for example, levels of water scarcity and deforestation.

Thus far, only a limited number of environment-poverty indicators have been developed to monitor environmentally based poverty, and little research has been directed at measuring the extent to which environmental improvements and poverty reduction are linked in the rural Chinese context. With environmentally based projects increasingly aimed at reducing poverty levels, it is important that appropriate indicators be developed in the near future to monitor their outcomes.[15]

## Targeting

Environment-poverty projects in China suffer from a number of problems: lack of transparency, inadequate dissemination of information and inequalities in the distribution of project benefits. To deal with these, targeting needs to be based much more on poverty identification and needs assessments, undertaken in partnerships with villagers who represent poor communities. These would provide information essential for more detailed targeting. In addition to specifying the salient features of poverty, they could analyse the specific needs and priorities of villages, as well as those of vulnerable and marginalized groups. The particular ways in which poverty affects women could also be detailed, together with an assessment of household coping strategies under conditions of vulnerability. Such assessments might provide more effective means of identifying the poorest and ensure a more equitable allocation of resources. Hopefully, they might also increase awareness of the difficulties faced by poor households in accessing projects, and suggest ways in which these difficulties might be overcome.

## Gender impact

As our analysis repeatedly shows, in many aspects of their lives, women in project areas continue to be disadvantaged. Furthermore, they appear to be particularly disadvantaged in areas where improvements can be facilitated through environmental interventions. Despite this, gender impact is neither assessed nor monitored in any meaningful way in the projects examined, nor are potential improvements in women's lives facilitated by seriously assessing their needs or enhancing their participation within projects. When this is achieved, for example, through the work of local ACWF organizations, it is often done without project assistance and, at times, despite the project.

Taking gender issues more seriously would not only improve the efficiency of projects, but might also result in women participating more fully in decisions that have a profound effect on their lives. Consequently, such areas as those outlined above need to be monitored, investigated further through social assessments and targeted for replication; lessons must be learned from them and incorporated in training in environment-poverty projects. Based on these conclusions, there are a number of issues that need to be addressed in environment-poverty projects. These are:

- funding for women's development and capacity-building to enable greater participation in decisions over natural resource management;
- targeting micro-credit at women's groups, and allowing women a greater role in formulating financial conditions for credit provision;
- including local branches of the ACWF in project design, implementation and evaluation, and building on local networks set up by the ACWF;
- promoting and establishing a leading role for women in project monitoring.

There are existing donor projects in which gender access is prioritized in some of these areas, and these could be taken as component-type models. For example, in Inner Mongolia, the UNDP has been implementing a micro-finance scheme for 4000 women, managed by the local ACWF. Women receive training in project management, gender awareness and participatory methodologies. Again, in a slightly larger poverty alleviation project in north-west Sichuan, implemented during 1997 to 2001, the UNDP set up rural development associations in six poor counties to coordinate project components. The associations developed policies based on the needs of women in poor households, determined through participatory assessments. In a Sino-German project, the Sustainable Development of Mountain Areas, implemented since 1995 in Jiangxi Province, 30 per cent of loans were taken out by women, targeted through participatory assessments. It might also be useful to examine current WFP projects, in which food assistance is accompanied by effective gender-sensitive training in areas such as literacy, health and sanitation, crop production, water management, livestock keeping, fisheries, and economic tree cultivation. In these projects, women's needs are ascertained through participatory techniques, using interviews, developing profiles of project areas and devising village development plans upon which projects are then based. In the WFP approach, projects are implemented by provincial, prefectural and county-level PMOs, in close cooperation with local branches of the ACWF.

## Replicability

Within an important area of most environment-poverty projects in China, there is a paradox. Many of the environmental interventions – particularly small watershed rehabilitation – aim to establish models for combining environmental improvements with poverty reduction. However, despite providing examples of 'best practice', no detailed strategies are offered either for their dissemination or replication.

One project that does appear to take replication strategies seriously is a Global Environment Facility (GEF)/UNDP Biodiversity Conservation in Yunnan's Upland Ecosystems project, currently being implemented in Yunnan Province. From the outset of this project, there is a central aim of producing models that are community based, participatory and replicable. The linking framework established in this project enables a collaboration that aims to demonstrate the effectiveness of project interventions through teamwork in neighbouring watersheds. This is accompanied by campaigns to raise public awareness, improved coordination between local government offices and agencies in supporting village teams, and a continuing participatory monitoring of existing project areas. A strategy of clustering small watersheds further enables a pooling of experiences for improved dissemination. Such an approach may seem rather basic; but, at the very least, it is addressing a crucial absence in most environment-poverty projects and indicating directions for strategies that promote replicability.

## Sustainability

The extent to which implementation can create conditions for the continuation of project achievements is a crucial issue for environment-poverty projects in China. Hence, capacity-building for sustainability is one of the most important questions to be addressed in project design. Although this issue is approached in general terms in World Bank projects, there is little evidence of developing specific strategies for capacity-building. For example, in our discussions with project management staff during our field research, we found that little thought had been given to capacity-building to promote sustainability through village-local government cooperation.

However, there are some donor programmes and projects that address this issue directly, formulating strategies for improving integration between departments, clarifying sectoral tasks, identifying appropriate organizations for tackling post-project issues and maintaining participatory levels. For example, in Ford Foundation-funded programmes in the forestry sector, key features are forestry bureau officials acquiring indigenous knowledge of local silviculture techniques, and farmers working with local officials to integrate former project components. Similarly, the UK government's Department for International Development's (DFID's) Yunnan Environmental Development Programme, implemented during 2000–2004, suggests general strategies for promoting institutional sustainability through improved coordination between local departments and bureaus via county and provincial facilitators.

One of the most innovative approaches to promoting sustainability is in the design of a GEF/UNDP project, Multi-agency and Local Participatory Cooperation In Biodiversity Conservation in Yunnan's Upland Ecosystems.[16] The project aims to set up replicable models for community-based watershed and nature reserve management in Central Yunnan. Village councils organize elections for multi-village 'watershed management' and 'reserve co-management' councils. Representatives on these councils then work with coordinators chosen from county officials in the reserve and watershed areas, selected on the basis of their expertise. These 'co-coordinators' link with relevant local departments in implementing project components. A provincial office is established, with staff from local government agencies, institutes, universities and bureaus (such as forestry and agriculture) to oversee developments within this framework of linked institutions. During project implementation, the Watershed and Reserve Councils prioritize and recommend site-based interventions, removing threats to biodiversity and improving watersheds. Baseline surveys, social assessments and targeting are undertaken by teams of villagers, local officials and specialists from bureaus and research institutes. Once this collaborative framework is established, it is maintained after the duration of the project, with an increased role given to the co-coordinators. Dissemination of the results of the project to adjacent watersheds and neighbouring reserves, together with 'training of trainers', is undertaken by teams of villagers and county officials, organized by the provincial office. Agreement to be involved in this dissemination is a precondition for villagers participating in the project.

## Participation

In several of the donor projects examined, participation of project beneficiaries has been important in increasing effectiveness. This can be illustrated in the following examples.

A GEF/World Bank Nature Reserves Management Project, implemented from 1995–2000,[17] aimed to improve reserve protection and management by introducing community resource management plans, based upon the participatory involvement of villagers living in communities within, and bordering, reserves. Environmentally, the project succeeded in rehabilitating watershed protection forests, natural forests and nature reserves, as well as in developing timber plantations in areas of Hubei, Yunnan and Fujian provinces. Socially, it provided employment for farmers either heavily involved in grazing or cultivating reserve areas, or formerly employed in the logging industry. It aimed to provide farmers with incentives to become involved in the monitoring and protection of reserve areas, while at the same time still being able to engage in cultivation and grazing. The project is run by a co-management team (comprising forestry/reserve, marketing, community and social development experts), in conjunction with a leading group (comprising a nature reserve village, and forestry district/county and prefecture leaders, together with members elected from key and primary stakeholder groups). In consultation with households in pilot villages, targeting and monitoring through social assessments were organized by the leading and co-management groups, assisted by a facilitator. Additionally, a co-management forum was set up for each area, with members elected by villages, in order to implement each of the project components in consultation with members of the leading group and co-management team.

In a follow-up project, funded by the GEF and the World Bank, and entitled Sustainable Forest Development,[18] participation is again a key element. The project involves a series of participatory elements: collection and evaluation of baseline socio-economic data for area selection; interviews with village leaders and households, identifying participants and developing a menu of project activities; interviews with household members and extension staff to finalize afforestation models; stakeholder group and village meetings on organization, production and land tenure arrangements; and village meetings to decide on the role of communities in monitoring and evaluation.

Concluding our assessment of frameworks that promote participation, it is worthwhile to point again to the Sino-German project, Sustainable Development of Mountain Areas. Implemented since 1996 in Jiangxi Province, it has implemented a simple, effective and successful design for linking environmental improvements with poverty reduction. Based on watershed rehabilitation – combining reforestation, terracing and warping dams – it also set up bio-gas digesters and provided revolving-fund credit and training for farmers' associations, which were the main organizations for project implementation. Building upon the 'mountain-river-lake' model adopted in 1994 by the Chinese government in Jiangxi Province,[19] it has been highly participatory in all areas, notably in land-use planning. A key feature has been its successful cooperation with rural credit cooperatives, targeting low-income households, and its promotion of close involvement of local line departments with farmers' associations in area selection, participatory rural appraisals, participatory land-use planning, monitoring and evaluation. A further feature has been its attention to gender issues. Thirty per cent of project loans have been disbursed to women, who also reportedly play leading roles in the project.[20]

## PARTICIPATORY ASSESSMENTS

The increased use of participatory assessments in Chinese projects during recent years, illustrated above, has been notable not only in environmental areas, such as forestry, water and nature reserve projects, but also in poverty reduction planning and even in resettlement projects.[21] This increase has been accompanied by the extension of community participation at the village level, and by the growth of civil society organizations, enabling increased participation of Chinese society in a number of areas, notably in service delivery. It is important to examine these developments, not only for their importance for contemporary Chinese society, but also for the effects that they are likely to have on environment-poverty projects, with greater decentralization enabling increased participation by villagers in projects that affect their daily lives. The following section briefly puts these developments in context in relation to changes occurring in Chinese society during the post-1978 reform period and, particularly, to changes occurring at the village level since the mid 1980s.

## Participation: The context

China's post-Mao reforms began during 1978, in the rural sector, with agricultural de-collectivization and the expansion of the scope of market operations. Alongside the restoration of family farms, the government sanctioned a rapid development of rural enterprises and a huge increase in rural-urban migration.[22] This led to substantial increases in farmers' incomes in most provinces.[23] Changes in urban areas proceeded more slowly. The state owned most urban factories, relying on them both as a source of revenue and as a means of welfare provision for factory workers – the so-called 'iron rice bowl' of housing, education, maternity leave and pension benefits provided to each worker. However, into the late 1980s, it became clear that many of these enterprises, with their technology surviving from the 1950s, were neither sustainable, nor could compete as China increasingly opened up to the world – hence, the processes of transformation and privatization of state enterprise, taken up in earnest from 1987 onwards.

While China's transformation since 1978 has led to continuing high growth rates, rising incomes, increasing levels of investment and massive strides in technology, there remains a problem for the state in delivering adequate social services to the population, notably in health, education, unemployment and pension benefits. The demise of the agricultural collective and the ending of the 'iron rice bowl' have left many insecure. As the state has withdrawn from its involvement in many economic areas, so, too, has it withdrawn from much of its previous commitment to deliver, or assist in the delivery of, social services. This has meant that, increasingly, civil society organizations have emerged to fill the gap left by the state, which in turn has encouraged this development. In addition, for similar reasons, the state has given greater independence to civil society organizations that have been in existence for some time.

These trends have created possibilities for increased participation by Chinese people in decisions that affect their daily lives. This is especially the case with the development of private enterprise associations, specialist organizations in trade, industry, commerce or agriculture, and with the growth of welfare organizations in areas such as pensions, social security, health and education. Furthermore, as we have seen, for example, in the case of water-user associations, there are areas in which participation is enhanced through the government's attempts to promote greater efficiency in implementing its policies in key areas. Consequently, there is a growing awareness that many of the functions performed previously by local government will have to be taken on by local communities and their associations.

These possibilities for enhanced participation are also being accompanied by changes in the political decision-making process at the local level, produced largely by the introduction of village committees. The post-1978 demise of agricultural collectives and rural communes left village leaders with unclear authority and limited resources at the very time when, in the mid 1980s, economic reforms were having a substantial impact on the countryside. The response of the government was to revamp and restructure village committees, which had first been introduced in 1982, but allowed to languish. The Organic Law on villagers' committees, promulgated in 1987, empowered villagers to elect committees as self-governing local-level organizations. The committees comprise three to seven members, elected by the villagers for three years, and responsible for all issues relating to the village, addressing the problems of welfare services, managing village lands and settling disputes.[24]

Since 1987, 25 of China's 31 provincial congresses have passed measures implementing the Organic Law, and villagers' committees now exist in virtually every Chinese village. Most commentators have noted progress in implementation. There remain major flaws: in some areas, the ballots are not secret, and there is a marked tendency for candidates to come from communist party members, from entrepreneurs and from clan leaders within the village.[25] However, overall, there is little doubt that the committees and assemblies have actively pursued villagers' interests. In many reports, there are accounts of committees successfully reducing charges and levies, securing funds for village services, arranging infrastructure improvements, publicizing financial allocations and details of the use of village resources, reducing illegal land seizures, defraying hospital charges, and mobilizing uncompensated workers for local employment. Village codes and charters, detailing the rights and responsibilities of villagers and their leaders, have been used to settle water and irrigation disputes, to curb illegal tree cutting, and to set up and distribute funds to village households.

In general, the establishment of village committees has created a new basis for political power through popular election. It also appears to be producing a changing distribution of power within China's villages, with political authority increasingly having three sources: the villagers' committee, the villagers' representative assembly, and the village communist party branch. Consequently, as a result of the development of village committees and assemblies, not only has the basis for involvement in decision-making become broader, but the focus of power within villages has also changed. Both of these processes have had a marked effect on levels of participation in the village and within the rural sector, in general.

## POVERTY REDUCTION, ENVIRONMENT AND PARTICIPATION

Both the increased involvement of civil society organizations and the possibilities for enhanced participation at the local level via village committees are likely to create an improved participatory and enabling framework for implementing environment-poverty projects in China. As we have already noted, this is particularly apparent in the government's recent village poverty-reduction planning, and is being extended further in areas mentioned earlier, such as community forestry and nature reserve management. The key problem for these projects is rapidly becoming one of capacity-building for participation, focusing on the need to change attitudes, and to develop appropriate systems of management and staff skills.[26]

On the one hand, the reform process and the need for efficient delivery of environment-poverty project outcomes have created greater possibilities for participation. On the other hand, particularly in China's poorer areas, participatory techniques in project design, implementation and monitoring have been introduced largely in a top-down way – through the implementation of donor projects, the programmes of the leading group for poverty reduction, the strategies of the Ministry of Finance, and so on. As in most areas of civil society, the Chinese government will attempt to restrict participation largely to this instrumental level, channelling the actions of village committees into strictly developmental, apolitical areas, and trying to ensure that projects do not concern themselves with sensitive political issues. However, evidence from other areas of civil society – as seen in recent protests on unemployment, social security and pensions[27] – indicates that the government may not be able to confine participation.

The success or otherwise of this attempt will have profound consequences, beyond the needs of both poverty reduction and environmental improvement. In the short term, however, it is vital that donors incorporate participatory approaches and assessments, together with strategies for developing and building capacity for community participation, within their projects. This will not only enable increasing control by villagers over project design and implementation, and promote project sustainability, but – under current conditions – may also facilitate the development of decentralization and improved local governance during the post-reform period in China.

# ENDNOTES

1   Poverty is defined here as a set of multiple deprivations experienced by individuals, households and communities. This set comprises low income and consumption, combined with serious disadvantages in most areas of human development (e.g. low literacy levels, poor health and nutrition, and high rates of infant mortality). It also includes the feelings of powerlessness, voicelessness and vulnerability so eloquently expressed by poor people in participatory assessments. The set of deprivations has a crucial gender aspect: one in five of the world's population lives in poverty, and two-thirds of this fifth are women.

2   A recent study of poverty in China concluded that the risk of being poor for an average person living in a poor area in the west in 1995 was as much as 12 times higher than for an average person living in a non-poor area in the east. See Gustafson and Zhong (1995, pp983–1006). The main, defining feature of these poor areas is that they are located in environmentally resource-constrained areas: the karst areas of the south-west, the mountainous central areas, and the loess regions of the north-west.

3   This poverty line is based upon the World Bank's international poverty standard of US$1 per day (in 1985 purchasing parity dollars) for cross-country comparisons of poverty. If the Chinese government's definition of US$0.66 is taken as the basis, rather than the World Bank standard, then 42 million (or 5 per cent of the population) are living in poverty. Based on the government standard, the number living in poverty has declined from 260 million in 1978 to the current 42 million.

4   Environmentally focused interventions aim to improve access to, and management of, natural resources (water, land, forests and energy resources), mediated by engineering, agricultural, institutional, financial, social and economic measures.

5   The research team comprised Dr John G. Taylor, Professor Li Xiaoyun, director of the Centre for Integrated Agricultural Development (CIAD), China Agricultural University, and Wang Haimin, researcher, CIAD.

6   For example, in the four villages researched in the irrigation component of the Shanxi project, during meetings with villagers, improved irrigation was cited as having contributed to diversification into crops such as cotton, wheat and maize. Irrigation had also resulted in the release of labour time, leading to improvements in levels of productivity. Greenhouse development had become possible from increased incomes during the project. For further details, and for information on the results of our investigations into the four World Bank projects, see Taylor (2002).

7    For example, in project villages in Ningxian County, Gansu Province, annual average per capita incomes increased from 302 to 987 yuan, during 1995–2000, based on data collected by the project management office. By comparison, in non-project villages, they increased from 302 to 550 yuan. In project villages assessed during our fieldwork in Jing Ning County, Gansu Province, where the project was implemented from 1997, household incomes had similarly increased, on average, from 650 to 1200 yuan during 1998 to 2001.

8    Enrollment rates for children aged 7 to 15 show relatively small increases in project villages in Guangxi and Guizhou, and a more substantial increase in Yunnan, but from a much lower base. Guangxi increased its enrollment rate from 91.1 to 91.4 per cent, Guizhou from 84.7 to 88.2 per cent, and Yunnan from 74.7 to 83.8 per cent during the years of the project. In the health subcomponent, child immunization levels declined 74.8 per cent to 73.7 per cent during 1997–1999, and immunization rates remained low in Guizhou, at 56.4 per cent in 1999. In a participatory poverty assessment (PPA) conducted in clinics in project areas during July 2000, poor villagers stated that in education and health, their needs were still not being met. Medics in local clinics were inadequately trained, resulting in villagers having to travel to county hospitals (data taken from the 1999 Monitoring Report for the project). For the PPA, see Beynon and Baohua (2000).

9    In the Yangtze project, of the 33 counties covered, only two were poor counties. By contrast, in the other three World Bank projects, the majority of the counties had poor status, as defined by the Chinese government through a set of indices covering a wide range of areas, from security to household incomes, market access, and levels of health and education.

10   This represented a decline from 580,000 to 170,610 households. The data is taken from the Project Monitoring Office report on the project (World Bank, 1999).

11   Foreign Capital Project Management Centre (FCPMC) of State Council and Leading Group Office of Poverty Alleviation and Development (LGOP), *World Bank Southwest Poverty Reduction Project in China: Poverty Monitoring Report*, p43, Table 2.

12   Both WUAS and WSCs form part of a new organizational concept piloted in the Yangtze project – namely, self-financing irrigation and drainage districts (SIDDs). The latter, replacing existing diverse authorities, such as local water resource bureaus, and water management stations and townships, are comprised of water supply corporations (WSCs) and water user associations. The WSCs operate and maintain reservoirs and branch canals, with the aim of providing and regulating supplies of water to farmers grouped together in water user associations. WSCs sell water to WUAs, aiming at recovery of operation, maintenance and some capital costs. Water is purchased according to the number of cubic metres used, and the WSC measures water deliveries, which are regulated by water sales agreements. Because water deliveries are charged by volume, farmers in the WUAs have an incentive to use water efficiently and less wastefully. WUAs are responsible for the design, construction, maintenance and management of water delivery at the farm level.

13   For example, in WUAs visited in Hunan by a World Bank supervision mission during July 2000, water costs had fallen on average from 40 yuan to 32 yuan per *mu* (1 *mu* = 0.0667ha) since the setting up of the associations in 1996 (compared with no reductions in non-project villages). Similar trends were documented in a more extensive survey of SIDDs undertaken in the Tieshan Irrigation District,

Hunan, June 1998. In these areas, despite an increase in water charges, water delivered and consumed has decreased as a result of taking volumetric measuring as the basis of the water charge. See College of Water Resources et al (1998).

14   While levels of women's participation in the running of WUAs have increased during recent years, they should not be exaggerated. In Dongxiang WUA, Longhui County, Hunan, for example, during 2000, of the 31 WUA representatives elected, only 3 were women.

15   A recent and interesting attempt to build participation into the design of monitoring indicators for village development planning is being undertaken for the Asian Development Bank by the Centre for Integrated Agricultural Development (CIAD) at the Chinese Agricultural University, Beijing. Indicators are being developed on a participatory basis, with detailed stakeholder analysis, a specification of the relevant elements of 'non-income' poverty (both human and environmental), and the development of methodologies for participatory planning through the use of participatory assessments and workshops. A subset of indicators is selected by households in poor villages as a basis for identifying and ranking levels of poverty. The subset is based on indicators already selected by villagers in five poverty areas: environmental, resource-based, economic, institutional and socio-cultural. Each of the indicators in the subset is then assessed in importance through further village consultations, resulting in the development of a weighted poverty index, specifying degrees of poverty for targeting poor villages and households. For an introduction to this research, see CIAD (2001).

16   The project is still in the formulation stage, and information provided here comes from a project brief published in 2000.

17   For the most detailed statement of this project, see World Bank/GEF, 1995.

18   The China-Sustainable Forest Development Project was designed for implementation in 2000-2006. As with the Nature Reserves Management Project, it is primarily a GEF/World Bank operation. For full details of the project, see World Bank, East Asia and Pacific Region (1999).

19   The 'mountain-river-lake' model, implemented in Jiangxi Province for the last ten years, is based upon the following principle: 'to manage the lake, the rivers must be harnessed; to harness the rivers, the mountain must be developed; to develop the mountain, poverty must be alleviated'. It provides a simple, replicable model, in which afforestation, grazing control, commercial tree-planting, terracing, small dam building, irrigation and small-scale human development components are combined with small watershed management to improve environmental conditions and alleviate poverty. The Jiangxi project was selected as one of the priority projects in China's Agenda 21 in 1994, offering a simple strategy of 'combining the management of mountains and waters with poverty alleviation'.

20   This disbursement was described by participants from academic and practitioner organizations involved in participatory assessments at a DFID-hosted seminar, which was held to discuss environment-poverty linkages in poverty alleviation projects, Beijing, 26 April 2001.

21   For examples of case study research in these areas, see Plummer and Taylor (forthcoming).

22   Town and village enterprises currently contribute 40 per cent of national gross industrial output, and employ approximately 130 million workers. The high point of their expansion was from 1984–1994, when their output grew at an annual average rate of 33.9 per cent. By the mid 1990s, however, growth slowed, and their

output has declined since 1996 (on this issue, see Dernberger, 1999). China's migrant 'floating population' was estimated at between 80 and 100 million people in the mid 1990s (see Mallee, 2000, pp83–101). Most commentators variously estimated the 2002 floating population at between 150 and 200 million people.

23  Average per capita annual incomes of rural households increased from 133.6 yuan per year in 1978 to 544.9 yuan in 1988, to 2162 yuan in 1998. In real per capita terms, rural incomes increased by 63 per cent between 1985 and 1997 (see Oi, 1999). Against this should be set the considerable gap between urban and rural incomes – with GINI ratios above 0.40 since the early 1990s, and the rise in intra-rural inequality noted by most researchers during the 1990s, particularly the large gap between coastal and inland provinces.

24  The Organic Law also stated that the committees would be responsible to village councils, comprising all adult villagers, which would establish a charter for the village and codes of conduct for the committee and review all committee accounts. Since the introduction of the 1987 law, the Ministry of Civil Affairs has encouraged the additional establishment of villagers' representative assemblies (VRAs) to oversee the day-to-day work of the village committees. The VRA are staffed by representatives 'recommended' by groups of 10 to 15 village families.

25  See Pastor and Tan (2000, pp490–512) and Oi and Rozelle (2000, pp513–539).

26  On these issues, see Plummer and Taylor (forthcoming), particularly Chapter 11, 'Enhancing local government capacity for participation'.

27  In 1995, it was estimated officially that protest marches involving more than 20 people rose to a record high of 1620, including more than 1.1 million people and occurring in more than 30 cities. During 1997, officials reported more than 10,000 cases of 'unruly incidents in the rural sector – varying from petitions to demonstrations and the damaging of local government offices'. See Lee (2000, pp41–61) and Burns (1999).

# REFERENCES

Beynon, L. and Baohua, Z. (2000) *Understanding Rural Poverty and Poverty Constraints in China: An Analysis of the Causes of Poverty and Poverty Constraints in Poor Rural Areas in China and the Impact and Effectiveness of Poverty Alleviation Projects*, Department for International Development (DFID), July 2000

Burns, J. P. (1999) 'The People's Republic of China at 50: National political reforms', *The China Quarterly*, No. 159, September, Oxford University Press

CIAD (2001) *Preparing a Methodology for Development Planning in Poverty Alleviation under the New Poverty Strategy of the PRC: Mid Term Report*, CIAD, Beijing

College of Water Resources, WUHEE et al (1998) *The First Phase Evaluation on Performance of Self-financial Irrigation and Drainage District and Water User Association at Tieshan Irrigation District*, Beijing

Dernberger, R. F. (1999) *The People's Republic of China at 50: The Economy*, *The China Quarterly*, No. 159, Oxford University Press, Oxford

Gustafson, B. and Zhong, W. (2000) 'How and why has poverty in China changed? A study based on Microdata for 1988 and 1995', *China Quarterly*, No. 164, December, pp983–1006

Lee, C. K. (2000) 'Pathways of labor insurgency', in E. J. Perry and M. Selden (eds) *Chinese Society: Change, Conflict and Resistance*, Routledge, London and New York, pp41–61

Mallee, H. (2000) 'Migration, houkou, and resistance', in E. J. Perry and M. Selden (eds) *Chinese Society: Conflict, Change and Resistance*, Routledge, London and New York, pp83–101

Oi, J. C. (1999) 'Two decades of rural reform in China: An overview and assessment', *The China Quarterly*, Oxford University Press, No. 159, September, pp616–628

Oi, J. C. and Rozelle, S. (2000) 'Elections and power; the locus of decision-making in Chinese villages', *The China Quarterly*, No. 162, June, Oxford University Press, pp513–539

Pastor. R. A. and Tan, Q. (2000) 'The meaning of China's village elections', *The China Quarterly*, No. 162, June, Oxford University Press, pp490–512

Plummer, J. and Taylor, J. G. (eds) (forthcoming) *Community Participation in China: Issues and Processes in Capacity Building*, Earthscan, London

Taylor. J. G. (2002) *Environment-Poverty Linkages in World Bank Projects in China: An Assessment*, Research Report for the Environment Policy Department/China Programme, Department for International Development (DFID), January

World Bank, East Asia and Pacific Region (1999) *China: Sustainable Forest Development project, Protected Areas Management Component, Project Brief*

World Bank and Global Environment Facility (1995) *Nature Reserves Management Project, People's Republic of China, Project Document*

(1999) *China Statistical Yearbook*, China Statistical Publishing House, Beijing, p38

# The Evolving Roles of Environmental Management Institutions in East Africa: From Conservation to Poverty Reduction

*Claire Ireland and Godber Tumushabe*

There is a relationship between democracy and the protection of the environment. In Uganda, the worst abuses against the environment, including large-scale poaching, encroachment on forest reserves and game parks, draining of swamps, have all occurred under dictatorial regimes. (*Report of the Uganda Constitutional Commission: Analysis and Recommendations,* 1993 – also known as the Odoki Commission Report)[1]

## INTRODUCTION

In East Africa,[2] governance, in its broadest sense, is at the core of the debate between environment, poverty and politics – what a recent United States Agency for International Development (USAID) report refers to as 'nature, wealth and power'.[3] This argues that as political power is closely intertwined with wealth generated through the exploitation of nature, reducing poverty must squarely address the issue of power imbalances over ownership and access to key natural resource assets. In East Africa this is particularly pertinent given that poverty reduction strategies (PRS) in all three countries are based on the use of the environment and natural resources, notably through the development of their agricultural sectors, to foster economic growth as a means of poverty reduction.

In this chapter we examine the key institutional reforms for environmental management in East Africa, and the political context in which they have taken place. We assess the key drivers for these institutional reforms and analyse the adequacy, or inadequacy, of these institutions to act in their new role as agents for poverty reduction. The following are the key emerging messages:

- *Balanced interventions are needed if poverty eradication is to be achieved.* The majority of the poor in East Africa depend upon natural resources, not only as assets for production but also as safety nets during times of stress and vulnerability. It can therefore be argued that in order effectively to implement their respective poverty reduction strategies, the three countries must balance their interventions along the premise of the 'nature, wealth and power' philosophy.

- *Environmental management institutions are well placed to scale up successful small-scale natural resource management initiatives.* There are a number of documented sustainable natural resource management success stories at the local level in East Africa that have led to increased incomes for the poor and other contributions to poverty reduction. These need to be scaled up to maximize benefits and to optimize outcomes for the poor. Environmental management institutions, particularly when working in partnerships with other government institutions are well placed to take leadership in demonstrating such success stories.

- *Good governance is fundamental to achieving sustained poverty reduction.* The nature of politics and governance systems has significant implications for the role that the environment and natural resources can play in poverty eradication. Decentralization, participation and public-private partnerships are all central to ensuring integrated poverty reduction and environmental management in East Africa.

- *Environmental management can be used as a tool to promote good governance.* Natural resources are the 'bread and butter' for the poor in East Africa. The impact of poor governance can often be visibly seen by the degradation it can cause to the resource and by the impact it can have on people's livelihood strategies. Environmental management can be used to tangibly demonstrate good governance, which means it is also a compelling vehicle for promoting and consolidating key good governance principles of participation, vertical and horizontal accountability, and representation.

- *Governments are taking environmental management more seriously as a foundation for economic growth and poverty reduction.* In the changing era of democratic governance in East Africa, there appears to be more attention given to the environment as a key pillar to economic growth and poverty reduction. This has been evidenced by the approach to public participation in government processes (Uganda), the recognition of the environment as a cross-cutting issue in poverty reduction strategies (Tanzania) and the appointment of environmental activists into key government positions (Kenya).
- *However, environmental decision-making is increasingly taking place in the political arena.* There is growing concern over the shift of environmental decision-making from mainstream environmental policy institutions to the political arena. Furthermore, while decentralization holds better promise for locally owned and people-driven public investments, the current capacity limitations need to be addressed in order to be able to effectively meet this new demand for local environmental management.
- *The judiciary is beginning to play a key role in preventing environmental abuse.* Numerous changes in political systems in East Africa over the last few decades have seen the evolution of constitutions as a foundation for governance systems. These constitutions are increasingly recognizing the rights of individuals to live in a clean and healthy environment and have led to a number of court cases over environmental mismanagement.
- *Environmental management has moved from historically being community led, through to centralized government management, and is now moving back to somewhere in between.* Over the last few centuries environmental management in East Africa moved from being solely a traditional system where the community self-managed the resource, to colonial governments introducing central legislation and new institutions to manage environmental resources. Today, as greater attention is being given to learning lessons, space is being created for more public involvement in environmental management that combines these two historical approaches.
- *Finally, underpinning all of these issues is the fundamental question of who should pay for environmental management, given its public good nature.* With more and more management responsibilities being devolved to local levels in East Africa, there is an assumption that the costs of meeting this local management should be derived from local government budgets. This is increasingly being challenged by various stakeholders who argue that the public good nature of the environment means that central government and/or international institutions should meet this growing cost.

## BACKGROUND AND CONTEXT

The institutional and political landscape for environmental management in East Africa has undergone significant changes over the last century. These changes can best be described in three major phases. The first, the pre-colonial phase, saw traditional institutions largely dominated by chiefs and headmen, providing members of the community with the opportunity to participate in managing key natural resources for the common good of society. These systems could often be extremely hierarchical and, at times, exclusionary. During the second phase, at the dawn of colonialism, the colonial governments introduced legislation and new institutions for managing key natural resources. The key characteristic of these reforms was the shift from consumptive use to an era of protection, often enforced through draconian legislation. This heavy protectionism took the form of large-scale biodiversity conservation. This situation remained through independence until the mid 1980s, when a new phase of laws and institutions began to emerge. The third phase, largely characterized by reforms aimed at creating new environmental management institutions and creating space for more public involvement in environmental management, began around the mid 1980s.[4]

A series of international policy processes such as the Stockholm Conference on the Human Environment in 1972, the World Charter for Nature in 1982 and the United Nations Conference on Environment and Development (UNCED) in 1992 led to major institutional reforms in many countries. In East Africa, these processes have provided some of the political impetus and context within which environmental management reforms have taken place. At a general level, the environmental institutions started looking back to how environmental management could be achieved by involving all major actors, including local communities. However, although there are significant similarities between the three East African countries, considerable differences exist in both the approaches and the pace of reforms at the national level.

This chapter analyses the key institutional reforms for environmental management, and the political context in which they have taken place, in Kenya, Uganda and Tanzania (referred to as East Africa). We assess the key drivers of these reforms and analyse the adequacy or inadequacy of these environmental institutions to act as agents for poverty reduction. Box 5.1 illustrates the multiple ways in which the environment matters to the poor in the region.

## BOX 5.1 WHY THE ENVIRONMENT MATTERS TO THE POOR

'In the 1950s, the soils were still fertile; the village was still covered with natural vegetation. We had plenty of food in this village. Generally, the world was good. Yields from the garden were very high and food security was guaranteed. Hunger and famine were unheard of'. (participant, Mukungu, Kisoro)

'The youths are the most desperate because they are poor. They deliberately go out to catch the immature fish because they know that is all that is remaining and they should catch it before another person gets it'. (community member, Hamukungu)

'My father allocated me a very small piece of land which has now become infertile. I am now getting money by working with two other people pit-sawing timber on other people's land'. (young man from the Bushenyi farming community)

'People are wondering how to abide by the fisheries laws when one catches very few fish legally'. (Maseruka Adonia, Katunguru)

'The Uganda Wildlife Authority contradicts itself. It has carved out land for the community, but at the same time restricts them from cultivating it'. (community development officer, Bushenyi sub-county)

*Source:* cited in Government of Uganda (2002)

The East African Community is comprised of three countries covering an approximate area of 1.7 million square kilometres. Between them, they have an estimated population of 80 million people sharing a common history, language, culture and infrastructure, as well as common resources that include national parks,[5] water bodies,[6] wetlands and diverse forest ecosystems.[7] This is in addition to more localized water bodies, rivers, national parks, forests, wetlands and a rich biodiversity largely found on private lands.

There are three key features to environmental management in East Africa that need to be emphasized in the context of institutional reforms and poverty eradication. First, most of these resources are under tremendous pressures – largely arising from an increasing population, increasing demand for various resources such as forest products and water, declining public investments, poorly defined property rights, and exclusionary policies and macro-economic policies that provide incentives for overexploitation. Second, in spite of this tremendous natural resource wealth in the region, environmental institutions have struggled to create the necessary incentives that promote wealth creation through the sustainable use of these resources and, as a result, have failed to

**Table 5.1** *Poverty-environment data for East Africa, 2000*

| Indicator | Kenya | Uganda | Tanzania |
|---|---|---|---|
| Total population | 30.1 million | 22.2 million | 33.7 million |
| Proportion of the population living in poverty | 56% | 35% | 35.7% |
| Proportion of the population with access to an improved water source | 57% | 52% | 68% |
| Mean distance travelled to collect water | na | 1.1 km[9] | na |
| Mean time taken to collect water | na | 26.07 minutes[10] | na |
| Proportion of land area covered by forest | 29% | 17.39% | 41.06% |
| Mean distance travelled to collect firewood | na | 0.9 km[11] | na |
| Proportion of diseases attributed to environmental causes | na | 33% | na |

*Note:* na = not available.
*Source:* World Bank, country profile tables in www.worldbank.org information.[12]

create an environment where the poor, who depend upon these resources, can sustainably lift themselves out of poverty. It is possible to argue that one reason for the failure of environmental institutions in the region to use this natural wealth to transform rural livelihoods and build prosperous communities is the political governance systems in place.

Third, while all three countries see their route to economic growth and poverty reduction through the use of these natural resources (whether through agriculture exports, increased tourism or mineral extraction), they have consistently failed to adequately involve environmental management institutions in developing these growth policies; therefore, the sustainability of these policies can be seriously questioned.[8] Table 5.1 shows a selection of poverty-environment indicators that are now being collected by the three countries in order to monitor the impacts of growth on the poor.

## SOME REFLECTIONS ON GOVERNANCE IN THE CONTEXT OF THE EAST AFRICAN COMMUNITY

A number of environmental policy practitioners in East Africa[13] have used Hyden's definition of governance[14] as a foundation for defining environmental governance in the region. Environmental governance is defined by these practitioners as being a body of values and norms that guide or regulate state-civil society relationships in the use, control and management of the natural environment.[15] It is argued that these norms and values are expressed in a complex chain of rules, policies and institutions that constitute an organizational mechanism through which both the broad objectives and the specific planning targets of environmental management must be articulated.

If we understand environmental governance in the above context, it is then important to recognize that within East Africa there are generally two accepted systems of environmental governance: informal and formal.[16] Informal environmental governance is composed of unwritten, traditional and systemic taboos, rituals and rules that regulate the interaction between the individuals and the natural environment. These informal environmental governance systems emerged from within the social system and were locally responsive to changes in the ecology upon which they were based. Decision-making on natural resource planning included the involvement of informal organizations and households,[17] although this could still often be exclusionary to some members of the community.

By contrast, formal environmental governance in East Africa is mainly composed of written and formal policies; environmental plans; legal instruments; and formal laws, rules of practice and institutions that explicitly or implicitly impact upon environmental management. For example, all three countries have national environment action plans (NEAPs). Uganda and Tanzania also have national environmental policies and all three have environmental statutes/laws in place (Uganda's National Environment Statute was passed in 1995, Kenya's Environmental Management and Coordination Act was passed in 1999 and Tanzania's National Environmental Management Act was passed in 1983 – although a new environmental framework is currently under development in Tanzania). As already alluded to, the informal systems of environmental governance tended to be more inclusive and responsive to people's demands at the local level. On the other hand, the history of formal institutional arrangements has tended to be rather exclusive, non-responsive and less participatory.

It is important to note that these formal and informal institutions operate in a political context. The politics and the political systems determine the degree of space available for these institutions to play their roles as managers, innovators and transformers. In order to fully understand the challenges and opportunities involved in making environmental institutions effective drivers for poverty eradication, it is worthwhile reflecting on the politics and political processes within which they operate.

# CURRENT TRENDS IN GOVERNANCE

The political upheavals in Uganda, the political mismanagement in Kenya and a failed socialist system in Tanzania, coupled with often gross economic mismanagement at all levels, have left the three countries with deep economic, social and environmental problems. Although there are significant disparities between them, a number of generalized conclusions can be made with respect to the socio-economic and political situations that occur in the three countries, especially to the extent that these situations affect environmental management institutions and poverty eradication.

First, the three countries are considered to have particularly high levels of corruption. According to Transparency International's 2002 *Corruption Perception Index*, Kenya and Uganda are both listed amongst the ten most corrupt countries in the world. While Tanzania is not perceived as 'bad' by the same index, the *World Bank Governance Indicators* suggest that 'control of corruption' is a more significant problem in Tanzania than in Uganda. Kenya appears to be, again, the worst of the three. Since natural resources form a substantial portion of the national cake, it is reasonable to assume that much of this corruption is linked to the access, control and exploitation of the environment and natural resources.

Second, when looking at the results that country governments are managing to achieve against basic indicators, Uganda and Kenya appear to be doing significantly better than Tanzania. Their infant mortality rates are around 80 per 1000 births compared to over 100 in Tanzania, and enrolment in primary education is also higher for these two. Tanzania does not lag so far behind, however, and has a significantly better adult literacy rate than Uganda, probably due to the relative stability of Tanzania compared to Uganda over the last 30 years.

The third and perhaps most important of the similarities on the political front consists of the various constitutional reforms that the three countries have undergone during the last ten years. Although the degree of reform has varied in each country, the environmental significance of these political/constitutional reforms has been the incorporation of environmental management provisions within the national constitutions. A key driver for this has been the growing realization of the importance of the environment, in general, and natural resources, in particular, in renewing and sustaining national socio-economic and political structures.[18] Another important driver involved the ruthless and dictatorial regimes that had dominated the region during the 1970s and 1980s. The gross mismanagement under these regimes resulted in unprecedented decline in the stock of natural resources and wildlife (in Uganda) and massive deforestation (in Kenya), which increased dramatically the hardships of survival for poor resource-dependent communities. Incorporation of environmental safeguards is therefore increasingly seen as a major safeguard towards natural resource exploitation and expropriation through greed and political patronage.

It is also increasingly being recognized that environmental sustainability can be pursued and achieved if there is a national scheme of governance that specifies state responsibility to provide a clean and healthy environment for its citizens. Incorporation of such rights within the national constitutions and framework environmental laws has more or less been accepted as a norm, although this process follows the process of constitutional reforms. In 1995, Uganda became the first East African country to make specific provisions on the right to a clean and healthy environment both in its framework environmental legislation and in the constitution.[19] The major constitutional reform process that Uganda went through (1986–1995) provided a significant opportunity for incorporating comprehensive provisions in the constitution.[20] Almost four years later in 1999, Kenya incorporated far-reaching provisions on the right to a clean and healthy environment in its own framework environmental law (see Box 5.2).[21]

---

## BOX 5.2 ENVIRONMENT MANAGEMENT COORDINATION ACT, 1999 (KENYA)

### Part II: General Principles

3 (1) Every person in Kenya is entitled to a clean and healthy environment and has the duty to safeguard and enhance the environment.

(2) The entitlement to a clean and healthy environment under subsection (1) includes the access by any person in Kenya to the various public elements or segments of the environment for recreational, educational, healthy, spiritual and cultural purposes.

(3) If a person alleges that the entitlement conferred under subsection (1) has been, is being or is likely to be contravened in relation to him, then without prejudice to any other action with respect to the same matter which is lawfully available that person may apply to the High Court for redress and the High Court may make such orders, issue such writs or give such directions as it may deem appropriate to:

(a) prevent, stop or discontinue any act or omission deleterious to the environment;

---

(b) compel any public officer to take measures to prevent or discontinue any act or omission deleterious to the environment;

(c) require that any ongoing activity be subjected to an environmental audit in accordance with the provisions of this act;

(d) compel the persons responsible for the environmental degradation to restore the degraded environment as far as practicable to its immediate condition prior to the damage; and

(e) provide compensation for any victim of pollution and the cost of beneficial uses lost as a result of an act of pollution and other losses that are connected with or incidental to the foregoing.

More comprehensive provisions have now been enshrined in the September 2002 draft bill for the constitution of the Republic of Kenya. Section 63 of this draft constitution provides that everyone has a right to:

- live in an environment that does not jeopardize one's health and well-being;
- have the environment protected for present and future generations;
- freedom of access to environmental information;
- compensation for damage arising from the violation of the rights recognized under the act.

Given this trend, it could be argued that the ongoing process to formulate a framework environmental law in Tanzania will provide an opportunity to incorporate similar provisions in statute. Tanzania's judiciary has already moved far ahead in its interpretation of the right to life as including the right to a clean and healthy environment (see Box 5.3). There has also been increasing public-interest environmental litigation in Uganda and Kenya; in both cases, the courts are handing out what appear to be 'favourable' decisions for environmental management and public-interest environmental litigation.[22]

The final point to note with respect to governance relates to the emergence of 'predatory states' in the region. Particularly in Kenya, the practice of rewarding political patronage through political and other appointments has seen the tremendous growth of a highly bloated public administration. Key parastatal agencies during the Moi regime were run down by incompetent and corrupt public officials protected from accountability because of their political loyalties. It is important to note that improvements in governance like those we have seen in Kenya because of change of leadership could increase efficiency, cut down on wastage and enhance service delivery systems that focus on the poor rather than on the predatory state.

## BOX 5.3 THE RIGHT TO LIFE INCLUDES A RIGHT TO LIVE IN A CLEAN AND HEALTHY ENVIRONMENT

In Tanzania, the courts have extended the interpretation of the right to life in the constitution to include the right to live in a clean and healthy environment. In 1998, the Tanzania Court of Appeal demonstrated just how powerful the constitution could be in ensuring that the vision of a clean environment was upheld for its citizens. The court of appeal in Joseph D. Kessy and Others versus Dar es Salaam City Council[23] interpreted the constitutional right to life as encompassing the right to an environment free from pollution.

In this case, some residents of the Tabata area applied to the High Court to prohibit the council from continuing to dump waste in Tabata, an area designated as residential under the city master plan. The Court dismissed the council's application and gave a wide interpretation of the right to life as encompassing the right to live in a clean and healthy environment. Reading the judgement of the court, Justice Rukangira stated:

> I have never heard it anywhere for a public authority, or even an individual, to go to court and confidently seek permission to pollute the environment and endanger people's lives regardless of their number. Such wonders appear to be peculiarly Tanzanian; but I regret to say that it is not given to any court to grant such a prayer. Article 14 gives every person the right to life and to protection by society. It is, therefore, a denial of this basic right to deliberately expose anybody's life to danger. It is also clearly monstrous to enlist a court's authority in such infringement.

The Court restated the above decision in the case of Festo Balegele and 794 Others versus Dar es Salaam City Council, which also concerned waste dumping. In this case, then Justice Rubana observed, *iter alia* that people's health and enjoyment of life were 'dependent on living in healthy surroundings'.

There have also been more proactive attempts towards regional economic and political integration in the context of the East African Community. The coming into force of the Treaty Establishing the East African Community in July 2000 provided a new beginning for the three East African countries in the areas of political, economic, social and environmental cooperation. At a broad level, the treaty in its objectives provides three pillars that should guide regional integration. The regional integration is supposed to be 'people centered, market driven and private-sector led.' While analysing the extent to which these pillars are being applied in the integration process is beyond the scope of this chapter, it will be worth watching how these pillars are applied, in practice.

Finally, the three countries have adopted macro-economic policies that are largely characterized by liberalization and private-sector led growth. This approach to economic management is likely to be the key driver in the ongoing institutional and policy reforms in the environment sector. Yet, if the private sector is understood in the neo-classic economic context, liberalization of natural resource management could lead to further deprivation of assets and exclusion of the poor from having control over resources that form a basis of their livelihood security. Over the last few years, there have been a number of cases where private-sector projects have displaced or threatened to displace communities, including developments in marginal environments. For example, in 1997 a proposed extension of the Kakira Sugar Works sugar cane plantation in eastern Uganda led to the disenfranchisement of over 1000 tree farmers in Butamira Forest Reserve (see Box 5.7, p121), and in Kenya the Tiomin project has resulted in the displacement of poor people in Kwale, rather than securing their livelihoods (see Box 5.4).

The following section analyses the major regional and national environmental policy reforms, reflecting on key drivers of these reforms and implications for poverty reduction strategies.

---

## BOX 5.4 TITANIUM MINING PROJECT IN KWALE, KENYA

A Canadian company, Tiomin Resources Inc., has received a concession from the government of Kenya to mine titanium in Kwale district in the Coast Province. At the time, serious concerns were raised by a cross-section of civil society organizations of the potential environmental and socio-economic impacts. The area is said to have a potential of 200 million tonnes of titanium and zirconium-bearing sands containing ilmenite, rutile and zircon. It is estimated that when operational, the mining works will produce over 300,000 tonnes of ilmenite, 75,000 tonnes of rutile and 37,000 tonnes of zircon each year during the first six years of production. This will represent approximately 4 per cent of the current world consumption.

The company is reported to be investing US$137 million in the project that is expected to run for 14 years and to generate up to US$50 million to $60 million of foreign exchange earnings a year.

The project has not started extraction yet, as issues relating to compensation, resettlement and benefit-sharing with the local community remain unsolved. About 10,000 peasant farmers are affected by the project. They will have to be resettled elsewhere as their land will be taken over for the mining works.

Apart from having to move from their ancestral homes, there are concerns that the mining project may disrupt access to sacred sites. It will also have a large negative impact on the biodiversity of the area and there are serious concerns about other environmental impacts that are yet to be settled to the satisfaction of all stakeholders.

The company has, in the past, offered the local farmers compensation packages that include relocation and the promise of a return to their land at the end of 21 years, together with 11,000 Kenyan shillings a year for each acre of land and additional money for buildings and crops lost. The farmers have refused these offers, complaining that the monetary compensation is too low.

*Source:* Michael Ochieng Odhiambo, Resources Conflict Institute (Reconcile), Kenya

# REGIONAL ENVIRONMENTAL GOVERNANCE PROCESSES

Since the mid 1980s, there have been several attempts to adopt a regional approach to environmental management. At the regional level, these efforts have focused on creating institutions and programmes that emphasize coordination of environmental management efforts.[24] Consequently, there have been continuous efforts to ensure commonality in policy and institutional coordination at the ecosystem level.[25] However, the biggest initiative for regional environmental cooperation can be traced back to 1993 when the three countries identified and agreed on key areas in which they would cooperate to facilitate regional integration. The *Common Text on Identified Areas of Cooperation between the United Republic of Tanzania, the Republic of Kenya and the Republic of Uganda* included conservation and the management of shared resources as one area for further cooperation.[26]

Regional efforts for environmental management were further crystallized in the memorandum of understanding (MoU) on environmental issues. The MoU was signed in October 1998, and it has some striking features that, prima facie, could have significant implications for its implementation at the national level. First, it was signed at the level of heads of environmental management agencies, and there is no evidence of involving the ministries of foreign affairs that would normally be responsible for signing such instruments. Second, it was negotiated and adopted with the facilitation of the United Nations Environment Programme (UNEP)/Dutch Project on Environmental Law and with no known public involvement.

This MoU has since been incorporated within the treaty establishing the East African Community.[27] Perhaps the most significant feature of the MoU is its emphasis on environmental rights. Article 7(1)(a) of the MoU explicitly provides for 'the right of the people of the partner states to a clean, decent and healthy environment'. Although very little is known about the process to develop this MoU, it has been stated that the inclusion of the right to a clean and healthy environment in the final documents was largely informed by previous international and national developments with respect to the right.[28] At the time of its adoption in October 1998, it was only Uganda that had incorporated the right to a clean and healthy environment in its constitution.[29] The regional recognition of the right to a clean and healthy environment therefore acts as a stimulus for further constitutional and legislative development.[30]

Furthermore, the MoU also contained a comprehensive elaboration of the environmental procedural rights adopted under Principle 10 of the Rio Declaration (see Box 5.5).[31] In what could be referred to as a 'legislative revolution'[32] in the history of environmental legislation in East Africa, the MoU makes provisions for access to justice in environmental matters. As part of the mechanisms for implementing the objectives of the MoU, article 16(2)(d) obliges the partner states to 'develop measures, policies and laws which will grant access, due process and equal treatment in administrative and judicial proceedings for all persons who are or may be affected by environmentally harmful activities in the territory of any of the partner states'. These provisions for locus standi are not just confined to citizens or the national borders of the respective partner states. The effect of the provisions of Article 16(3) is 'to grant rights of access to the nationals or residents of the other partner states to their judicial and administrative machineries to seek remedies for transboundary environmental damage.'

---

## BOX 5.5 PRINCIPLE 10 OF THE RIO DECLARATION

Environmental issues are best handled with the participation of all concerned citizens, at the relevant level ... each individual shall have appropriate access to information concerning the environment ... and the opportunity to participate in decision-making processes. States shall facilitate and encourage public awareness and participation by making information widely available. Effective access to judicial and administrative proceedings, including redress and remedy, shall be provided. (Rio Declaration, 1992)

These principles are well articulated under the East Africa MoU on the environment.

---

It is important to appreciate the significance of these rights in the context of sustainable development and poverty eradication. It can be argued that:

> ... effective governance based on transparent decision-making
> and public access to government decisions is the foundation of
> fair, legitimate and sustainable economic and development
> choices. Effective governance permits transparent, participa-
> tory and accountable decision-making; promotes the integra-
> tion of social and environmental concerns in economic
> development decisions; and allows for the management of
> risk.[33]

Decision-making, built on the pillars of access to information, public
participation and access to justice, not only gives an opportunity to the
public to make informed choices and influence decisions, it also creates
a stable and predictable investment environment for business.

There have been other regional initiatives that clearly demonstrate
attempts at both the political and the policy level to address problems
of environmental management. Other initiatives include the Lake
Victoria Environmental Management Programme, the Lake Victoria
Fisheries Organization and the operation of the Ministerial Committee
on the Environment of the East African Community.

Although there are demonstrable efforts of regional integration and
improved approaches in environmental management, a few conclusions
can be made with respect to regional policy and political processes for
environmental management. First, the three countries have distinct
national policy-making structures, and the processes of policy and
institutional reforms take place at different paces. Consequently, while
we saw Uganda enacting a framework environmental legislation as early
as 1995, the legislative process in Kenya was not completed until 1999
when the National Environment and Coordination Act was finally
enacted. A similar process to enact framework legislation for environmental management has just begun in Tanzania.

Second, environmental policy and institutional reforms in all of the
three countries began under the umbrella of structural adjustment
programmes. Yet, by the early 1990s, there was increasing recognition
that 'mitigation approaches' to environmental management reforms did
not create the enabling conditions for long-term sustainable development. Around the same period, the World Bank and other key lenders
were willing to move away from 'business as usual' investment in
economic growth towards a more sustained investment in long-term
strategic national policy and legislative reforms.[34] Consequently, building on the NEAP (national environment action plan) processes, the
World Bank and many other bilateral donors have been significantly
involved in institutional reforms in the environment sector, including

bank-rolling the establishment of the national environment management authorities (NEMAs).[35]

It is therefore no surprise that across all three countries, a key characteristic of these reforms has been the restructuring of public institutions for environmental management from mainstream public-service institutions to semi-autonomous and often statutory agencies. For example, as early as the 1990s, the Uganda national parks and game departments were merged to create the Uganda Wildlife Authority. Similar reforms took place in Kenya with the creation of the Kenya Wildlife Services. Currently, similar institutional reforms are occurring in the forestry sector. For example, the forestry department in Uganda has just been wound up to give way to the National Forestry Authority, created under the 2003 National Forestry and Tree Planting Act.

Third, although there is growing emphasis on 'brown' environmental issues, including transboundary pollution and transboundary movement of hazardous waste, there is little evidence to suggest that, at the regional level, progress is being made to address these issues in earnest. In particular, the continuing pollution of Lake Victoria from industrial and other land-based sources could threaten the livelihoods of many people and undermine national economic growth. For all of the three countries, Lake Victoria is one of the most important inland water fisheries.

Fourth, if there is a tendency to think regionally, the tendency to act locally is more evident. While existing literature suggests consensus on the need to harmonize national policies and legislation, especially with respect to managing shared natural resources, evidence suggests that actions to reform policies, legislation and institutions are generally driven and dictated by local political and economic circumstances, rather than the need for further integration, coordination and harnessing of economies of scale.

Finally, most observers of the regional policy reform processes would argue that there is limited evidence of public participation in initiatives of a regional nature. While we see the private sector, such as the national Chambers of Commerce and Industry, being actively involved in the process of regional integration, there are no equally deliberate efforts to involve poor resource users in these processes. Even in the field of environment and natural resources there are currently no known deliberate efforts to engage the public in regional policy processes, such as the work of the Ministerial Committee on the Environment.

# NATIONAL ENVIRONMENTAL GOVERNANCE IN THE CONTEXT OF POVERTY ERADICATION

As already noted, over the past 15 years, all three countries have seen major political, economic and governance reforms at the national level. Towards the end of the 1990s, the poverty reduction strategy papers (PRSPs) became the broad policy frameworks within which major reforms and public investment decisions were being made. Under the enhanced Highly Indebted Poor Countries (HIPC) framework, debt relief and access to international development assistance resources required all recipient countries to submit PRSPs to the boards of the international financial institutions (IFIs). With the exception of Uganda which had already developed its Poverty Eradication Action Plan (PEAP) in 1997, Kenya and Tanzania developed their first PRSPs in 1999. Under this new arrangement, actual financial flows became dependent upon the joint assessments of country-prepared PRSPs by World Bank and International Monetary Fund (IMF) staff in consultation with the national governments. As Kenya, Uganda and Tanzania are all regarded as HIPC countries, they were required to prepare PRSPs.

It is important to note that the PRSP process in East Africa was not the first experience in developing national poverty reduction strategies. In Uganda, a national process[36] was already well advanced when the idea of PRSPs emerged and Uganda was eventually successful in persuading the boards of the IFIs to accept its PEAP as its poverty strategy. In Kenya, the National Poverty Eradication Plan (NPEP) had been formulated through extensive participation of civil society and private-sector organizations, NGOs and government agencies, although implementation had not begun. In Tanzania Vision 2025 had laid out the long-term development goals and perspectives against which the National Poverty Eradication Strategy (NPES) was developed.

Set against this backdrop, government institutions had to realign their programmes to be more poverty focused. This included environmental management institutions. Environmental agencies that until then be-haved largely as conservation agencies had to embark on efforts to align themselves with the poverty reduction priorities set out in the poverty reduction strategies.

The following sub-sections analyse the key elements of environmental reforms at the national level, the key political and economic drivers, and the extent to which this realignment has made it possible (or not) to make environmental and natural resources key drivers in poverty eradication.

# Reorganization of environmental management institutions

One of the key reform processes in all three countries has been the reorganization of environmental management institutions. As already mentioned, Uganda and Kenya now have national environment management authorities and Tanzania has embarked on a similar process.

One of the key guiding principles for the creation of national environmental management authorities was to increase horizontal and vertical coordination among institutions with an environmental remit in these countries. At the horizontal level, coordination needed to be improved among environmental institutions, on the one hand,[37] and between environmental and other agencies, on the other.[38] Conceptually, the national environmental management authorities are supposed to be apex environmental agencies that foster coordination and interaction among sectoral agencies and planning institutions, such as ministries of finance, planning and agriculture.

It is still too early to asses how the National Environment Management Authority (NEMA) in Kenya has performed since it was established less than two years ago. However, the National Environment Management Authority of Uganda, which was created in 1995, has had clear successes and challenges in meeting this coordination function. The following observations can be made with respect to the operations of Uganda's NEMA during the last seven years.

First, the political and economic context within which the institution operates has significant implications for its performance. NEMA has had to make difficult decisions between conserving the environment and approving investments that may destroy some of the country's natural resource wealth. Investments such as the Vegetable Oil Development Project and the development of hydropower at Bujagali Falls are key examples. In both these cases, NEMA was often under strong political pressure to approve environmental impact assessments to allow the projects to proceed before proper scientific and economic analysis had actually been undertaken.[39] The issue here is not that economic development is necessarily bad for the environment; rather, it is that NEMA's decisions were based on political pressure, thereby undermining its own autonomy and reducing the public's faith in it as an independent regulatory institution.

Second, Uganda's NEMA is almost entirely funded by the World Bank. Although efforts are ongoing to explore ways of obtaining sustainable funding for the authority, the implication of the current funding situation is that NEMA remains functioning largely as a World

Bank project. As an institution, therefore, it has to struggle with working alongside its under-resourced government counterparts, while fulfilling its mandate as an agency of the Ugandan government.

Third, in the absence of a clearly designated agency for addressing brown environmental issues, such as pollution control and hazardous waste management, NEMA has been proactive in developing regulations and standards in these areas.[40] Consequently, NEMA has provided the missing link between environmental assets and environmental quality in the face of glaring institutional gaps.

Perhaps more important is the way in which these new institutions are reorienting their roles from purely conservation objectives, to addressing issues of poverty eradication and integration of environment and natural resource concerns within various sectors of the economy. Increasingly, we are seeing more progress in the way in which these institutions are interacting with the macro-economic sectors and the agriculture sector. There is also evidence of these institutions beginning to link up their interventions with those institutions that focus on governance and conflict. Nevertheless, these efforts are still evident at the dialogue level, and what remains to be seen are actions – especially by the governance practitioners – to address the critical links between natural resources and political processes.

## Sectoral policy and legal reforms

In the three countries, there have been reforms in all key environment and natural resource sectors, especially wildlife, tourism, forestry, agriculture and fisheries. Certain aspects of these reforms need to be highlighted. First, the new policies emphasize the role of the private sector and the scaling down of the role of government in managing natural resources. Consequently, corporate social responsibility and transparency will be critical if this approach is to engender poverty reduction.

Second, there is more policy emphasis on public participation in environmental decision-making. Public participation in this respect is meant to ensure that the voices of the poor are heard through effective civil society representation. In an assessment conducted by civil society in Uganda,[41] a number of findings showed how public participation in environmental management can contribute more effectively to poverty eradication. The report found that, although government agencies are increasingly enlisting public participation in the policy-making processes, the practice is less common with respect to decision-making of a more economic nature. The assessment found less participation, for example, in the processes to grant forest concession permits, fish-processing licences and wastewater discharge permits.

This assessment also found that there was a complete lack of access to information with respect to these key economic aspects of natural resource management. This, coupled with poor administrative and judicial redress and remedial mechanisms, undermines the ability of the poor to take advantage of new or alternative economic opportunities. It is therefore evident that future policy directions should focus on strengthening mechanisms for public participation, access to information and access to judicial and administrative redress and remedy, especially for the poor.

---

## Box 5.6 The case of de-gazetting Kenyan forests

In October 2001, the government of Daniel Arap Moi in Kenya issued a gazette notice communicating its intentions to de-gazette 67,600 hectares of forest reserves in different parts of the country. The official government position was that it needed land in order to resettle many landless people.

A number of public-interest organizations raised objections to the proposed de-gazetting and challenged the efforts by government. Many of them saw the efforts as being politically motivated and argued that government was trying to find a cheap way of buying votes by using the country's dwindling protected forest estate. At this time, a number of public-interest law groups in Kenya challenged the proposed de-gazetting in court and events were halted until the disposal of the main suit. As the court battle was going on, the government of Daniel Arap Moi was defeated in a general election in 2003.

Although the court process is still ongoing, public-interest groups in Kenya are convinced that the new government is keen to protect the country's natural resources capital more than the previous government. The government has also expressed its willingness to withdraw the de-gazetting notice.

*Source:* Maurice O. Mak'Oloo, Institute for Law and Environmental Governance, Kenya

---

## Mainstreaming environment and natural resource management

To date, all countries' PRSPs emphasize the need to mainstream environment and natural resources in their various poverty eradication objectives. What the PRSPs and stakeholders involved in environmental and natural resource management have failed to achieve, however, is a clear understanding at the policy level as to why environmental mainstreaming is important for economic growth and poverty reduction, what needs to be mainstreamed and how. We have seen that the majority of the people in the three countries is poor, that the economies are predominantly agriculture based and that poverty is intricately linked to a dependence upon the environment and broader questions of governance. We therefore argue that in order for mainstreaming to be effective, it needs to occur within the context of all three issues.[42]

The Tanzanian PRSP[43] explicitly recognizes the importance of the environment to the survival of the poor. While it does not go into great depth about poverty-environment links or strategies for addressing this issue, it does commit to future iterations of the PRS, including better integration of poverty-environment linkages and incorporating environmental quality indicators within its poverty monitoring strategy.

In Uganda, the Plan for Modernization of Agriculture (PMA) is seen as the key strategy for eradicating rural poverty. From the outset, the PMA has sought to integrate environmental and natural resources concerns within central government policy reforms and local government development grants. With over 85 per cent of Uganda's population living in rural areas and employed in natural resource-based activities, the PMA sees environmental integration and sustainable natural resource utilization as key elements to its successful implementation and to the sustainability of its interventions.

## The changing landscape of environmental decision-making

Another key observation is the changing landscape of environmental decision-making. Increasingly, environmental decision-making is shifting away from the mainstream environmental policy institutions to the political arena. Consequently, decisions on whether to de-gazette protected areas (e.g. the Karura forest in Kenya); on the changing land use of an area; on extinguishing the rights of poor farmers (e.g. the Butamira Forest Reserve in Uganda; see Box 5.7); and on compensating victims of unfair treatment (e.g. the Bunyahulu Gold Mines in Tanzania) are more politically motivated and not necessarily driven by scientific rationality or socio-equity considerations. What we have seen in many of these cases is that political decisions are made in favour of particular individuals or businesses, and the environmental agencies are compelled to work backwards to legitimize them as policy decisions. In such cases, decisions are not necessarily guided by scientific information and social-equity considerations, but by political expedience and, more often, by political patronage.

# BOX 5.7 THE CASE OF BUTAMIRA FOREST RESERVE IN KAGOMA CONSTITUENCY, JINJA DISTRICT, UGANDA

Frank Nabwiso is MP of Kagoma constituency in Jinja district, eastern Uganda. Within his constituency lies Butamira Forest Reserve, a forest that has become well known in Uganda due to the extensive press coverage of the intense battle of ownership and user rights that has taken place over the last decade. Butamira Forest Reserve is known to be the single largest forest reserve in Jinja district, and accounts for approximately 20 per cent of the entire forest estate. It was established by the then Busoga Kingdom government in 1929 and was leased, in 1939, to Kakira Sugar Works.

Although Kakira Sugar Works had the lease of the forest, it did not have the right to change the use of the land from forest to plantation, and all through the 1950s and beyond, attempts were made to gain the right to utilize the Reserve to grow sugar cane. In 1997, as the lease was set to expire, Kakira Sugar Works, which had made repeated attempts over the previous 50 years to exploit the reserve, applied to the forestry department, once again, to utilize the Reserve for its operations.

Kakira Sugar Works was, on this occasion, granted permission, and the new permit gave the company the rights to put the entire forest reserve under use for general purposes. With this new permit, but without having undertaken an environmental impact assessment (EIA), as required by law, the company embarked on a scheme to clear the existing forest estate and replace it with sugar cane plantations. This enraged the local community, who depended upon the forest for their livelihood in terms of fuelwood and other forest products. The reserve also serves as a catchment for an important water source for the community. The community formed itself into a group known as the Butamira Pressure Group, which sought to prevent the destruction of the reserve. As a result of pressure from this group, and other alleged mismanagement of the forestry sector, the parliament of Uganda instituted an investigation of the issues surrounding the issuance of the permit. This found that the permit was issued fraudulently and recommended that it be cancelled with immediate effect.

In November 2001, the concerns of the local people led to a petition being presented to parliament by the Honourable Frank Nabwiso on behalf of three organizations: the Advocates Coalition for Development and Environment, the Uganda Wildlife Society and the Butamira Pressure Group. Throughout this period, individual members of the Butamira Pressure Group were constantly harassed by government leaders in Jinja district. The petition was immediately referred to the Sessional Committee on Natural Resources, who uncovered reports that the resident commissioner for Jinja working with the chief government valuer had started a process to value the permits of the tree farmers for subsequent compensation. They strongly argued that the reserve should be protected. However, the report was delayed in order to allow the addition of an addendum by Uganda's environment minister at the time, Ruhakana-Rugunda, effectively overturning the findings of the committee.

In the subsequent debate, the environment minister went on to assure parliament that the government had shelved the idea of de-gazetting the Forest Reserve. However, he requested parliament to pass a motion allowing the government to issue a permit to Kakira Sugar Works, allowing it to grow sugar cane – claiming this to 'be in line with government policy on poverty eradication and sustainable development'. The debate on the report was so heated that, for the first time in the history of the Ugandan parliament, the matter concerning forest reserves had to be decided through a division lobby. When the matter was put to vote, 32 members of parliament opposed the motion, 86 supported it, while 5 members abstained.

The people of Butamira may have lost this battle; but the sustained pressure that they and their MP applied during their fight was not in vain. Issues concerning forest reserves and the protection of natural resources received an enormous amount of sympathetic attention in Uganda, and while it cannot be claimed that the incident weakened the government, those involved would certainly look back on it as a highly embarrassing episode (see Figure 5.1).

*Source:* ACODE (2003)

The implications of this situation are that the poor will continue to be deprived of their core productive assets and coping strategies, leading to further vulnerability, environmentally related stress and increased deterioration in the quality and quantity of environmental goods and services. Therefore, if environmental management institutions are to act as drivers for poverty eradication, political governance frameworks must enable them to regain their political space, become champions of the poor and provide avenues for more cost-effective administrative redress and remedial systems.

## Decentralization of ENRM responsibilities to local governments

The restructuring of environmental management institutions has proceeded hand in hand with efforts to decentralize environmental and natural resources management (ENRM). In all three countries, districts and lower local government units are increasingly being asked to take up managing key environmental resources, including forests, wetlands, water and sanitation. Yet, local authorities in each of the three countries are heavily dependent upon central government for financing. Despite stated government commitments, central governments and environment ministries have resisted transferring appropriate and sufficient powers to local authorities. In the narrowest view, this can be seen as resistance by political leaders who fear losing current economic benefits, including rent-seeking opportunities that they currently have over natural resources.[44]

*Source:* ACODE file photo

**Figure 5.1** *The Butamira Pressure Group meeting the Parliamentary Sessional Committee on Natural Resources in Jinja*

More widely, there is a genuine concern over the lack of capacity to plan, budget and implement environmental programmes effectively at the local level. This has been exacerbated by the increasing number of conditional grants to local governments who are overstretching their capacity to plan and allocate resources efficiently in priority poverty reduction activities. Consequently, problems of financial, human and infrastructure capacity remain. Unless these constraints are addressed in order to enable targeted investments in environmental management, we are unlikely to see sustained improvements in the quantity and quality of the natural resource capital. This could undermine efforts for poverty eradication.

Furthermore, there are still problems of governance at the local government level, as well as concerns about corruption. In Uganda, for example, tendering processes involving natural resources are becoming major business for politicians who are trying to cash in on their electoral successes; therefore, there is less emphasis on utilising such resources for poverty eradication. Addressing these problems will not only require capacity building for local governments, it will also be necessary to build a strong civil society that can independently monitor and hold local government officials to account.

## Democratization can lead to improvements in environmental integration

Greater democratization in all three countries, as described earlier, is leading to better integration of environmental issues within government programmes. At the most obvious level was the recent appointment of Professor Wangari Maathi, an environmental activist during the KANU administration and now Nobel Peace Prize winner, as deputy minister in the Kenyan Ministry of Environment. In Tanzania, the government has given due recognition to the issue of institutional and legal reform in the environmental sector in order to promote good environmental governance at the national level, and is on course to develop a new environmental governance framework. Equally, in Uganda, the government has committed to wide stakeholder participation during the revision of the PEAP, including explicitly seeking representatives from environmental civil society organizations to participate in sector working groups (SWGs) and the formation of a team of experts on cross-cutting issues, including the environment and natural resources.

## Governance issues are at the core

Governance in its broadest sense is at the core of the debate between environment, poverty and politics. There is no doubt that the environment and natural resources will be the key catalyst to poverty eradication in the region. Because political power is closely intertwined with wealth generated through the exploitation of nature, reducing poverty must squarely address the issue of power imbalances over ownership and access to key natural resources assets. It is also tenable to argue that, because natural resources are the bread and butter for the poor, they offer compelling cases for promoting and consolidating key governance principles of participation, vertical and horizontal accountability, and representation.

## Public-interest civil society organizations can make a difference

Over the last ten years, we have seen the evolution of public-interest organizations in the three countries working together to improve governance in the context of poverty eradication.[45] These organizations, many of which operate with an environmental perspective, have invested in programmes to promote accountability, transparency and responsiveness in the way that the environment is managed, in the way that political decisions with environmental implications are made, and in the way that the private sector conducts business. These organizations have initiated and conducted training programmes for the judiciary;[46] engaged in policy advocacy to strengthen environmental procedural rights in both policy and legislation;[47] challenged governmental decisions that deprive the poor of their environmental assets, including by providing pro bono legal services to the poor;[48] and worked with government and parliament to develop new policies and laws.[49]

In all of these cases, public-interest organizations with active policy and advocacy programmes in the environment and environmental rights are proving to be effective vehicles for promoting the triple objectives of good governance, poverty reduction and environmental protection. By holding government accountable in environmental decision-making, they are providing a voice for the poor in policy- and decision-making. By protecting the environment, they are contributing to protecting poor people's assets. And by advocating for responsible and responsive decisions and pro-poor policies and laws, they are helping to build a strong foundation for good governance.

Many of the above cases have demonstrated that the poor are unable to access judicial and administrative mechanisms for redress and remediation because they are powerless, can be ignored or are unaware of their rights. Current experiences suggest that, in the foreseeable future, poor people will rely on public-interest advocacy organizations to act as a bridge to formal judicial and administrative redress systems. Yet, as in all other cases, these public-interest advocacy organizations are also limited by capacity constraints and funding constraints, which affect their long-term viability, independence and autonomy.

## LOOKING TO THE FUTURE

In this chapter, we have seen how environmental management institutions in East Africa are expanding their mandate beyond the traditional conservation activities to embrace the new development policy framework that focuses on poverty eradication. We have also described the political context within which this process is taking place and the key drivers of policy change that influence the progress that can be achieved by these institutions. Based on the foregoing analysis, it is possible to draw some general conclusions about the trends in this intricate relationship between poverty, politics and environment.

First, if the growing interest in the environment and natural resources (ENR) continues, and if environmental institutions keep focusing their interventions on poverty reduction, we could see more commitments at the macro-economic policy level to channel additional public financial resources into the ENR sector. This should result in more positive and direct impacts on poverty reduction, and the building of a strong foundation for sustainable economic growth and development. Yet, for this change to happen there is need for more specific quantitative data to demonstrate how ENR contributes directly to poverty reduction. And this will require initial public investments to generate quantitative data and document key trends in the ENR sector.

Second, the contribution of the environment and natural resources to national economic growth and to a reduction in poverty is intricately linked to the democratization processes in the region. As observed in this chapter, undemocratic and corrupt states can abuse the natural resource base, inflate transaction costs for doing business in the sector, and limit the economic opportunities available to the poor. In a situation where ENR institutions are not functioning properly and have limited financial and human capacity, all actors end up transfering these costs to the environment and natural resources either through illegal exploitation or dumping of waste to offset their costs.

However, ongoing political processes in the three countries could be managed to change this situation. The political and constitutional reforms in Kenya and Uganda provide an opportunity for strengthening political accountability, for reviewing the political costs of public administration, and for empowering institutions in environmental governance and accountability. It is important to recognize that setbacks in the democratization process, especially in the area of natural resources, could become a harbinger for environmentally related conflicts. This would, in turn, undermine political stability and democratic progress, and divert much needed public resources to fighting insecurity and insurgency.

Third, because of the macro-economic policies being pursued by the three countries, we are likely to see a more dominant role of the private sector in the exploitation of natural resources. While the private sector is driven by markets and profits, creating win-wins for poverty reduction and natural resources management will require more social responsibility on the part of the private sector. We are therefore likely to see the continuing influence of public-interest civil society organizations in trying to fill the accountability vacuum that could emerge in the absence of strong and autonomous public ENR institutions that can effectively regulate the private sector.

Finally, the good news is that policy-makers are clearly beginning to listen. In the environment sector in East Africa, we are seeing increased dialogue among policy-makers on means to integrate the environment and natural resources in the poverty reduction strategies. Although efforts are still needed to 'win over' the decision-makers in areas of governance and in the macro-economic policy arena, there are indications of progress. What are needed are very specific measures and actions that can be implemented in the context of overall governance reforms.

# ENDNOTES

1 Also cited in Tumushabe and Bainomugisha (forthcoming).
2 In this chapter, reference to East Africa refers to the countries of Kenya, Tanzania and Uganda only.
3 See USAID et al (2004), where the authors argue that 'while the fate of Africa's natural resources cannot be separated from the broader context of economic and development challenges, neither can Africa's economic and development future be separated from the management of its natural resources'.
4 For example, Uganda created its first ministry of natural resources in 1987.
5 For example, the famous Masai-Mara defies the colonial national boundaries between Kenya and Tanzania.
6 Lake Victoria, the biggest freshwater lake in the world with its unique trademark fish, the Nile perch, is shared between the three countries.
7 For example, the Sango Bay-Minziro Ecosystems is a rich biodiversity area crossing from the Rakai district of southern Uganda to the Bukoba district of northern Tanzania.
8 See respective PRSPs for all three countries. Available on the World Bank website: www.worldbank.org.
9 See Ministry of Finance, Planning and Economic Development (2003).
10 See Ministry of Finance, Planning and Economic Development (2003).
11 See Ministry of Finance, Planning and Economic Development (2003).
12 Derived from www.worldbank.org information obtained for the year 2000.
13 See, for example, work by John Mugabe and Godber. W. Tumushabe
14 In his study of governance in Africa, Hyden (1992) defines governance as 'the conscious management of regime structures with a view to enhancing the legitimacy of the public realm'. He argues that this incorporates three principle dimensions of governance – citizen influence and oversight; responsive and responsible leadership; and social reciprocities among citizens.
15 See Okoth-Ogendo and Tumushabe (1999).
16 See Okoth-Ogendo and Tumushabe (1999).
17 Informal institutions and norms for environmental management were a dominant feature of the phase, as described above.
18 See poverty reduction strategy papers for Kenya, Uganda and Tanzania. Available on the World Bank website: www.worldbank.org.
19 See Section 4 of the 1995 National Environment Statute (Uganda) and Article 39 of the 1995 Constitution of the Republic of Uganda.

20  Article 39 of the 1995 Constitution of Uganda provides for the right to a clean and healthy environment. See also the national objectives and directive principles of state policy in the constitution.

21  See Part II of the 1999 Environmental Management Coordination Act.

22  See, for example, Greenwatch versus Golf Course Holding Ltd, HC Misc. Application No. 390/2001 (arising out of HCCS No. 834/2001, Uganda); Siraji Waiswa versus Kakira Sugar Works Ltd. Misc. Application No. 230/2001 (arising out of HCCS No. 69/2001, Uganda).

23  Civil Case No. 24 of 1998. HC, (Dar).

24  See the East African Cooperation Development Strategy (1997–2000), available at www.eastafricaweb.com/EAC/strategy.php.

25  The East Africa Cross Borders Project, which is jointly implemented by Kenya, Uganda and Tanzania, with funding from the Global Environment Facility, is one such initiative that focuses upon ecosystem-level institutional coordination.

26  See *Common Text on Identified Areas of Cooperation between the United Republic of Tanzania, the Republic of Kenya and the Republic of Uganda* (November 1993).

27  The treaty came into force on 7 July 2000. Available from www.eachq.org/eac-TheTreaty.htm.

28  Personal telephone conversation with Robert Wabunoha, senior legal counsel, National Environment Management Authority, Uganda.

29  See Article 39 of the 1995 Constitution of the Republic of Uganda, 1995, and Section 4 of the 1995 National Environment Management Statute.

30  For example, the right to a clean and healthy environment has now been incorporated under section 3(1) of the 2000 Environmental Management and Coordination Act.

31  The Rio Declaration is the political statement that came out of the United Nations Conference on Environment and Development (UNCED) held in Rio de Janeiro, Brazil, in 1992.

32  The MoU represents the first expressions of intent to grant citizens access to the judicial process in each of the partner states.

33  See Tumushabe and Bainomugisha (2002).

34  See Mugabe et al, 1997, supra note 12. See also Frances (1996).

35  For more detailed discussions on World Bank policy on adjustment lending, see World Bank (2003).

36  Uganda's PEAP was first established in 1997, two years before PRSPs emerged as a conditionality for HIPC countries. The PEAP was revised in 2000 to include the development of sector-wide approaches, the participatory research carried out by the Uganda Participatory Poverty Assessment Project (UPPAP), the constraints identified in the *Poverty Status Report* and the development of costings of public actions and indicators that could be monitored.

37  In Uganda, efforts are currently underway to develop a sector-wide plan for the environment and natural resources sector (SWAP) in order to ensure coordination in budgeting and more poverty-targeting in public expenditure (Claire Ireland and Godber Tumushabe are members of the Environment and Natural Resources Sector Working Group, or ENR-SWG).

38  The National Environment Statute of Uganda, for example, establishes a policy committee on the environment chaired by the prime minister as the key structure to ensure coordination.

39  In the case of the hydro-power development project by Nile Independent Power at Bujagali, the power purchase agreement (PPA) had to be 'bulldozed' through

parliament for approval even before the environmental impact assessment (EIA) for the project was approved.

40 For example, standards or regulations have been developed for air quality, hazardous waste management and ozone depleting substances.

41 See work undertaken by the Advocates Coalition for Development and Environment.

42 For a detailed discussion on mainstreaming, see Tumushabe (forthcoming).

43 See United Republic of Tanzania (2002).

44 See Ribot (2002).

45 For example, the work being done by the Advocates Coalition for Development and Environment (ACODE), www.acode-u.org, and Greenwatch in Uganda; the Lawyers Environmental Action Team (LEAT) and the Human Rights and Legal Resource Centre in Tanzania; and the Greenbelt Movement and Reconcile in Kenya.

46 To date, Greenwatch and ACODE have been conducting judicial training programmes in environmental law and public interest litigation issues for the Ugandan judiciary.

47 For example, ACODE's engagement in the forestry legislation processes was a key factor in ensuring that the provisions on access to information and access to justice were retained in the 2003 National Forestry and Tree Planting Act.

48 LEAT in Tanzania provided pro bono legal services for the community in the Rufiji Valley when their environment was being threatened by an alleged multi-billion dollar investment in prawn farming. In Uganda, ACODE helped the Butamira Pressure Group to prepare and present the first-ever petition by a community challenging a government proposal to de-gazette Butamira Forest Reserve, extinguish the tree-farming rights of its members and allocate the reserve to Kakira Sugar Works in order to turn it into a sugar plantation. Although the petition was partly unsuccessful because of apparent manipulation by the government, it was a precedent-setting petition in public-interest advocacy work.

49 In all of the three countries, public interest groups are working with government agencies on abroad range of policy, legal and institutional reforms for environmental management.

# REFERENCES

AICAD (African Institute for Capacity Development) and JICA (2003) *Examination of the Needs through the Study of Poverty Reduction Strategy Papers for Kenya, Uganda and Tanzania*, Report prepared by Taiyo Enterprises Ltd under the general instructions of AICAD

Government of Uganda (2002) *UPPAP/MFPED Participatory Poverty and Environment Assessment (PPEA)*, Briefing paper, GoU

Ministry of Finance, Planning and Economic Development (2003) *Uganda Poverty Status Report 2003: Achievers and Pointers for the PEAP Revision*, Government of Uganda

Mugabe J., Seymour, F. and Clark, N. (1997) *Environmental Adjustment in Kenya: Emerging Opportunities and Challenges*, Ecopolicy 9, ACTS Press, Nairobi

Okoth-Ogendo, H. W. O and Tumushabe, G. W. (1999) (eds) *Governing the Environment: Political Change and Natural Resource Management in Eastern and Southern Africa*, ACTS Press, Nairobi, Kenya

Ribot, J. C. (2002) *Democratic Decentralisation of Natural Resources: Institutionalising Popular Participation*, World Resources Institute, Washington, D.C.

Seymour, F. (1996) *Lending Credibility: New Mandates and Partnerships for the World Bank*

Tumushabe, G. W. (forthcoming) *Poverty, Agriculture and Environment: Learning through Case Studies*

Tumushabe, G. W. and Bainomugisha, A. (forthcoming) *Environment and Parliamentary Representation in Africa: The Case Study of Uganda*

Tumushabe, G. W. and Bainomugisha, A. (2002) *Consolidating Environmental Democracy through Access to Justice*, Information and Participation, ACODE Policy Series No. 5, ACODE, Kampala

United Republic of Tanzania (2002) *Poverty Reduction Strategy Paper*, October

USAID et al (2004) *Nature, Wealth and Power: Emerging Best Practice for Revitalizing Rural Africa*

World Bank (2003) *From Adjustment Lending to Development Policy Support Lending: Key issues in the Update of World Bank Policy*, www.lnweb18.worldbank.org/SCSL+Dev/OD+8.60/CW-OD-860

(1998) *World Reference Atlas 316*, second edition, Dorling Kindersley

# 6

# Stories on the Environment and Conflict from Northern Nigeria

*Jean-Paul Penrose, Hassan Bdliya and John Chettleborough*

## INTRODUCTION

In conflict situations not everyone is a loser. The Hadejia Nguru Wetlands in northern Nigeria provide a fascinating insight into the complexity of issues surrounding access to, and use of, environmental resources such as land and water. Through the experiences of ordinary people living in and around the wetlands, we explore how political processes and decisions, often made far away from the wetlands themselves, have profound impacts on those living there. The role of national policies, processes of 'agricultural modernization', the dismantling of traditional institutions and political marginalization will be examined in the light of recent social, environmental and economic changes in the wetlands.

In 1998, Alhaji Musa became the *Dagaci* or traditional village leader of Pandim, a village in the Hadejia Nguru Wetlands (HNW) in northern Nigeria. It should have been a special year to remember for Alhaji Musa. And, indeed, it was, but for all the wrong reasons. In his first months as *Dagaci* he had to help his community through a period of unprecedented violence that broke out between villagers, predominantly farmers from Pandim and Fulani cattle herders in the area.

For several days, farmers and cattle herders fought pitched battles that resulted in the burning down of three villages, and the killing of 19 farmers and, according to some sources, up to 50 cattle herders. As well as lives lost, the conflict resulted in the loss of resources that were vital to local livelihoods such as irrigation pumps, farm implements and bicycles. All of the village food stores were destroyed and, as Alhaji Musa recalls, 'we were left without food and without clothes'. The state government intervened by providing 900kg of maize in order to prevent starvation. The impacts of the conflict remain today, with constant tension between farmers and herders. This tension makes it hard for the nomadic Fulani, the predominant cattle herders in the area, to find grazing and they are pushed into areas where grazing is more marginal. This situation is now commonplace across the HNW.

Conflict between cattle herders and farmers over access to land and water has been a feature of rural life in Nigeria for centuries. However, during the last 30 years the scale and violence of this conflict has escalated significantly. The issue now receives regular attention in the Nigerian media (see Box 6.1). The government response to conflict tends to be reactive. It varies from under- to over-reaction and is typically heavy handed, involving armed police or the army. This has done little to diminish the risk of violent conflict.

---

## BOX 6.1 NEWSPAPER HEADLINES ON FARMER-PASTORALIST CONFLICT IN NIGERIA

'Crop farmers and herdsmen clash imminent in Enugu' (*This Day*, 5 March 2002)

'Thousands of Nigerian herdsmen flee into Cameroon' (*This Day*, 11 April 2002)

'Nine killed as farmers and herdsmen fight in Plateau' (*Punch*, 29 May 2002)

'Seven killed as herdsmen farmers battle in Borno' (*Daily Trust*, 10 December 2002)

'Clash claims ten lives in Adamawa (Fulani herders/Yingu farmers)' (*Daily Trust*, 10 December 2002)

'8 killed in Adamawa (farmers/*Fulani* herders)' (*Daily Trust*, 3 March 2003)

---

The HNW provide a fascinating insight into the role of environmental resources in situations of conflict. This chapter will underline the critical role that access to political space plays in such conflict situations. It will illustrate that the environment itself is rarely a true *cause* of conflict. Rather, it is a *trigger* and reflects underlying tensions related to the amount of power held by different stakeholders at national, regional and local levels over access to a range of goods and services, including natural resources. We shall see that for some groups, particularly elites, conflict is not necessarily a bad thing and helps to strengthen their power base and ensure continued resource capture. For this elite minority, conflict management and avoidance may act against their interests and may therefore be opposed.

In our analysis, personal stories and the viewpoints of stakeholders will be used to demonstrate how political marginalization and institutional structures and processes contribute to conflict situations in the HNW, in which the environment is often a pawn.

In particular we shall see that:

- The wetlands' population has become marginalized from the regional and national political arena. This has allowed natural resource capture by political and urban elites outside of the HNW, leading to increased resource scarcity for those within the wetlands.
- Within the wetlands, the marginalization of certain groups, especially cattle herders, has led to inequitable access to resources.
- The shift of power from traditional authorities and institutions to local government has reduced the capacity of traditional conflict prevention and management mechanisms, and has often contributed to conflict.

These and a range of other factors, including migration into the area and population growth, have all contributed to a situation in the HNW in which the level of conflict has escalated significantly during the past 30 years.

# THE HADEJIA-NGURU WETLANDS

The Hadejia-Nguru Wetlands are part of the Komadougou-Yobe river basin in north-eastern Nigeria (see Diagram 6.1). The wetlands were formed where the waters of the Hadejia and Jama'are rivers met lines of ancient sand dunes and split into multiple channels, lakes, seasonal ponds and zones of seasonally flooded land. Precipitation feeding the wetlands follows a distinct pattern, with 80 per cent occurring between August and September (Hollis et al, 1993). Prior to the construction of a series of dams, the area was characterized by extreme flooding during the August–October period, inundating up to 2000 square kilometers, and massive recession of floodwaters during the 'dry season' so that by April water would be found only in a few river channels (Lemly et al, 2000). Under this hydrological regime the HNW became a site of high floral and faunal value. The Nguru Lake and Marama Channel have been designated as Nigeria's only Ramsar site. Within the wetlands, Dagona Sanctuary and Zurgum Baderi Reserve have been designated components of the Chad Basin National Park. The Baturia Wetlands form a state government-designated nature reserve. Within the national park, no grazing, farming, fishing or harvesting of wild products are permitted, although enforcement of these restrictions is patchy. Within the Baturia Wetlands, fishing is allowed with permission from the local government, which provides some regulation and control.

The wetlands have a high level of natural resource productivity largely because of the ecological effects of seasonal inundation. They consequently support approximately 1.5 million people (Bdliya, 1998).

The population of the HNW is ethnically diverse, with Hausa, Manga, Bade and Fulani making up the dominant ethnic groups in descending order of population size. The majority of the region's population is Muslim. Less than 5 per cent are Christian, typically migrants with government jobs. Cattle herders are predominantly of Fulani origin, although increasingly Tuareg camel herders are found seeking grazing. Traditionally, migration was seasonal, with herders and fishermen coming to the HNW during the dry season for grazing and fishing and leaving during the rainy season. However, the past three decades have seen increased levels of permanent settlement in the HNW, encouraged by government policies.

For communities in northern Nigeria, the wetlands have, for generations, provided valuable resources and formed an important part of their livelihoods. Under natural conditions the area provides an abundant habitat for fish, a variety of valuable forest products and, as floodwaters recede, luxuriant grazing resources and fertile agricultural land. Eaton and Sarch (1997) estimate that in a typical year 250,000 head of cattle may be reared in the wetlands, and livestock markets in the area provide an income of 416 million naira (US$5.2 million at 1995 prices). Rice provides a revenue of some 250 million naira (US$3.2 million); 6000 metric tonnes of fish are caught each year with an annual turnover of 454 million naira (US$ 5.6 million); and the marketing of doum palm fronds provides some 35 million naira (US$0.5 million) (Okali and Bdliya, 1998).

At 353 people per square kilometre, population density is significantly higher than in the surrounding areas (Ibrahim and Chiroma, 1998). Until the mid 1990s, population growth in the HNW was estimated at 3.3 per cent per annum as a result of permanent in-migration from neighbouring arid and degraded areas (Chiroma and Polet, 1996). Although the population is growing within HNW, increased competition over resources means that it is less rapid than before. Some villages have even witnessed population decline.

In addition to supporting local populations, the wetlands have had a central role in the regional economy for centuries (Hollis et al, 1993), providing a food source for key cities such as Kano. Critically, the

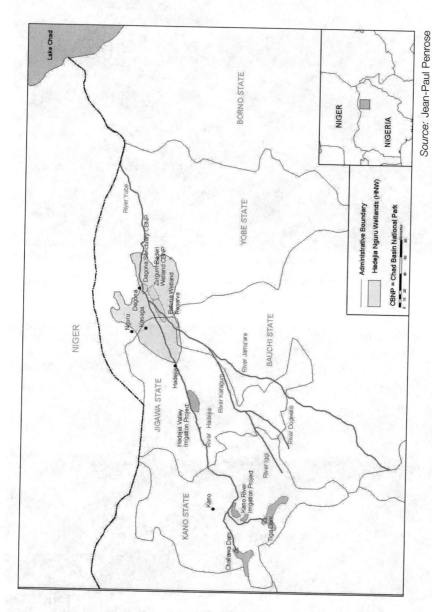

**Diagram 6.1** *Location of the Hadejia Nguru Wetlands*

*Source:* Jean-Paul Penrose

**Figure 6.1** *Land for grazing is increasingly scarce in the Hadejia Nguru Wetlands*

**Figure 6.2** *Fishing in Hadejia Nguru Wetlands*

HNW are responsible for recharging aquifers that cover much of north-eastern Nigeria and that supply water to communities in some of the most arid parts of the country.

However, since the early 1970s, this picture of wetlands productivity has changed considerably. While still productive, yields for agriculture, fisheries and cattle have fallen considerably. In addition, there has been increased competition for access to, and use of, natural resources, leading to high levels of conflict.

So, what has brought about this change in the HNW? The following section explores, from the perspective of a local farmer and a cattle herder, the issues which have led to this situation of reduced productivity and increased conflict over environmental resources.

# Through the Eyes of a Farmer
## and Cattle Herder

### The farmer

> Before, I could easily obtain 100 bundles of millet a year. Now I can only obtain ten, and other poorer villagers who are unable to protect their crops from birds can obtain even less. (Mohammed Grema, *Wakili* – village head, of Kasaga).

During the 1960s, Mohammed Grema, like most of the villagers of Kasaga, farmed land to the south of the village. This was where the best agricultural land was found. He practised a combination of wet season upland farming and recession agriculture on the floodplains, utilizing the residual moisture from the receding floods (*fadama* farming). Settled and Fulani (nomadic) herders were an integral part of the system. They would pay Mohammed to allow their cattle to graze upon the crop residues on his farms, thus helping to fertilize soils as well as providing him with an additional income. Mohammed's income was supplemented by fishing, using traditional *sankiya* traps in the dry season river channels. Fishing rights were clearly issued according to a comprehensive set of traditional regulations. Often individuals or families would have rights to particular ponds, and visiting fishermen would pay fees to use them.

The system of farming, fishing and grazing which Mohammed describes worked in a reasonably integrated way. However, he is the first to admit that there were times when conflicts occurred – between farmers and herders, farmers and fishermen and between other stakeholders. It was the role of the *Wakili*, as village head, to resolve such issues. Mohammed notes that this was almost always achieved without resorting to violent conflict. The situation began to change during the 1970s, when the federal government embarked upon a programme of dam construction and water management projects. This programme would significantly and adversely affect Mohammed's livelihood. Yet, the financial driver for this programme (substantial oil revenues) and the motives (demands by a political elite in Kano for water for urban and agricultural use) were issues that were very remote from Mohammed's existence in the wetlands.

## A new focus on dams

By 1970, Nigeria had turned from an agrarian-based to an oil-based economy, with petroleum making up 58 per cent of export value. The oil price hike of 1973 ensured that the government was awash with money. Public spending priorities focused upon investments in infrastructure, prestige projects, investments in 'modernization', public salaries and military expenditure. Probably the single most significant element was investment in infrastructure, including dams. A rapidly growing population in Kano in northern Nigeria with a powerful political voice (see Box 6.2) demanded investment in water resources infrastructure to ease growing urban water shortages and to support 'modernization of agriculture' programmes through irrigation (Wunder, 2003). The importance and power of Kano in Nigerian politics should not be underestimated. At a time of high oil revenues, the opportunity for the federal government to buy political influence in the Kano region through a programme focused upon the construction of water resources infrastructure and agricultural modernization must have seemed politically attractive.

First constructed was the Tiga Dam on the upper reaches of the Hadejia River (see Diagram 6.1). Built in 1972, it provided irrigation for 14,000ha of land near Kano (the Kano River Irrigation Project) and water for the city. Most of the beneficiaries were landowners and investors from Kano who derived considerable benefits from the profits of irrigated agriculture, as well as from contracts for constructing the irrigation infrastructure. During the 1980s, two other dam projects were started, although they were not completed until 1992: the Hadejia Valley Barrage, built just upstream of Hadejia town to irrigate 8000ha of land and the Challawa Gorge Dam, located further upstream as a dry season storage facility. As a result of these dams, the Hadejia River is now artificially controlled over 80 per cent of its length (Goes, 1997).

The dams retain water, preventing the natural flooding cycle, and instead ensure a more constant year-round flow in the local rivers, suitable for irrigation purposes. As a result, the typical flooding of the wetlands has declined by over half. While, during the late 1960s, more than 2000 square kilometres of land flooded in the rainy season, this had fallen to less than 900 square kilometres during the early 1980s. Some claim that the Tiga Dam has led to a 50 per cent decrease in the wetland habitat and reduced groundwater levels by 25m in places (Pearce, 1992).

---

## BOX 6.2 WHY THE POWER OF TRADITIONAL GOVERNMENT WAS REDUCED IN NIGERIA

Under the British colonial administration, Nigeria was divided into three administrative regions (north, west and east), representing the dominant ethnic groups (Hausa, Yoruba and Igbo). A different system of administration was used in each region. While the British introduced their own administrative structures to the western and eastern regions, in the north they practised 'indirect rule' and handed responsibility for governance to the traditional system of government: the Emirates. The Emirs presided over a cohesive and subservient hierarchy, right down to village leaders such as the *Wakili*. This approach led to the development of a northern power base not matched by the other two regions. Northern regional power was focused upon Kano city. The north regularly displayed its power during the 1960s by voting *en masse* on specific issues, giving it considerable influence over national policy.

In an attempt, partly, to reduce the dominance of the Northern power block, a process of state creation was introduced in which the powers of traditional authorities, the bedrock of northern political power, were transferred to newly created states and local governments. Kano, nonetheless, retains a high level of political importance within Nigeria and most federal governments have contained at least one minister from Kano. Within the northern region Kano is politically, commercially, industrially and culturally dominant, ensuring that the needs of Kano interests are met before those of rural areas such as the Hadejia Nguru Wetlands (HNW). As one local leader describes it, 'the Emir of Kano can raise more dust than the five Emirs of the HNW put together'.

---

## Livelihood impacts of the dams

The impacts on local livelihoods in the wetlands have been complex and have varied both spatially and temporally.

During the late 1970s, Mohammed Grema recalls that it became clear to local farmers that the area flooded in the wet season was declining in size and that this was reducing the availability of land for both

*Source:* JP Penrose

**Figure 6.3** *Typha grass is colonising the Hadejia Nguru Wetlands affecting fishermens' livekihoods*

*fadama* farming, using the residual moisture of the floods, and for dry season cattle grazing. This was the first impact of the new dams.

During the early 1980s, Mohammed noticed the second impact – the arrival of a new grass species taking hold in the wetlands. *Typha australis* is an invasive grass which grows aggressively where water is permanent. Under the new hydrological regime established by the dams, *typha* spread rapidly across the HNW. It began to block river channels, reducing the flow to some areas, causing desiccation of the flood-plain and destruction of its grazing potential. Ironically, rapid *typha* growth began to block the channels supplying Kano with water, requiring the Kano River Basin Development Authority to increase releases from the Tiga and Challawa Dams in order to ensure adequate water supply.

In other areas, the *typha* grass had the opposite effect. By diverting the releases from the dams into confined areas, it actually led to a new phenomenon: dry season flooding. In 1995, this dry season flooding destroyed the *Wakili*'s prized mango orchard and began to inundate agricultural land used by other farmers. Eventually, all of the farmers were forced to move to less productive land, leading to an inevitable fall in agricultural productivity. This was compounded by rapid population growth of *quelea* spp. – birds which thrive in the breeding grounds provided by *typha*. *Quelea* are infamous in northern Nigeria for decimating crops such as sorghum and millet. Poorer households that cannot afford crop protection particularly suffer from the birds.

The new hydrological regime adversely affected fisheries in the HNW. The change in flooding patterns led to ambiguity over fishing rights. Greater levels of floodwater in the dry season often meant that pond boundaries were no longer distinguishable or that new areas, over which no one had fishing rights, were created. These ambiguities mean that conflict between fishermen is now a common occurrence in the area.

In those parts of the HNW experiencing reduced flooding, fish catches began to fall and their value dropped, as fish scarcity increased. Alhaji Abubahar Gambo of Dagona village recalls:

> In the past we used to have a lot people coming (and paying) to fish all around the village; but because of the lack of water, many of these people and even Dagona villagers have migrated out. Most able-bodied men have migrated elsewhere to find some other work. As for the women, they have resorted to weaving mats or harvesting doum palm fruits or tamarind to sell in the village.

As the quantity and quality of land and water available for farming declined, conflict over access to these resources became inevitable. Conflict has been most evident between herders and farmers. However, Mohammed notes that there is now conflict between farmers themselves over access to water for small-scale irrigation. Much of this conflict results from upstream farmers abstracting water to the detriment of downstream users. As a *Wakili*, Mohammed says that he is spending an increasing amount of time helping to resolve conflicts between a greater range of stakeholders than was ever the case in the past.

As a counterbalance to the increase in conflict involving farmers and fishermen, the declining availability of resources in Kasaga eventually forced many of the pastoralists to graze their cattle elsewhere, leading to a decline in, but not cessation of, the frequency of farmer-cattle herder-related conflict. The pastoralists did not leave the wetlands, they just relocated to another area. Consequently, while conflict between farmers and pastoralists in Kasaga lessened, the overall picture in the HNW during this time was one in which both pastoralists and farmers were forced into smaller and smaller pockets of land. One such pocket was Pandim, the location of the conflict described in the introduction to this chapter.

## The poverty dimension

Changes to the hydrological regime, *typha* invasion and increased conflict have combined to increase poverty in most wetland communities. Recent studies in the HNW (JWL, 2003) indicate that in many communities, householders' perceived level of poverty has increased significantly during the last five years. In 1998, households regularly produced surpluses of crops and fish that could be traded across northern Nigeria. Today households more frequently subsist, producing little in the way of surpluses for trading, and the incidence of families surviving on one main meal a day has increased tenfold. This is mainly the result of lack of water in the wetlands system for small-scale irrigation and fishing. It is compounded by restrictions on farming, fishing and grazing in the national parks, although enforcement is inconsistent and liable to small-scale corruption. Chiroma (pers. comm., 2003) notes that in Kabak, on the Marma Channel in the HNW, the community correlates its increasing poverty with an inability to marry off young women from the village.

## The economics of the dams

Investment in projects such as the Tiga and Challawa dams were opportunities for the federal government to demonstrate its strength and buy political favour from political elites in the Kano region. The economic benefits of improving water supplies to the urban population and providing water for irrigation were not challenged when the projects were implemented. Recent analysis, however, indicates that the upstream benefits (water supply for Kano and irrigation) are not matched by the downstream losses (crop and fisheries production losses in the HNW). In fact, the dams cause an estimated US$6.4 million deficit to the Nigerian economy each year through lost agricultural and fisheries production (Barbier and Thompson, 1998). Despite these economic losses and the significant rise in poverty in the HNW, a second phase of the Kano River Irrigation Project has been commissioned. The impacts of this second phase upon the HNW are unknown, although it is clear from official documents that there is continued focus upon benefits to upstream users in the Kano region and little consideration of the need for parallel downstream projects to enhance livelihoods in the HNW.

The environmental, social and economic impacts of water resource schemes in northern Nigeria should be considered in the light of trends across Nigeria where the costs of environmental degradation were estimated in 1990 to be US$5 billion annually (World Bank, 1990), reflecting a national problem in effectively managing key natural resources. Given that some 60 per cent of Nigeria's population is rural and that they are directly dependent upon natural resources for their livelihoods (Government of Nigeria, 2004), the impact of such degradation upon the lives of millions of Nigerians is substantial.

## The cattle herder

> I recall a time when farmers would welcome our cattle on to their land. (Mallam Y'au Mohammed, Fulani herder from Hadejia town)

### Changing farmer-cattle herder relations

Mallam Y'au Mohammed is now a respected Fulani elder, settled in the town of Hadejia. During the 1960s, however, he was a traditional nomad, grazing his 115 cattle to the south-west of Hadejia town. During the wet season, like most of the Fulani in the region, Mohammed kept his cattle on the fringes of the wetland away from the flooded areas. As the flood receded in the dry season, Mallam Y'au moved his cattle onto the floodplains. The floodplains provided a wide variety of different grasses suitable for grazing cattle. Irrigation in the area was very basic, utilizing traditional technologies such as the *shadouf*, a system employing a cantilevered bucket. Consequently, irrigated agriculture was not widespread and large areas of the floodplain were available for grazing.

Mallam Y'au generally enjoyed a good relationship with farmers in the areas he visited. After the harvests, farmers would invite him onto their land, ensuring that there were crop residues for his cattle. During this time, artificial fertilizers were not available; therefore, cattle manure played a vital role in maintaining soil fertility. In addition, and perhaps more importantly, farmers benefited from payment by herders of *jangali*, a cattle tax for grazing their land. In return for these grazing rights, Mallam Y'au ensured that his cattle did not stray anywhere near farms while crops were still in the fields.

The relatively peaceful – and mutually beneficial – relationship between farmers and pastoralists began to deteriorate during the 1970s. In part, this was due to the changes in the hydrological regime of the HNW which so dramatically affected farmers such as Mohammed Grema. It was also due to national policies that aimed to modernize agriculture and promote permanent settlements of herders.

During the 1960s, agriculture formed an important part of the Nigerian economy. This changed during the 1970s as oil revenues began to fill the government coffers. The share of agricultural exports was 80.9 per cent in 1960, progressively declining to 30 per cent in 1970, 7.2 per cent in 1975 and 2.4 per cent in 1980 (Ezeala-Harrison, 1993). Successive governments allowed the economy to be driven by the oil sector and little or no investment was made in other productive activities such as agriculture.

Rural areas suffered as a result of continued neglect and under-investment, leading to increased poverty. The emphasis placed by successive governments on services, construction and industry rein-forced a pre-existing urban bias that would increasingly draw labour out of agriculture (Wunder, 2003).

## Agricultural modernization

In the wake of erratic and often declining oil revenues, and dependence upon food imports and rapid urbanization, the fragility of the agricul-tural sector finally began to be recognized during the late 1970s. In an effort to revive rural areas and the economy in general, the government set ambitious agricultural growth targets of 3.5 per cent per year (Milligan, 2000). If these targets had translated into strategic and poverty reducing investment in the agricultural sector, they would have been good news for cattle herders and farmers, alike. However, during this period of military governments, governance was characterized by short-term solutions and 'quick fixes'. In the agricultural sector, these included the wide-scale promotion of irrigated agriculture and commit-ment to increased permanent farming, including a policy of forced settlement of nomadic cattle herders. The 1979 Land Use Decree provided for legal title to be given for settled farming, but not entitlement for continued rangeland grazing by pastoralists.

## Forced settlement of nomadic herders

Settlement of cattle herders had been official policy since colonial times, and during the 1970s and 1980s, the process was supported by the international community. The approach had very limited success due to reluctance on the part of nomadic herders to settle and evidence that nomadic pastoralism was often a more efficient and productive use of dryland resources.

Mallam Y'au recalls that at the time of the resettlement programmes, the pastoralists were very sceptical of the security of tenure of any land allocated to them. He also notes that land allocations were not made in accordance with cattle herd sizes so that those with larger herds would have been given insufficient grazing land. This challenged both the cultural and economic imperatives of pastoralists to have larger herds and was thus strongly resisted. The friction between pastoralists and government exists to this day. It is certainly one reason that explains the continued marginalization of herders in the Nigerian political landscape.

## Promotion of farm irrigation

During the 1980s it was determined that small-scale irrigation provided one of the simplest ways to increase agricultural production. The government introduced measures to support irrigation, including continued support for dams and water management programmes. It also obtained a World Bank loan of US$67.5 million for the National Fadama Development Programme (NFDP). Unlike previous irrigation policy that had concentrated on large-scale irrigation schemes, the NFDP specifically targeted small-holder farmers on floodplain areas.

The impact that these developments in agricultural policy had on the wetlands can only be understood if considered alongside changes in local-level governance that were taking place at the same time. These changes marginalized cattle herders further from local political structures by destroying the basis of their relationship with traditional authorities.

## The role of traditional authorities

During the 1960s, the governance of land and water resources in the wetlands was firmly in the hands of the traditional authorities. Traditional rulers such as the *Wakili* of Kasaga worked with local *Alkali*, or judges, to enforce their decisions regarding natural resources allocation. This system was largely funded by taxes paid by all resource users. In the case of farmers, this consisted of a formal tax, *haraji*, and a portion of each year's harvest known as an 'allegiance due', or *gara mulki*. The latter was distributed to all tiers of the traditional government, right up to the Emir himself. On the part of the herders, this consisted of a cattle tax, known as *jangali*. During the 1960s, Mallam Y'au recalls paying *jangali* of 50 kobo per head of cattle. Such was the economic importance of cattle herding that monies from cattle tax often exceeded that from agricultural taxes. The system existed across the wetlands and provided a framework benefiting the interests of both farmers and pastoralists.

Under this system the traditional rulers benefited from the presence of Mallam Y'au's cattle through the payment of *jangali* and, to a significant extent, were accountable to him. Mallam Y'au recalls that he could request an audience with the local leaders on issues that he thought were important and the leaders would attend. In fact, at times, the cattle herders, as a result of their wealth, may actually have had more influence over traditional rulers than farmers. In return for the payment of *jangali*, traditional rulers ensured that the areas traditionally set aside for grazing and stock routes were not encroached by farmland. Although not demarcated on the ground, these areas were well known and accepted for generations.

## Reducing the power of traditional authorities

The situation changed during the 1970s. Under the government of President Yakuba Gowon, traditional authorities were stripped of their powers to have their own policemen and judges. This was followed by the abolishment of the *jangali* and *haraji* taxes, although the *gara mulki* (allegiance due) paid by farmers still exists. The process culminated in the 1975 Local Government Act and the 1979 Land Use Decree that finally took away any statutory powers that traditional authorities had in land and water management. These were transferred over to local government. The Land Use Decree, in particular, has exacerbated the risk of conflict by making it possible for farmers to occupy rangelands and apply for certificates of occupancy for exclusive agricultural use. There is no provision for herders to apply for use of rangelands for cattle grazing, thus further disenfranchising them from land management opportunities.

These changes had a fundamental impact on the equity of land management at a local level. They created an imbalance whereby local leaders no longer benefited from cattle taxes but still profited from the *allegiance due* paid by farmers. This, coupled with the fact that local leaders dealt with farmers on a daily basis, gradually led to a bias in local government towards farmers and farmland expansion.

The erosion of the powers of traditional authorities meant that even when leaders wanted to ensure equitable management of resources, they could do little to stop farmland expansion. In theory, formal local government institutions should have filled the void on issues such as conflict management. In reality, the responsibilities previously held by traditional institutions were often transferred to corrupt officials with no vested interest in the local area or its people. Such officials were often motivated by the short-term financial gains possible from promoting farmland expansion.

## Marginalization of herders

As a result of the convergence of the two processes of promoting irrigation and transferring power from traditional authorities to local government, cattle herders became increasingly marginalized. Farmers thus started to capture land and water resources at an increasing rate. Traditional grazing areas, stock routes and access to water were reduced and lost as the rapid expansion in irrigated land proceeded. By 1993, 70 per cent of the pasture lands that had existed 20 years before in Hadejia Emirate were lost (Hadejia, 1993). In the face of this encroachment there was nothing that the politically marginalized cattle herders could do.

Mallam Y'au vividly remembers the first time this new situation affected him: 'We came to a farm where a route to the water used to be. We tried many times to find a way through. It was impossible. The cattle were desperate for the water and in the end they just ran through the crops.' In areas such as Pandim and others all over the wetlands this scenario has become increasingly commonplace.

# BRINGING THE STORIES TOGETHER

The previous discussion has attempted to summarize the impacts of 30 turbulent years of government policies, economic trends and stake-holder activities in the context of the HNW. This is no more than a somewhat simplistic overview of complex political, social, economic and environmental interactions, most of which are undocumented. There are, however, some clear trends that emerge and which have, ultimately, affected the management of environmental resources and peoples' livelihoods in these critical wetlands.

## National, regional and local politics – supporting elites

Government in Nigeria is characterized by a constant tension between federal and state tiers for influence and power. We have seen that the federal government has frequently used large-scale infrastructure projects to demonstrate its potency and to gain regional political support. This was strongly characteristic of the 1970s when it financed dam and water resource infrastructure projects, but continues today with renewed commitments to upgrade these infrastructure schemes. However, there is little or no consideration of the environmental and social impacts. Nor is the economic justification for such schemes sufficiently robust. The environmental degradation resulting from these projects, and leading to agricultural and fisheries losses, warrants rigorous assessment of continued project implementation. Such issues need to be considered in the light of power structures. In northern Nigeria, this applies particularly to the politically powerful city of Kano, whose urban and political elites are able to influence decisions on such schemes and thereby gain from them through enhanced resource capture. This is usually to the detriment of rural communities such as those in the HNW.

Recent trends have de-emphasized the role for local management of resources and have significantly undermined traditional social structures which, although by no means ideal, provided mechanisms to ensure more equitable access to, and use of, natural resources such as land and water. Traditional authorities also provided a mechanism to prevent and manage conflict. Institutions such as the police, courts and local government are often criticized for reacting to and policing conflict, rather than preventing it. Coupled with population growth, the risk of continued conflict over access to natural resources remains high with no clear solution in sight.

## Environmental degradation and poverty – volatile links

Agricultural and water resource management policies aiming to induce economic growth in northern Nigeria have been largely unsuccessful. In part, this is because of the massive environmental degradation that they have caused. Barbier and Thompson (1998) undertook an economic assessment of the benefits and costs of further water diversion projects. They estimated that such projects would generate upstream benefits from irrigated agriculture of US$29 per hectare, but by affecting the existing flood regime, would significantly and adversely reduce the current downstream benefits by US$167 per hectare.

A clear link exists between this environmental degradation, reduced productivity and increased incidence of poverty in the HNW. In the wetlands, 43 per cent of households depend upon agriculture and 28 per cent upon fishing for their principal income (World Bank, 2003), although most families subsist through a range of activities that might include a mix of farming, fishing and livestock rearing. The clear trends in falling agricultural and fisheries productivity are thus affecting the majority of households in the area. Falling productivity and household income inevitably place increased pressure on agricultural and fishing communities to compete directly for land and water resources between themselves and with pastoralists. The World Bank's poverty and environment study (2003) indicates that increased incidence of conflict, primarily between farmers and pastoralists, but also between farmers and fishermen, reflects worsening environmental quality and should be taken as a warning sign requiring action. In a country in which 10,000 lost their lives during the 1990s because of violent conflict (NIPC, 2002) it is evident that the causes of conflict are a serious issue that require urgent attention in Nigeria.

What is clear is that, at a national and regional level, farmers such as Mohammed Grema and pastoralists such as Mallam Y'au have little say in the decisions affecting the management of the HNW and, thus, their livelihoods. They suffer from a policy and legislative environment that is decidedly urban-biased and which, at the local level, is predisposed towards settled farmers rather than pastoralists. Decisions affecting access to, and use of, land and water are played out at a national and regional level. The adverse impacts are faced locally, but not by the key decision-makers.

## CONCLUSION AND RECOMMENDATIONS

The political marginalization of Nigeria's Hadejia Nguru Wetlands at national and regional levels has been detrimental to the lives of the vast majority of the area's 1.5 million inhabitants. Within the wetlands, certain groups have fared better than others; but the overall trend is one of worsening poverty. The prognosis for the communities of the HNW is not particularly promising without a commitment from federal-level and state-level government to address the political issues that underlie rural poverty. To date, there has been limited evidence of such commitment. However, there are glimmers of hope, with government at all levels leading new programmes with donor support. The World Bank's Local Empowerment and Environmental Management Programme and the UK Department for International Development's (DFID's) Joint Enhancement of Wetlands and Livelihoods Programme are two examples where federal and state governments have committed to work with local and traditional institutions to improve equity in access to, and use of, environmental resources in order to tackle rural poverty. Over and above such programmes, some key areas that need to be addressed include:

- development of democratic institutions that empower communities to engage more effectively with both local and state government and elected representatives in order to influence decisions affecting their livelihoods and to redress existing biases in decision-making (this would involve capacity-building initiatives, including awareness-raising; increasing community recognition of the rights to good and effective governance; access to justice; and support of negotiating skills for community leaders when dealing with decision-making authorities);

- support for rural communities to diversify their livelihoods, and to reduce their vulnerability to environmental and economic shocks, coupled with support for increased access to markets to increase household income;
- development of effective mechanisms for conflict resolution and management, drawing upon the breadth of institutions capable of supporting such processes, including local government and traditional authorities;
- commitment by government to address poverty-environment linkages in order to promote equitable and sustainable economic growth, by building this into processes such as the Poverty Reduction Strategy;
- revision of Nigeria's Land Use Law to enable herders, individually or collectively, to secure rights for access to, and use of, rangelands for their cattle similar to those allowing farmers rights for agricultural activities;
- review of the potential for land-use planning and zonation to allocate areas for farming, herding and other activities which currently compete for the same resources;
- review of water resource management at the catchment level in the Komadougou-Yobe river basin in order to optimize allocations, distribution and efficiency of water resource use for the benefit of both urban and rural populations (this should include a review of the role of river basin development authorities to ensure that there are no conflicts of interest in activities, and that decision-making on water resource management is based upon catchments rather than administrative boundaries).

# REFERENCES

Barbier, E. B. and Thompson, J. R. (1998) 'The value of water: floodplain versus large-scale irrigation benefits in northern Nigeria', *Ambio*, vol. 27, no. 6, pp434–440

Chiroma, M. J. and Polet. G. (1996) *Population Estimate of the Hadejia-Nguru Wetlands*, Report to the Hadejia-Nguru Wetland Conservation Project, Nguru, Nigeria

Eaton, D. and Sarch, T. (1997) *The Economic Importance of Wild Resources in the Hadejia-Nguru Wetlands*, CREED Working Paper 13, Collaborative Research in the Economics of Environment and Development, London

Ezealea-Harrison, F. (1993) 'Structural readjustment in Nigeria: Diagnosis of a severe Dutch disease syndrome',' *American Journal of Economics and Sociology*, vol. 52, no. 2, pp193–208

Goes, B. (1997) 'Introduction', in *Water Management Options for the Hadejia – Jama'are – Yobe River Basin, Northern Nigeria*, IUCN, HNWCP

Government of Nigeria (2004) *Draft National Economic Empowerment Development Strategy*, March, Government of Nigeria, Abuja

Hadejia, I. (1993) 'Socio-economic basis of farmer-pastoralist conflict in Jigawa State', Paper presented to seminar on effective land tenure systems in Jigawa State, 2-5 August 1993, Office of Deputy Governor of Jigawa State

Hollis, G., Adams, W. and Aminu Kano, M. (1993) *The Hadejia Nguru Wetlands*, IUCN, Gland

Ibrahim, U. S. and Chiroma, M. J. (1998) 'Socio-economic characteristics of the wetlands', in D. Okali and H. Bdliya (eds) *Guidelines for Wise Use of the Hadejia-Nguru Wetlands*, Hadejia-Nguru Wetlands Conservation Project mimeo-graph, IUCN, Gland, Switzerland

JWL (2003) *Poverty, Environment and Livelihoods in the Hadejia Nguru Wetlands – Report of Training and Fieldwork Exercise May 2003*, JWL, Dutse

Lemly, A. D., Kingsford, K. T. and Thompson, R. (2000) 'Irrigated agriculture and wildlife conservation: conflict on a global scale', *Environmental Management*, vol. 25, pp485–512

Milligan, S. (2000) *Desk Review of Herder-Farmer Conflicts in the Hadejia-Nguru Wetlands, Nigeria*, Unpublished report submitted to the UK Department for International Development, London

NIPC (National Institute of Peace and Conflict Resolution) (2002) *Strategic Conflict Assessment for Nigeria*, IPCR, Lagos

Okali, D. and Bdliya, H. (eds) (1998) *Guidelines for the Wise Use of the Hadejia-Nguru Wetlands*, Hadejia-Nguru Wetlands Conservation Project mimeograph, IUCN, Gland, Switzerland

Pearce, D. (1992) 'Death of an oasis', *Audubon*, May–June, pp66–74

World Bank (1990) *Towards a National Environmental Action Plan for Nigeria*, World Bank, Washington, D.C.

World Bank (2003) *Nigeria: Poverty-Environment Linkages in the Natural Resources Sector*, World Bank, Washington, D.C.

Wunder, S. (2003) *Oil Wealth and the Fate of the Forest*, Routledge, New York

# The Sea is Our Garden:[1] Coastal Resource Management and Local Governance in the Caribbean

*Yves Renard*

## INTRODUCTION

This chapter[2] tells the story of a very small place that finds itself, like so many other communities in the Caribbean and other parts of the developing world, the victim of forces and processes that are beyond its control, and that have direct impacts upon its present and future well-being. It is the story of a community that is forced to look for alternatives, for responses to the challenges of globalization, economic marginalization and environmental degradation, and for ways of combating the poverty that these processes generate. It is also the story of an attempt to shape the contours of modern democracy – to answer a growing demand for improved mechanisms for popular participation in policy-making and in governance.

The case study presented in this chapter specifically describes planning processes and institutional arrangements for natural resource governance in a coastal context in a small island developing state in the Caribbean. The focus of the study is on the institution of local governance, defined as the sum of all local organizations and practices of public governance (Box, 1998). It presents and discusses two of the main lessons that have emerged from a research project carried out in the community of Laborie, Saint Lucia, over the past three years. These lessons are that:

- local empowerment in natural resource governance can happen, and can have positive impacts on livelihoods and poverty reduction, even in the absence of a formal delegation of management authority and without changes in formal property rights; and

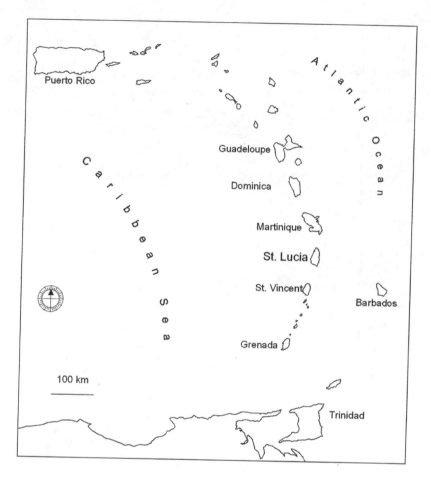

Diagram 7.1 *Location of Saint Lucia*

- natural resource management, especially in a coastal context, requires an integrated and functional system of local governance that incorporates a multiplicity of actors and processes, including formal local government agencies, in order to perform the wide range of roles involved in environmental management and social and economic development.

# A SMALL ISLAND AND ITS INTERNAL POLITICS

## Saint Lucia: An overview

This study focuses on the island of Saint Lucia, in the eastern Caribbean. Saint Lucia is located in the Windward Islands, a chain

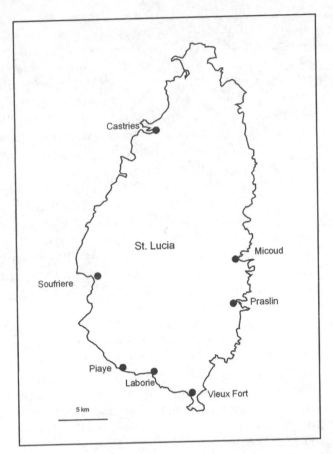

**Diagram 7.2** *Saint Lucia*

of predominantly volcanic islands in the south of the Antillean archipelago that includes two French territories (Guadeloupe and Martinique) and four states (Dominica, Grenada, Saint Lucia, and Saint Vincent and the Grenadines) that gained their independence from the UK during the 1970s, and which are now part of the Organization of Eastern Caribbean States (OECS).

Saint Lucia is an island of 616 square kilometres, with a total population of approximately 160,000 people. Its modern history mirrors that of most of the other islands in the Caribbean, with European colonization having resulted in the almost complete elimination of indigenous Amerindian populations, the creation of an industrial plantation system and an economy based on the intensive use of slave labour, and the radical transformation of the natural environment. Sugar cane production dominated the local economy from the late 18th century until the 1950s, when bananas became the main commercial crop and when the tourism sector began to develop.

Social and economic conditions have changed radically over the past few years, with dramatic transformations in the economy and society resulting from new global trade arrangements. Saint Lucia, like the other independent countries in the Windward Islands, has suffered significant declines in production and earnings in the banana sector over the past ten years as a result of the loss of preferential access to the European market. Consequently, there has been significant economic contraction, rapid transformation of the economy from agriculture to services, and an increased reliance on tourism as the only potential growth sector in the economy.

## Coastal resource use

Throughout history, the coastal zone and its natural resources have occupied a very special place in the island's economy and in the livelihood strategies employed by its people. Before European colonization, most human settlements were located on the coast, and archaeological evidence indicates that Amerindian populations depended primarily upon coastal resources for food and tools. In the colonial era, the coastal zone remained important for human settlements and transportation, but it only had a marginal role in a production system – the plantation – that was based almost exclusively on the monoculture of crops for export to metropolitan markets. In contrast to a rural landscape that was dominated by large agricultural estates and to a plantation economy characterized by slave labour and industrial production, the coastal zone offered freedom and diversity. To many, including the freed and runaway slaves, it offered the opportunity to create or reconstitute livelihood strategies based on the use of diverse coastal resources.

In many respects, the processes that happened in the coastal zones of the Caribbean throughout modern history were similar and parallel to those that took place in the region's mountainous rural areas, where former slaves and plantation workers resisted the dominant system and created peasant communities that survived and prospered on small-scale farming. The history of the Caribbean is the history of a struggle for power between plantation and peasant adaptations (Mintz, 1974). In this struggle, the coastal zone played a central role, outside the control of dominant political and economic forces. It is a role that remained largely unchallenged until the advent of tourism 50 years ago, when the coast began to perform new functions, functions that often came into conflict with traditional uses and users.

## The political system

The political system that was introduced in Saint Lucia at the time of independence in 1979 is based on the Westminster model, with a governor general who serves as head of state and is appointed by the UK, and with a parliament that includes an elected house of assembly made up of 17 members. The prime minister, who serves as head of government, is appointed by the governor general, and is the leader of the party that commands a majority in the house of assembly. Elections are normally held every five years, but can be called at any time in the event that parliament is dissolved. The constitution provides for a multiparty political system.

This political system is functioning well in that Saint Lucia has a good track record of democracy, with an overall respect for the rule of law, with the holding of free and fair elections, and with a regard for those human rights and civil liberties that are guaranteed by the constitution. Voter participation is high, but has declined significantly between the last two general elections (1997 and 2001), reflecting a trend that is prevalent throughout the Caribbean region. While the political system functions well, there remain a number of political issues that impact upon democracy and governance at the national level, including the absence of formal mechanisms for popular participation in policy-making, the inflated power of the state as a regulator, employer and provider of basic services, and instances of corruption and abuses of authority, particularly as this relates to police brutality and barriers to accessing justice.

The national political landscape is dominated by two political parties that find their origin and political base in the social movements of the 1930s and 1940s at a time when the island was still under direct colonial administration, again reflecting the experience of most other Commonwealth Caribbean states. The current government was formed by the Saint Lucia Labour Party, which won the general elections of 1997 and 2001. This party has a popular base in both rural and urban areas; it was created in 1950, after an intense period of social and industrial unrest led by the Saint Lucia Workers Co-operative Union, and in anticipation of the introduction of universal adult suffrage in 1951. The opposition United Workers Party was created in the early 1960s as a result of a split within the ruling Labour Party. It went on to win the general elections of 1964 and remained in power until 1997, save for a two-year period of Labour Party rule between 1979 and 1981, immediately after independence. Its popular base is in the rural areas that were the focus of social movements during the 1950s, and among the urban middle class.

In addition to formal political processes, there are a number of institutions and forces that are important in guiding and shaping the structure and functioning of Saint Lucian society. Strong patterns of inequity and dependency have been inherited from the island's colonial past; but these have been partially eroded in recent times, thanks mainly to political independence and moves towards regional integration, to changes in the land tenure patterns inherited from the colonial era, and to increased social and economic mobility. Race remains an important determinant of personal identity, and a key factor in social and power relations. While there have been positive changes during recent years, thanks to the efforts of cultural activists and progressive community leaders, there remain strong prejudices and informal mechanisms of social exclusion against predominantly Creole-speaking rural people.[3] There also remain strong patterns of gender inequity, and gender relations and roles have significant impacts upon the socio-economic vulnerability of women.

## Local government and local governance

Decentralized local government was established by the colonial administration in 1947, with the enactment of a Local Government Authorities Ordinance that was complemented, in 1967, by a second piece of legislation dealing specifically with the establishment of an authority in the capital city of Castries. During the early days, these elected local government authorities were responsible for a range of services and functions related primarily to solid waste management and sanitation, infrastructure and public utilities. Since the late 1960s, the powers of these authorities have been eroded by the gradual concentration of management responsibility in the hands of central government agencies, and by recent moves towards privatization. In 1979, local elections were suspended, following the election of the Saint Lucia Labour Party, and town and village councils have since been appointed by central government.

Shortly after its return to power in 1997, the government of the Saint Lucia Labour Party embarked on a process of local government reform, which aimed to reintroduce an elected system of local government. A task force was established and studies and consultations were carried out (Aubrey Armstrong Management Associates, 1999), leading to the preparation of a Green Paper (GOSL, 2000) containing specific recommendations. While this process professed the intention to empower communities and to create mechanisms of popular participation, it remained focused on a specific administrative model and failed to examine the broader issues of, and opportunities for, participation and empowerment. The process has not yet delivered on its original promises, and there remains a need for improved local governance that demands innovative and creative solutions.

The situation that prevails in Saint Lucia reveals some of the specific issues of local governance in a small state. On the one hand, many argue that the small size of the country and the financial constraints that it faces do not justify elaborate processes of decentralization. At the same time, there is an implicit and explicit demand for improved local governance, coming primarily in response to the challenges of social and economic development, and to the cultural and economic impacts of globalization. In Saint Lucia, this demand currently manifests itself in both positive and negative ways through the vitality of several community organizations and the strength of many informal networks and support mechanisms, but also through a growing cynicism towards established patterns of governance and political life, and the disengagement of many citizens from formal processes and institutions.

## Natural resource management

In the field of natural resource management, Saint Lucia has experimented with and implemented a range of participatory approaches to planning and management, and there are a number of valuable cases of collaborative and decentralized institutional arrangements in the country, including the well-documented Soufriere Marine Management Area (Brown, 1997; Geoghegan et al, 1999), the case of the Mankòtè mangrove (Geoghegan and Smith, 2002) and the experience of the Praslin Protected Landscape (Romulus and Ernest, 2003). Public-sector management agencies, notably the Ministry of Physical Development, the Department of Fisheries and the Department of Forestry, are all committed to, and have significant experience and capacities in, participatory and people-centred approaches to conservation and natural resource management.

This trend towards the decentralization of authority for the management of protected areas in Saint Lucia came as a result of a number of converging factors. Conventional approaches to planning and managing protected areas that were employed during the 1970s and 1980s had not been very effective, and had often exacerbated resource use conflicts. Over the past two decades, the policies and programmes of international agencies, including donors, have become explicitly supportive of participation and decentralization, and these agencies have often placed participation as a formal or informal condition of their support to local programmes. Lastly, the serious fiscal constraints that have been faced

**Figure 7.1** *View of the Laborie Bay*

by the state since the mid 1990s have made decentralization and devolution even more necessary in order to reduce the financial burden of management on government agencies. During the past 15 years, the policy context has become openly favourable to participation and decentralization.

# THE CASE STUDY: CONTEXT AND STAKEHOLDERS

## The place

The site on which this study focuses is a coastal area that includes three small bays on the south-west coast of the island of Saint Lucia. The coastal village of Laborie is at the centre, with one small bay on each side, giving a total of 3.2km of coastline. The bays have sandy beaches and are separated by rocky outcrops. There are no permanent rivers that drain directly into Laborie Bay; but several gullies and ravines drain into the sea during the rainy season. Two of these drain into a small basin mangrove. The hills surrounding the village have a moderately steep terrain, rising to a maximum of 280m above the Laborie Bay watershed approximately 1km inland. They are covered by low scrub and dry forest vegetation and have not been severely affected by recent clearing for agriculture. The small Laborie watershed is surrounded by two

159

**Figure 7.2** *Boats in Laborie Bay*

larger watersheds; higher elevations are covered by rainforests, while the middle and lower parts of these watersheds are cultivated and include several rural settlements.

The local society and economy are characterized by mixed livelihood strategies. Laborie, with a total population of approximately 5000 people, has traditionally been a fishing village and a small commercial centre serving a number of surrounding rural communities. Following the major social and economic transformations of the mid 19th century (emancipation of slaves; industrial revolution and advent of new technologies, notably steam power; influx of European capital to the Caribbean; and resulting concentration of land and industry into large sugar estates and central factories), Laborie and its environs underwent a number of profound changes. Because of the topography of the area, large-scale sugar cane cultivation was abandoned, and many estates were fragmented and devoted to mixed agricultural production, including subsistence farming by smallholders, squatters and tenants. The expansion of banana farming during the 1960s and 1970s brought tangible social and economic benefits to the area, with bananas being produced on small farms and constituting the main source of income for most rural households.

As a result of economic decline at the national and regional levels, there have been noticeable increases in incidences and levels of poverty, and new social issues have emerged. At present, employment opportunities are scarce, unemployment is high,[4] and emigration has been, and remains, one of the popular responses to economic difficulties. As a consequence of emigration, there has been a continued contraction of the population over the past three decades in this community.[5] While there are no recent data to quantify poverty levels, all indications are that they have increased, and that more people and households have become vulnerable to poverty.

## Coastal resource use and local livelihoods

Social and economic changes have had, and continue to have, direct impacts on and implications for natural resource management, and local livelihoods increasingly depend upon the natural resource base in two ways. First, there is now a higher level of dependence on natural resources for subsistence as people have had to diversify their production and sources of revenue, and are no longer able to count on the revenue from export crops and the formal commercial sector to sustain themselves. At the same time, natural resources have begun to provide opportunities for economic diversification, particularly in support of tourism, but also in agriculture and fisheries. In this site, as in many other coastal areas in the Caribbean, it is tourism that defines the balance between these two trends: wherever tourism is significant, large-scale commercial interests prevail; elsewhere, subsistence strategies remain important for large sections of the population.

Coastal resources in the study area include beaches, reefs, sea-grass beds and small mangroves. Commercially important species include reef fishes, lobsters, seaweeds and sea urchins. The main environmental issues that affect the ecosystems and species in the area include pollution, with high levels of bacterial contamination and extensive habitat degradation in near-shore areas, habitat destruction, and severe depletion of the stocks of commercially important species as a result of over-harvesting and reductions in the natural productivity of ecosystems.

These resources support multiple livelihood strategies, and most people in these coastal communities depend, to some extent, upon these resources. Laborie Bay is particularly important for pot-fishing, spear-fishing (mainly by people from surrounding rural areas) and for casting nets. Sea-urchin harvests also provide an important source of cash and have had historical importance in the area (Smith and Koester, 2001). Seaweeds constitute another economically important resource, and harvests have been important sources of income for decades (Smith and

161

Gustave, 2001). Most of the very poor households depend primarily, and in some cases entirely, upon marine-related activities (occasional fishing and resource harvesting, fish cleaning, illegal sand mining, and occasional labour at the service of fishers and other coastal resource users) to sustain themselves because they have no other physical assets (especially land) and few opportunities for employment in other sectors.

During the 1980s, as a response to concerns over the depletion of wild seaweed stocks because of over-harvesting, and in recognition of the economic potential of a new aquaculture industry as a source of income for households in coastal communities, the Department of Fisheries in Saint Lucia began a research and development project aimed at promoting seaweed cultivation in the country. Laborie Bay was one of the sites where experiments were conducted in the early 1990s, and where technical assistance was provided to farmers and processors. As a result, seaweed farming is now one of the economic activities carried out in this community.

While there is a range of marine-based economic activities that contribute to local livelihoods, marketing is perceived as a major constraint to the generation of household income. For example, people who had been involved in early seaweed farming initiatives have mentioned that marketing arrangements were inadequate and did not allow them to generate sufficient revenue to sustain these initiatives, while sea urchin harvesters have encountered difficulty in accessing local and national markets during recent harvests. More generally, fishers in the area express concern over the effectiveness of current marketing arrangements for fish, and over their inability to affect market prices (Hutchinson et al, 2000).

Laborie Bay and its resources are particularly important to younger and older persons. First, this is the place where marine-based skills and rules are learned, and where young people learn to swim and fish, but also where many of them learn how to manage and share resources, how to collaborate, and how to avoid and manage disputes and conflicts. In a sense, these near-shore resources are those that support traditional apprenticeships. At the same time, the bay and its resources play an important role in supporting the livelihoods of older persons, particularly fishers who are no longer able to fish for pelagic species far from shore and to take the physical punishment inherent in deep-sea fishing. The bay and its near-shore resources may therefore not generate large economic benefits; but their social functions are critical, and they are threatened by environmental degradation.

# PROMOTING SUSTAINABLE COASTAL LIVELIHOODS

## Community planning

This case study must be placed in the context of the community development processes that have taken place in the village of Laborie over the past few years. Against the background of the national political processes that were briefly described earlier, this community finds itself in a peculiar situation because it has persistently, over the past four decades, supported the Saint Lucia Labour party, which was in opposition for most of the time between the early 1960s and the time of its accession to power in 1997. In a political culture that is based largely on patronage and favouritism, this meant that the community felt marginalized and excluded from many of the benefits of state-sponsored projects and programmes. Several observers attribute some of the community's strength and cohesion to the resilience and autonomy that it was forced to develop in response to this marginalization.

The elections of 1997 that took the Saint Lucia Labour party to power brought much hope to this community, which expected that it would rapidly see the benefits of its indefectible support. Indeed, several projects were conceived, largely on the initiative of the member of parliament, but also through a number of national agencies and programmes. In particular, the community began to benefit from a number of poverty reduction initiatives and programmes that were established or strengthened by the government, with funding from external donors. These included the Poverty Reduction Fund and the Basic Needs Trust Fund.

But the focus on infrastructural projects did not fully meet the needs of the community, especially since there appeared to be little concern for issues of ownership, participation, management and sustainability. Several projects were conceived and some were implemented, but they brought little change on the ground. In 1999, largely as a result of frustration with the dominant approach to local development, a group of community leaders who had been brought together by a government agency precisely for the purpose of managing an infrastructural project realized the limitations of this approach and decided to embark on a participatory strategic planning process that would look holistically at development challenges, options and priorities for the area. This process led, after two years of extensive research and consultation that included sector workshops, focus group sessions and informal discussions, to the formulation of the *Strategic Development Plan for Laborie* (Laborie

Development Planning Committee, 2001). This initiative was spearheaded and facilitated by an informal group called the Laborie Development Planning Committee, which comprised 25 individuals coming from all of the main social sectors and geographic communities in the area. The plan was formulated by the committee, in consultation with relevant government agencies.

The strategic development plan defined a vision for the community, identified a number of priority programmes and actions, and recommended the establishment of a new community organization – the Laborie Development Foundation – that would lead the implementation of the plan. Since then, the foundation has been formally established as a federation of community-based organizations and groups. Following several months of membership mobilization and institutional networking, it is currently in the process of finalizing short-term work plans, recruiting staff and raising funds. Meanwhile, central government agencies and local actors in other communities are looking at this experiment as a model that could be replicated in other locations. Thanks, in part, to its position on the national political landscape, the community of Laborie has produced concepts that may receive broader acceptance and warrant wider application.

This strategic development plan places emphasis on natural resource management, and on the relationship between environmental management and social and economic development, including poverty reduction. In its vision statement, the plan expresses the goal of 'coordinating the conservation and management of natural resources, a clean and healthy environment, equitable access to resources, and equitable distribution of the benefits derived from the use of these resources'. In its various programmes, the plan identifies strategies and actions aimed at optimizing the use of natural resources, enhancing sustainability and promoting equity.

## People and the Sea: A research project

In 2000, while the *Strategic Development Plan for Laborie* was being finalized, a three-year research project was initiated through a partnership between a community organization (the Laborie Development Planning Committee), a national governmental agency (the Department of Fisheries in the Ministry of Agriculture) and a regional organization (the Caribbean Natural Resources Institute) for the purpose of exploring technical and institutional options for coastal resource governance in support of livelihoods and poverty reduction. This project was funded by the UK Department for International Development (DFID) through

**Figure 7.3** *The office and gas station of the local Fishers' Co-operative, with a sign describing the People and the Sea project*

its Natural Resources Systems Programme (NRSP), and the Caribbean Natural Resources Institute coordinated its implementation.

The primary objective of the project was to test and develop specific tools and methods, as applied to the management of coral reefs and other coastal resources, particularly in relation to the design of participatory institutions and to the development of technologies and management tools that can enhance the social and economic benefits derived from the sustainable use of coastal resources. At the same time, the project sought to evaluate the impact of participation on the sustainability of resource use and on the livelihoods of people. Although it was recognized that time and resources available to this project would be too limited to undertake a comprehensive evaluation exercise, the project sought to identify and monitor concrete links between institutional and technological change on the one hand, and the well-being of both the people and the reefs on the other.

Third, and perhaps more importantly, the project aimed at providing guidance towards identifying alternatives to marine protected areas. Throughout the developing tropical world, coastal conservation and management initiatives have tended to emphasize marine protected areas as the most appropriate management instrument for conserving reef resources. While it cannot be disputed that these areas have made, and continue to make, a significant contribution to biological

165

**Figure 7.4** *School children explore the reefs from a glass bottom boat*

conservation and sustainable development, it is now becoming increasingly evident that they are not appropriate to all circumstances. Typically, in Saint Lucia and other parts of the region, marine protected areas are established in the coastal regions of greatest biological diversity and economic potential, especially in the tourism sector, while other coastal zones continue to suffer from inadequate management. The project therefore sought to define management instruments that were suited to the conditions of coastal areas where the resource may not warrant, nor be able to support, marine protected areas.

This research project began with a baseline study of natural resources and livelihood strategies, and was then structured around four main

*Source:* Julian Dubois

**Figure 7.5** *Monitoring sea urchin stocks with a sea-egg caliper*

activities that looked, among other things, at institutional arrangements and options. Using specific management initiatives that had the potential to contribute directly to poverty reduction, the project examined the forms and types of governance arrangements that appeared best suited to the conditions of this small community.

## Managing the sea urchin fishery

One of the main activities of the project focused on the management of the edible white-spined sea urchin, *Tripneustes ventricosus*, locally known as the sea egg. Traditionally, this resource has been an important source of income for people in coastal communities in Saint Lucia, especially since periods of harvest coincide with the start of the school year (August–September), thus providing cash income to poor households at a critical time. In 1986, in response to over-exploitation and declining stocks, a national management programme was implemented by the Department of Fisheries (Smith and Berkes, 1991; George and Joseph, 1994). A co-management arrangement was established as a result, and it functioned well for a number of years until stocks declined severely in the mid 1990s. The cause of the decline was uncertain; but

167

it was probably not due to over-harvesting, as a similar trend was seen in other islands where the species was not exploited.

At the start of this research project in 2000, there were indications that sea urchin population levels were beginning to rise for the first time since 1994, and illegal harvesting had already resumed in some communities around the island, threatening sustainability. Baseline surveys were therefore conducted jointly by harvesters and management agencies, and meetings were held for the purpose of sharing information and deciding on a course of action. These activities revealed the need for improved information sharing between harvesters and management agencies, and provided an interesting forum for interaction between popular and scientific knowledge. On the basis of these discussions, negotiations were held between harvesters, the Department of Fisheries and community organizations in order to arrive at decisions regarding the timing and conditions of harvests in 2001 and 2002.

The processes of data collection and monitoring, information sharing and participatory planning that were used in this activity demonstrated an effective approach to adaptive management. A large number of people with very diverse backgrounds and with conflicting interests came together to share information and make decisions on a matter of common concern. Two key local actors, the president of the Fishers' Co-operative and the representative of the Ministry of Social Transformation, played essential facilitating roles. Without a formal structure or organization, stakeholders defined procedures and created opportunities that allowed them to negotiate amongst themselves, to influence the decisions of state management agencies and to define the terms of their collaboration.

These meetings and discussions on the issues of sea urchin management specifically raised the matter of access rights, with a number of people, especially the younger harvesters, advocating formal rules to guarantee exclusive rights to nearby stocks by local harvesters. This generated heated and difficult debates, with more experienced harvesters and other fishers expressing the view that such exclusion would not be desirable because the people from other communities who would be excluded would inevitably retaliate and prevent access to another fishery. In the end, it was agreed by all parties that formal exclusion was not possible, but that a number of informal steps could be taken to ensure that local harvesters would be given priority access to local stocks.

During the 2002 harvest season, continued dialogue between all stakeholders revealed that there was a large stock of urchins and that the harvest had begun successfully. However, a number of participants noted that because of the level of production, marketing options for the processed sea urchins needed to be improved. A specific promotion and marketing event was therefore proposed, to be held on the last day of the open season, and was advertised nationally as *Lafèt Chadon*.[6] The local Fishers' Co-operative, which was not previously involved in resource management initiatives, hosted the event, using it to generate a significant increase in sales of sea urchins. In a subsequent review of the event, it was decided that it should be held annually and promoted widely.

The results of this project – a partnership between state agencies and local resource users; the use of both popular and scientific knowledge in the formulation of management decisions; a greater community control over resource access and use; and improved marketing arrangements – are expected to last beyond the life of the project as all the management functions have since been integrated within the work of existing organizations.

## Seaweed farming

A second project activity focused on seaweed farming and, more specifically, on the feasibility of cultivating species of *Gracilaria* that are known to have market potential, examining the economic feasibility of cultivation, as well as the conditions under which the technology can be adopted as a means of income generation for disadvantaged people in the local community. This experience, coupled with lessons learned from other seaweed farming initiatives in other parts of Saint Lucia over the past two decades, revealed a number of issues and suggested a number of directions.

Among these issues, the project noted that while there were national organizations that were vested with resource management and development control responsibility, there were no organizations dedicated to providing technical and marketing assistance. It was felt that such support was needed, especially since production diversification and marketing offer specific opportunities to women. The project also noted the need for policies that preserve the rights and interests of the poor (e.g. secure tenure and access, assistance to small-scale producers to access planting materials and extension and marketing services, and involvement of producers in management and governance). In order to address these needs, stakeholders agreed to the establishment of a task force that would include the government's Department of Fisheries, as well as a number of local bodies, notably the Fishers' Co-operative and the local credit union. Since then, the Laborie Development Foundation

*Source:* Julian Dubois

**Figure 7.6** *A project workshop to assess requirements for the development of seaweed farming*

has begun to implement the recommendations of the study, with a focus on product development and marketing.

## Community-based tourism

The third component of the overall research project focused on tourism, and sought to explore some of the processes and conditions under which marine and coastal-based tourism brings benefits to people, especially the poor. It responded to a growing awareness, in Saint Lucia and other parts of the Caribbean, of the urgent need to develop and implement strategies and programmes that optimize the impact of tourism on poverty reduction and social development. It investigated the possibility of establishing an alternative form of tourism, one that does not mirror the dominant dynamics and relationships of the larger political economy.

This study was based on a number of premises and hypotheses. It recognized that tourism is a major economic sector, and that it was the only growth sector in the eastern Caribbean at this time. Many global and regional processes impact negatively upon traditional economic sectors, especially the banana industry that has been the mainstay of the economy for three decades, and tourism provides one of the few alternative economic options available to small island Caribbean states. Yet, in its present dominant form, tourism often brings negative social, cultural and environmental impacts, and may not be economically sustainable. At the same time, the natural and cultural assets of small Caribbean communities, including the common property resources located in the coastal zone, may provide a valuable opportunity for developing an alternative product that benefits poor people and the national economy (Renard, 2001).

A base line study was conducted to describe the natural and human capital available in the community and to assess the impact of tourism on local livelihoods. This provided the basis for a participatory planning exercise that involved three main steps, namely:

1 a visioning exercise, looking at various options and models of tourism development, but without developing full scenarios;
2 the dissemination of information to local stakeholders to enhance the community's understanding of the context of tourism; and
3 the design of institutional arrangements.

While these activities were being designed and carried out, two infrastructural projects were being implemented by central government, following the initiative of the member of parliament representing the area. One of these projects involved the construction of a jetty, proposed as a vehicle to attract tourism development in the area. The jetty has now been built; but in the absence of a clear plan for its use and management, it has not yet affected local development, and its future role in tourism development is unclear.

From this experience, and from its own planning process, the project concluded that four parallel and complementary directions were needed to realize the vision for tourism contained in the *Strategic Development Plan for Laborie*, namely:

1 product development in order to develop a product of quality that is attractive, meaningful and marketable, and that meets international standards; such a product should include a mix of public and private assets;
2 policy development in order to provide for the minimal standards of quality, to facilitate and secure access to key assets by poor people, and to prevent privatization of important resources and services;
3 governance and capacity-building in order to develop meaningful partnerships between state agencies, local stakeholders and the

171

private sector, to vest much of the planning and management functions in local organizations, and to equip local actors with the skills and resources they need to perform their roles effectively and efficiently;

4 marketing, bringing the visitor (both national and foreign) closer to the product, and ensuring that the product is sold under terms that are truly beneficial to the host communities.

Thanks to the results of this project, the community of Laborie has been selected as the location for a pilot project to be carried out under the auspices of the Saint Lucia Heritage Tourism Programme, and the Laborie Development Foundation has begun implementing the various components of the strategic development plan in this sector.

## Perceptions and awareness of pollution

The objectives of the project's fourth experiment were to study how increased awareness of, and access to, information on the status, causes and potential impacts of water pollution can contribute to a change in behaviour, and to identify the processes by which these changes occur.

This study should be seen against the background of an increasing focus, in Saint Lucia and other parts of the Caribbean, on the observed decline in the health of coral reefs and on the need for more information in order to be able to evaluate these negative trends. Near-shore reefs adjacent to population centres are the most directly affected, primarily as a result of human impacts. While pollution by agrochemicals remains a concern in some areas of Saint Lucia, their use is declining due to the changes in the type and extent of agriculture in the country, particularly the decline in banana production. Meanwhile, the problem of sewage pollution continues to increase as coastal communities expand without adequate wastewater treatment facilities. This can result in elevated nutrient levels and eutrophication of coastal waters.

Local residents have long been concerned with the decline in water quality in Laborie Bay, which they attribute to sewage pollution originating amongst a certain section of the population in the eastern corner of the bay; but no previous surveys of the type and level of contamination had been conducted. This project therefore conducted a number of analyses, as well as community surveys and interviews with key informants. The many meetings, discussions and presentations that took place to discuss and analyse results revealed or highlighted a number of important issues and results. They confirmed that the issue of sewage pollution, which local residents had identified as a primary concern and as a priority for research, proved to be a very serious issue, indeed. Moreover, they confirmed that it was an issue of immediate concern to poor people and households as it affects their health and the quality of life.

This research, however, contradicted the dominant perception in the community that the households located near the polluted corner of the bay were the source of the problem. In light of the social status of this community, created at the beginning of this century by former agricultural workers who migrated from a poor squatter settlement on the fringe of a nearby estate, it is possible that this environmental phenomenon was used by the larger community to forge, strengthen and change its social perceptions. Considering dominant forms of racial and social prejudice in Caribbean societies, it is not surprising that the wider community found it convenient to blame the people from this area for a problem that was considered serious and potentially dangerous.

Meanwhile, the surveys of perceptions and awareness that were carried out amongst relevant national and local management agencies revealed that, at the beginning of the project, most of these agencies had no knowledge of the pollution issues affecting the area. Responsibilities for dealing with these issues were also unclear. Thanks to the information disseminated by the project, national agencies such as the Ministry of Health have committed themselves to assist, the local village council has agreed that issues of pollution and coastal water quality should now be placed high on its agenda, and funding is being sought for the construction of a treatment facility that will serve new public baths and toilets.

## LESSONS LEARNED: LOCAL GOVERNANCE AND INSTITUTIONAL ARRANGEMENTS FOR COASTAL CONSERVATION AND MANAGEMENT

These focused activities have brought changes to and improvements in the use and management of some of the area's coastal resources, and they have brought tangible benefits to the poor. They have also provoked wider changes in local governance systems and institutions, and they have provided important lessons in this regard.

*Local governance requires complex systems and networks that involve a diversity of actors.* This research project has revealed that, even at the local level in a small locality in a small island state, there are many roles to be performed, and there are a number of organizations that could and should be involved in aspects of natural resource governance. Coastal zone management, because of the diversity of management issues, and because of especially high levels of ecological, economic and social complexity and uncertainty (Brown et al, 2002), is necessarily a local process that requires local rules and capacities. This project has confirmed that local governance is a system that involves a multiplicity of actors and institutions, both formal and informal, and that it is much more than simply having one local government agency. Local governance, therefore, includes both public- and private-sector agencies, it includes both formal and informal institutions, and it involves a myriad of actors who impact upon people and communities at the local level in various ways. In order to be effective, this system of local governance needs to be driven by a clear vision and shared strategic directions.

*Formal local government authorities are necessary constituents of the systems and networks of local governance.* At the same time, this project has confirmed the need for a legitimate and functional local government authority, and the fact that this authority would have an essential role to play in resource management, particularly as it relates to planning, and to the management of common property natural resources and other public assets. Indeed, this experience has shown that the natural resources that can be made available to the poor are often those that are held in public ownership. In the Caribbean, this is true in most coastal areas, where beaches, bays, reefs and other living marine resources have the potential to generate income and to create jobs, and are the only resources available to people who have no physical assets. But, in order to realize this potential, there is a need for policies that facilitate and secure access to these resources, and there is a need for local institutions that make it happen on the ground by setting rules and conditions of access and use, by providing training and financing, and by setting up suitable systems for product development and marketing. Since these natural resources are public resources, it is most appropriate to devolve their management to a public institution or, at least, to an institution that is accountable to the public.

*Within local institutional arrangements for natural resource management, attention needs to be paid to social and economic development issues.* Against this background, this study has also revealed that some very critical roles – especially those related to marketing, business development and other economic aspects – were not currently performed by any organization. While it had been established that seaweed cultivation was technically feasible, and while sea urchin harvests had become abundant, it was realized that people had no one to turn to in order to assist them with priority needs such as marketing. In many respects, dominant approaches to coastal resource management, in the Caribbean as in many other parts of the developing world, are concerned primarily with resource conservation, resource use control and conflict management. One of the lessons of this project is that local institutional arrangements need to give far greater attention to economic aspects, with a focus on poverty reduction and equity issues.

*Resource users and other local actors can play a meaningful role in natural resource management, even in the absence of a formal transfer of management authority.* This project has provided an interesting lesson with respect to property rights. In the case of sea urchin management, there was no de jure exclusion (and most resource users recognized that exclusive access would be undesirable, that it would be impossible to enforce, and that it would create conflicts over the use of other resources); but there was a de facto exclusive use for one resource (the sea urchin). This exclusion was based on the legitimacy and visibility of local decision-making and management processes, which discouraged people from other areas from harvesting near this community, and it was also based on the wider community support for, and endorsement of, the management process.

In many instances, what is needed for effective and equitable natural resource governance is not necessarily the devolution of management or policy-making authority, but transparency in the decision-making and policy-making process, the availability and credibility of the information used for decision-making, and the legitimacy of the persons and the organizations involved. The state does not necessarily need to transfer property rights for good governance to occur, and state agencies can be very effective facilitators of related processes. Such a positive role by resource management agencies does not happen automatically, it requires advocacy and representation, and it requires a constant monitoring of the performance of these agencies by those who are expected to benefit from management. This suggests that there is often a need to devolve political power and to build political influence, instead of devolving natural resource management authority. In this instance, the diverse group of people who depend upon the coastal resources to sustain their livelihoods did not claim the right to make their own management decisions independently from state agencies; but they demanded, and welcomed, opportunities to express their needs, to challenge the management agencies and to monitor the implementation of agreements.

*Local governance is a process, and this process needs to be facilitated and supported by deliberation and inclusion.* For good governance to occur there is a need for spaces and moments for sharing and discussing, and for formulating views and guiding decisions. Concretely, this means that institutions of local governance cannot be truly democratic and effective if they do not provide for the flow of information, transparency and accountability, and participatory decision-making. While the project used a range of standard techniques of participation, it also highlighted the need for deliberate methods and efforts to include those who are normally excluded. In particular, it concluded that regardless of the quality of the attention paid to the format of planning events, they are not sufficient to deliver genuine participation, as the very poor, the elderly or those who live on the margins of society do not, and cannot, participate in formal processes. While the literature on deliberative and inclusive processes (Holmes and Scoones, 2000) actually places much emphasis on events (i.e. citizens' juries, workshops or focus groups), the experience of this project brings two main lessons in this regard:

1   Events cannot be fully inclusive, and they inevitably exclude some people on the basis of social status, culture, sex, age or abilities.
2   Beyond the events, there are many other factors of inclusion and effectiveness of deliberation, such as transparency, legitimacy and information dissemination.

Local institutional arrangements are the product of, but can also impact upon, the larger political landscape. The project has highlighted the limitations and inadequacies of the dominant political structure and culture. It showed how the weaknesses of existing systems of local governance can give too much space to the political system, and too much power to the politicians who are at the centre of that process, resulting in actions that are motivated more by the desire to impress the electorate with tangible and visible achievements than by the genuine development needs of the people. Indeed, there are reasons to believe that current expressions of political resistance to local government reform in Saint Lucia can be explained by the fear of sharing power, and by the fear of systems and institutions that reduce the power of the politician. This suggests that one of the key challenges of local governance is to build the autonomy of local institutions, and to institutionalize and strengthen local networks and capacities, while preserving their diversity.

*Natural resource management can provide a good point of entry for wider improvements in local governance and for progressive political change.* Natural resource management, and especially common property resource management, has the potential to promote collective action, to allow for local revenue generation, to empower people to participate in decisions that affect their lives, and to give power and relevance to local agencies. In countries and societies where there is a desire or a commitment to strengthen local governance, natural resource management issues, while they deserve consideration for their own sake, can also serve as useful channels to demonstrate needs and to channel processes of change.

## CONCLUSIONS

The lessons of this project suggest that there is a need for new forms of local governance and participation, and for new channels and mechanisms that can involve people in the development process. New approaches to local governance must be part of a larger process to reinvent democracy and to build overall systems of governance (at local, national and international levels) that are truly participatory, accountable, efficient and effective. Processes and mechanisms of local governance are critical to social development and poverty reduction as they relate to key issues of empowerment, rights, democracy and participation, but also to practical issues of efficiency and effectiveness in the delivery of goods and services to people and communities.

Even in small island states such as Saint Lucia, the concept of local governance is relevant.

## ENDNOTES

1    In rural Caribbean societies, the 'garden' has important historic, symbolic and economic significance. It refers to the plot of land that people can farm on their own primarily for subsistence purposes, either as individual or communal owners, tenants or squatters, in contrast to the estate, or plantation, associated with slave or low-wage labour, export crops and large private landholdings. These words, *Lanmè-a sé jaden nou* in Creole, were used as the slogan for the project described in this chapter, on the suggestion of George Wilfred, a highly respected and talented fisherman of Laborie, Saint Lucia.

2    This chapter is largely based upon the outputs and products of a project funded by the UK Department for International Development (DFID) as part of its Natural Resources Systems Programme (NRSP). The project was known as People and the Sea, a study of institutional and technical options for improving coastal livelihoods in the Caribbean (NRSP reference R7559). The main contributors to these products and outputs were Ulric Alphonse, Mathias Burt, Lydia Charlemagne, Sylvester Clauzel, Gillian Cooper, Augustine Dominique, Julian Dubois, Lucius Ellevic, Sarah George,

Juliette Gustave, Gem Hutchinson, Rudy John, Grelle Joyeux, Stephen Koester, Yves Renard and Allan Smith. The project received technical and scientific support from Professor Melissa Leach of the Institute of Development Studies at the University of Sussex. This chapter has also been informed by the process to develop a Social Policy for Human Development for Saint Lucia, which is currently being implemented under the auspices of Saint Lucia's Ministry of Social Transformation, Culture and Local Government. Special thanks are due to Steve Bass, Lucius Ellevic, Stephen Koester, Vijay Krishnarayan and Paul Steele for their review of, and comments on, this chapter.

3  While English is Saint Lucia's official language, a French-based Creole remains the dominant language in Saint Lucia's rural areas. The majority of the population is bilingual.

4  Data from the National Population and Housing Censuses of 1991 and 2001 indicates that unemployment at the national level has increased from 7.22 per cent to 13.54 per cent during the ten-year period, while the Laborie area has witnessed an increase from 35.27 per cent to 40.06 per cent over the same period.

5  This phenomenon affects young people more directly. For example, census data show that there were 206 boys aged between five and nine in 1991; ten years later, there were only 79 males aged between 15 and 19.

6  'Sea Urchin Festival' in Creole.

# REFERENCES

Aubrey Armstrong Management Associates (1999) *St. Lucia Local Government Reform, Final Report*, Aubrey Armstrong Management Associates, Christ Church, Barbados

Box, R. C. (1998) *Citizen Governance, Leading American Communities into the 21st Century*, Sage Publications Inc., Thousand Oaks, London and New Delhi

Brown, K., Tompkins, E. L. and Adger, W. N. (2002) *Making Waves: Integrating Coastal Conservation and Development*, Earthscan Publications Ltd., London

Brown, N. A. (1997) *Devolution of Authority over the Management of Natural Resources: the Soufriere Marine Management Area, St. Lucia*, Caribbean Centre for Development Administration (CARICAD) and Caribbean Natural Resources Institute (CANARI), Barbados and St. Lucia

Geoghegan, T., Renard, Y., Brown, N. and Krishnarayan, V. (1999) *Evaluation of Caribbean Experiences in Participatory Planning and Management of Marine and Coastal Resources*, CANARI Technical Report No. 259, CANARI, St. Lucia

Geoghegan, T. and Smith, A. H. (2002) 'Conservation and sustainable livelihoods: Collaborative mangrove management in St. Lucia', *International Forestry Review*, vol. 4, no. 4, pp292–297

George, S. and Joseph, W. (1994) 'A new participatory approach towards sea urchin management in Saint Lucia, West Indies', *Proc. 46 Gulf and Caribb. Fish. Ins.*, vol. 46, pp197–203

GOSL (2000) *Green Paper on Local Government Reform*, Ministry of Community Development, Culture, Co-operatives and Local Government, Castries, Saint Lucia

Holmes, T. and Scoones, I. (2000) *Participatory Environmental Policy Processes: Experiences from North and South*, IDS Working Paper 113, Institute of Development Studies, University of Sussex, Brighton

Hutchinson, G., George, S. and James, C. (2000) *A Description of the Reef Fishery of Laborie, St. Lucia*, CANARI LWI Project Document No. 1, CANARI Technical Report No. 291, St. Lucia

Laborie Development Planning Committee (2001) *Strategic Development Plan for Laborie*, Laborie, Saint Lucia

Mintz, S. W. (1974) *Caribbean Transformations*, The Johns Hopkins University Press, Baltimore and London

Renard, Y. (2001) *Practical Strategies for Pro-poor Tourism: A Case Study of the St. Lucia Heritage Tourism Programme*, PPT Working Paper No. 7

Romulus, G. and Ernest. P. (2003) *Towards Environmental Action and Community Learning: A Case Study of the Praslin and Mamiku Communities on the Island of St. Lucia*, Saint Lucia National Trust, Castries, Saint Lucia

Smith, A. H. and Berkes, F. (1991) 'Solutions to the "tragedy of the commons": Sea urchin management in St. Lucia, West Indies', *Environmental Conservation*, vol. 18, no. 2, pp131–136

Smith, A. H. and Gustave, J. (2001) *A Description of the Harvest of Wild Seamoss in Laborie, St. Lucia*, CANARI LWI Project Document No. 2, CANARI Technical Report No. 292, St. Lucia

Smith, A. H. and Koester, S. (2001) *A Description of the Sea Urchin Fishery in Laborie, St. Lucia*, CANARI LWI Project Document No. 4, CANARI Technical Report No. 294, St. Lucia

# 8

# 'Working for Water' in a Democratic South Africa

*Phillipa Holden and David Grossman*[1]

## INTRODUCTION

The scourge of invasive species is a very significant consideration in the quest for an African Renaissance. (President Thabo Mbeki, March 2000)

The story of South Africa's Working for Water (WfW) programme is a story about a fortuitous, synchronous alignment of the goals and objectives of the new political order, environmental sustainability and the alleviation of poverty. Working for Water is an environmental initiative with significant social benefits, which emerged in post-apartheid South Africa. The expectation and general acceptance of change associated with the installation of a democratic government provided a unique window of opportunity for addressing an ecologically and economically critical issue that was aligned with the new government's Reconstruction and Development Programme (RDP) and the need for job creation, especially amongst the neglected rural poor. The total cost of invasive plants to South Africa is very high and includes a serious threat to biodiversity, as well as a loss of water through reduced in-stream flow and increased evapotranspiration, with significant economic ramifications. The WfW initiative was developed with the dual purpose of controlling alien invasive plants and providing an ideal opportunity for skills development and job creation. As a result of the support it received and the input from government, the private sector and, at a grassroots level, community and non-governmental organizations (NGOs), it flew, although not without the inevitable wobble.

# WHAT IS 'WORKING FOR WATER'?

Working for Water originated during 1995 as a state-funded public works programme aimed at controlling and, where possible, eradicating alien (and, in certain cases, indigenous) invasive plants that negatively affected the environment. The changing political climate as South Africa moved from apartheid to democracy, coupled with willing private-sector partners and donors, and further fuelled by the need for skills training, poverty alleviation and employment generation, provided the ideal opportunity for an innovative project satisfying multiple objectives. Prior to 1994, South Africa was minority ruled by the white Nationalist government, which resulted in huge disparities in power and access to land. In terms of the apartheid 'grand vision', over 80 per cent of the population was expected to be settled in so-called 'homeland' areas, which were to receive nominal independence. Furthermore, there were few opportunities for black involvement and leadership in conservation and natural resource management institutions. After the change to majority rule, South Africa embraced an open and innovative attitude to policy review, providing enormous opportunities for making forward-thinking and creative changes in order to address social, economic and environmental challenges and imperatives. Changes in governance structures also provided an opportunity for new partnerships and inputs from previously disempowered parties and interests.

Essentially, the thrust of WfW is to train and equip teams of unemployed local people to remove invasive alien vegetation. The means vary from location to location, with different species needing to be cleared and methods being appropriately adapted. For example, in the Western Cape, invasive alien species threaten the local endemic fynbos vegetation, recognized as one of the world's biomes. Steep and mountainous terrain requires specialized techniques for accessing and controlling the spread of alien species. Considerable technical expertise is required in order to access invaded areas safely. Species differ and so, accordingly, do removal methods. In mountainous terrain, previously unskilled, unemployed people have been trained in basic mountaineering techniques, including abseiling, and are equipped with the necessary kit to enable them to reach poorly accessible areas. In the North-West Province, teams are equipped with custom-made bush-cutters that are used to thin and reclaim land on cattle farms and conservation areas, encroached by an aggressive indigenous species, *Dichrostachy cinerea* (zebra wood). A herbicide is applied to the cut stump to prevent re-growth, wood is laid out to dry and is then bundled and sold as

**Figure 8.1** *Working for water team members*

firewood. Feasibility analyses revealed that this was the most efficient means of control and disposal of the wood. Adding value through charcoal production would not have been sustainable in this particular case, due to start-up and transport costs and irregularity of supply (Gore, 1997). Each team is trained both technically and in terms of business skills, enabling them to operate on an ongoing, revenue-generating basis. They charge the landowner on a per hectare cleared basis, and the wood is sold. Other examples differ in detail. In all cases, however, the basic principles of the project remain the same.

# WHY 'WORKING FOR WATER'?

## Needs of the natural environment

The country has a serious ecological problem with aggressive invasive alien plants that are rapidly spreading. The worst alien offenders were identified as pine trees from Europe and the United States, *Prosopis* spp. (mesquite) from Central America and several Australian *Acacia* species (Kasrils, 2000). The extent of this impact can be gauged from the following:

*Source:* Working for Water Programme, South Africa

**Figure 8.2** *Clearing invasive alien species from land near a water source*

- At least 161 invasive species cause problems in natural and semi-natural systems (Henderson, 1995).
- Ten million hectares, equivalent to some 8 per cent of the surface area of the country, is negatively affected (le Maitre et al, 2000).
- Dense stands of invasives intercept and use some 7 per cent of runoff water, exacerbated by the fact that much of this occurs in areas already subject to water scarcity.
- There is an, as yet, unquantified impact on groundwater reserves in arid areas.
- Invasive species result in increased biomass, leading to increased intensity and negative impacts of fire, including soil erosion and decreased germination of indigenous plants, as well as attendant risks to local people and negative influences on the burgeoning tourism industry ('Who wants to see fire scars on Table Mountain when we come to look at flowers?').
- The cost of controlling invasives is estimated at 600 million rand per year, escalating for each year that control is not implemented, given the rate of spread of aliens.
- Invasives also result in markedly reduced biodiversity due to competition, allelopathic effects (a situation where certain plant species exude compounds that prevent the growth of other plant

183

species, resulting in virtually monospecific stands) and increased fire intensity.

The cost of these to both the economy and the environment are significant, invading catchment areas and reducing in-stream flow, increasing evapotranspiration, and reducing biodiversity and associated use and non-use benefits. Studies have shown that species invasions have reduced the value of fynbos ecosystems by over US$11.75 billion. They have also shown that the total cost of invasion would be in the order of US$3.2 billion on the Agulhas Plain in the Western Cape and that the cost to clear alien plant invasions in South Africa amounts to approximately US$1.2 billion.

## Needs within the social environment

The socio-economic reality of apartheid South Africa meant that a vast number of people lived in very difficult circumstances, were neglected by the Afrikaner Nationalist government and suffered under a range of apartheid laws and policies. This situation was evident both in rural and urban areas, though the rural poor were perhaps most impoverished, with less access to infrastructure and employment opportunities and declining access to deteriorating natural resources that might otherwise sustain them. Many people faced a basic needs crisis and environmental degradation as a result of overcrowding in so-called 'homeland' areas. This social engineering included the manipulation and virtual disruption of customary and traditional resource management practices and the stripping of resources for survival by local communities and for commercial gain by others. In many ways, this is not dissimilar to what has happened elsewhere in the world, where ecologically sustainable land-use and resource-use norms and practices have been disrupted as a result of factors such as missionary or government intervention and political strife. These are often replaced by under-resourced, 'Western-style' institutions and controls that prove to be ineffective, while at the same time disempowering the very communities who critically depend upon the resource base and have the greatest interest in protecting it, leaving it and them vulnerable to the ravages of external pressures and interests. In the South African case, this was further exacerbated by the growing 'homeland' populations who were increasingly economically hamstrung.

Faced with the destructive legacy of these inherited social, environmental and economic problems, critical action had to be taken by the new government in power. The first Reconstruction and Development

Source: Working for Water Programme, South Africa

**Figure 8.3** *The WfW childcare initiative, which allows women to engage in labour for household income*

Programme (RDP) initiative of the democratic government was aimed at addressing these problems in a number of ways, and the WfW programme emerged against this background. While many of the RDP initiatives involved policy-level interventions, at least in their early stages, WfW was able to begin work on the ground relatively quickly, jointly combating the problems of ecological degradation through alien invasion and the need for economic activity in depressed rural areas. It has also raised the level of environmental knowledge and awareness in these areas, encouraging the sustainable use of natural resources and highlighting the need to keep these areas free of invasive alien plants.

## THE POLITICAL ENVIRONMENT: TIME FOR ACTION

As far back as 1945, invasive alien plants were identified as a great threat to indigenous vegetation, particularly in the Cape. At that point, the potential impact on water flow and supply was recognized, but had not been quantified. Subsequent hydrological experimentation in the Cape by the former South African Forestry Research Institute and its successor, the Council for Scientific and Industrial Research (CSIR), Division of Forest Science and Technology, revealed the extent of

185

*Source:* Working for Water Programme, South Africa

**Figure 8.4** *Invasive alien species use some 7 per cent of water runoff in South Africa*

increased water use and loss from the system as a result of afforestation and invasion, and the resulting impact on regional water supply in the Cape. Further government-funded research during the early 1990s revealed the significance of the likely increase in density and extent of invasions, resulting in reductions in stream flow of between 30 per cent and 60 per cent.

The scientific community had formed an interdisciplinary team that included ecologists, hydrologists, resource economists and engineers who could effectively analyse and illustrate the ramifications of the problem and possible solutions. However, publicizing these findings in scientific journals did not raise the profile of the problem enough; as a result, politicians needed to be approached directly in order to draw attention to the issue. A special working group was put together and charged with presenting the problem in non-technical language.

In 1995, this strategic attempt to raise the profile of the problem finally met with success. A presentation given to the ebullient Professor Kader Asmal, then Minister for Water Affairs and Forestry, resulted in the initiation of the WfW programme. The presentation emphasized not only the threat to water resources, but also the opportunity that a clearing programme would offer for job creation (van Wilgen et al,

2002). It also came at a time when major policy and legislative revisions were underway, including:

- the RDP, which was aimed at redressing past injustices and focused on the previously disadvantaged sector of South African society;
- the new constitution, which guaranteed people the right to basic needs and a 'healthy environment'; and
- the drafting of a New Water Law for South Africa.

The core objective of the latter was to 'manage the quantity, quality and reliability of the nation's water resources ... to achieve optimum long-term, environmentally sustainable, social and economic benefit for society from their use' and to reserve water to meet basic human needs and maintain ecological functions.

At the macro-political level, President Mandela's cabinet was faced with increasing pressure from the newly enfranchized electorate and from political and economic interests outside of the country to address the backlog of service provision, including housing, education, health services, and, importantly, water provision and job creation.

The programme kicked off with a budget of US$4 million to cover its first six months of operation and, under the guidance of a small, dedicated management team, was able to spend the budget within the allocated time, creating 6163 jobs and clearing 33,229 hectares of infestations in ten projects spread over six of the country's nine provinces. It is noteworthy that the project started without the usual 'bureaucratic delay', seemingly because Professor Kader Asmal was buoyed up by the enthusiasm generated by the scientific community, as well as by the 'good fit' with government RDP objectives:

> I well remember when I was confronted by the assertion that we should clear invading alien plants because of their threat to our water security. The argument put forward by Dr Guy Preston, then a researcher at the University of Cape Town, was that we should not build dams and (inter-catchment) transfer schemes until we have optimized the potential of ... catchment management. Central to efficient catchment management, it was argued, was the clearing of invading alien plants.
>
> ... I was intrigued by the arguments and we formed the National Water Conservation Campaign. Reinforced by the cogent arguments put forward by the WWF-SA [World Wide Fund for Nature, South Africa], I approached my dear colleague, Jay Naidoo, for funding. Jay was minister without

portfolio in the first democratic cabinet of South Africa, responsible for the Reconstruction and Development Programme.

... Perhaps it is safe to confess that I approached Jay Naidoo for initial funding [for WfW] without a business plan. Jay is a wise person and he saw the value of what was being proposed. (Asmal, 2000)

The programme, once started as a result of Asmal's bold decision and without bureaucratic delay (seeking donor funding may have delayed the start-up time and diverted the project's aim), was well publicized by an in-house communications team, highlighting the achievements and raising the profile of the issue amongst landowners and the general public, as well as gaining acclaim for a new government that was eager to prove itself and tangibly demonstrate its capability to deliver. This success and the clear demonstration of government's commitment to the concept led to further funding from local government, the private sector, foreign donors and the government's poverty relief initiative, aimed at creating employment amongst the poorest sectors of society. By 1999/2000 the programme's total expenditure had risen to US$120 million, with the creation of 21,000 jobs.

Key to the success of the project was the cabinet-level support and political backing that it received. Furthermore, a dedicated and persuasive 'champion' in the form of Dr Guy Preston was appointed through funds made available by the World Wide Fund for Nature (WWF-SA) to ensure ongoing support for the initiative at the appropriate level. Being accountable directly to a committed and somewhat innovative minister also ensured that the project did not get bogged down in bureaucracy. The successful marketing and publicity surrounding the project ensured ongoing awareness and support and, in turn, helped to secure more funding from a diverse range of sources. Nevertheless, alternative means of raising funds are still needed in order to avoid an over-reliance on funding from central government. Possibilities for such funding include levies from the growers of invasive plantations, users of water from alien-free catchments such as local municipal authorities, foreign aid and income from associated secondary industries. The cost of clearing invasions might also be reduced by implementing effective biological controls, and these are currently being investigated and researched.

Further partnerships were formed within WfW by developing complementary programmes to provide assistance to poor and marginalized people in a number of ways. WfW linked up with the National

*Source:* Working for Water Programme, South Africa

**Figure 8.5** *Construction activities under the WfW Secondary Industries programme*

Population Unit, the United Nations Population Fund and the Planned Parenthood Association of South Africa to set up a reproductive health programme. Social scientists working within the WfW programme also interact with the community youth in increasing awareness of HIV/AIDS. Furthermore, a childcare initiative is intended to enable women to engage in labour for household income. At its peak, WfW had over 42,000 workers in the field, drawn from the so-called 'poorest of the poor', primarily in rural (but also urban, e.g. Cape Town) areas. Fifty-four per cent of the beneficiaries were women, 26 per cent youth (16 to 25 years of age), and 1 per cent were people with disabilities. Particular attention was paid to single-headed households. It also allocated some 500 positions to ex-offenders.

A Secondary Industries programme was initiated to add value to the clearing of alien plants. Objectives include:

- maximizing the positive economic benefits of the WfW programme by creating extra jobs through the harvesting and processing of plant material, thereby creating further small, medium and micro-enterprise opportunities;

189

- reducing the net cost of clearing, thereby contributing to the sustainability of the WfW programme; and
- minimizing potential negative environmental impacts, such as fire damage, by leaving less biomass behind after clearing.

The small business and skills training that many workers on the programme receive enables them to exit the programme and run businesses on their own. Some of these are related to the utilization of products from the clearing of vegetation, and this secondary industries component of the project boosts the benefits that the programme is able to generate. Examples include firewood sales, as well as adding value to the cleared wood by charcoal and furniture manufacture, screens and blinds, décor items for interior/lifestyle shops, fencing arches and garden furnishings, and educational toys, where financial analyses indicate the viability of such projects. Another related business development and employment creation opportunity has been the start of indigenous nurseries to supply appropriate tree species for planting after clearing.

## IS EVERYTHING ROSY?

Despite its successes, the programme has faced a number of setbacks and problems. The causes of these are varied, and while some issues have been actively addressed and rectified, others continue to detract from the programme. However, many relate back to the political pressure for rapid delivery and the rapid growth of the programme, together with increasing 'bureaucratization'. For instance, the programme had no experience to draw on and insufficient attention was given to developing a strategy and to medium- and long-term planning. In the rush to implement them, projects were sometimes initiated without proper advance planning and were then poorly managed, with inappropriate or incorrect methods sometimes being used to deal with plant species. Stands were occasionally cleared with no or insufficient follow-up, making the situation worse, rather than improving it. In some cases, stands of indigenous trees were accidentally cleared due to insufficient training. This situation was further exacerbated by the desire for political expediency, and the need to satisfy political goals often superceded ecological objectives. As a result, projects did not necessarily target high biodiversity areas, and a number were undertaken in non-priority areas or targeted non-priority species in order to demonstrate that benefits could be delivered and in order to direct poverty relief to the poorest areas.

At the same time, despite cabinet support and the flexible approach demonstrated by Kader Asmal, spending of state funds is obviously subject to the usual rules and regulations associated with any government bureaucracy. Appropriate procurement procedures, auditing, compliance with statutory procedures relating to contracts, labour employment, complex tender processes, liability insurance and other time-consuming procedures led to frustration and division between state-employed actors and those relatively unshackled by the bounds of bureaucracy, working in the parastatal, private and NGO sectors.

It also emerged that investment in training is crucial. Low productivity and inefficiency often resulted from the push for affirmative action appointments that were supported in order to ensure that previously disadvantaged members of society benefited from the programme. As part of the package of innovations introduced to redress past inequities, the government is committed to 'Black Economic Empowerment'. However, in many cases this has not been accompanied by the necessary capacity-building and skills transfer, especially at a management level. Weakness in managing projects was further exacerbated by the lack of a cohesive, strategic approach to the initiative.

In other cases, over-committed and under-resourced staff were hard pushed to spend all available money in short time periods, a factor which was made worse by the sporadic nature of the funding (finishing at the end of the financial year with a delay before the next year's funds came in), with a resulting stop-start work programme and practical and motivational implications. A lack of support and enthusiasm from some key partners and implementing agents (particularly in mainstream government departments) who were not involved in conceptualizing the programme could have been avoided by ensuring wider buy-in and participation at the start.

A conflict of interests was also experienced between WfW and different user groups, especially where invasive species were of commercial or other value – for instance, exotic *Acacia* species that provide firewood, *Eucalyptus* that provides nectar for bees, plantation forestry and shade trees or windbreaks. This could, perhaps, have been mitigated through prior negotiation and discussion, with mutually acceptable solutions being identified:

> I think it is fair to criticize WfW as having been somewhat 'top down' in its focus on invasive alien plants. However, I also think that such a major cross-cutting (and, effectively, international) issue cannot be dealt with at a local level. It needs an overarching focus and design. However, within that, it has

been possible for us to engage with workers and communities regarding the structure of our work, and especially with respect to the social development considerations. We have had considerable support from local government and civic structures in the allotment of training/employment opportunities and our responsibilities as an employer. It is true to say, regrettably, that this has diminished somewhat, as other initiatives get up to speed and ask for similar support, and as volunteer fatigue sets in. More does need to be done to empower our workers and contractors to exit the programme successfully, and it is something we are trying to do in full partnership with them – improving the training, creating the enabling environment, reassessing our role in their emergence as independent contractors and workers, looking at collectives as alternatives, etc. Having faced the anger of workers who have been disadvantaged by the programme (e.g. late payments), they are not 'passive'. We do, however, worry about whether we have enough control over the emerging power of the contractors, who are not necessarily driven by the same commitment to the RDP as we idealists are. (Guy Preston, head of Working for Water Programme, personal communication, July 2003)

## OUTCOMES

### Lessons learned

Perhaps the most important lesson is that with a little creative thinking and the necessary will amongst key drivers, enormous success can be achieved. It cannot be disputed that the changing political climate in South Africa during the mid 1990s offered an unprecedented opportunity for such a programme to come into effect; but the innovative approach to satisfying an array of social, ecological and economic dilemmas, while involving public, private and community sectors and resulting in benefits for each, was noteworthy.

In order for this type of innovation to become more common, it is necessary for governance to evolve so that an environment is created that truly fosters partnerships between state, the private sector and communities. Parochial interests and political expediency often militate against such partnerships; but WfW provided a fortuitous alignment of the needs of politicians, environmentalists, government agencies, the private sector and community members. Politically astute and well-placed or empowered 'champions' often play a key role in promoting the agenda in the right places and in the right way by melding the needs of the various parties and by providing a crucial link between them.

Furthermore, political will and a supportive policy and legislative framework are required, including funding vehicles and partnerships which ensure that the funding cycle is commensurate with the project design so that it does not become a hindrance. Possible ways of diversifying funding sources also need to be found.

Increasing the stability of the programme is also essential to ensure a medium- to long-term perspective on the work that is done, something that is crucial for effective alien plant control, which requires regular follow-ups over a number of years. In order for this to happen, long-term funding needs to be available. If this is not the case, then the initial clearing is futile and available funds should be reallocated to where they will achieve the greatest long-term return, rather than increasing the area of operation.

The extension of the WfW model to other spheres requires that the goals of the governors at national, provincial and local levels also neatly coincides with the needs of the poor, as well as the environment. Similar initiatives in South Africa include the incorporation of the 'small grower' into forestry and sugar cane production, as well as attempts to start a National LandCare programme. Moderate success has been attained in the forestry and sugar cane sectors, affecting limited numbers of people relative to the WfW programme. The LandCare initiative has failed to gain momentum: it has not been championed at the political level and it has not enjoyed popular support due to limited funding and low impact on poverty levels.

The WfW programme has had an effect at the policy level and has aided the revision of legislation such as the Conservation of Agricultural Resources Act, enabling it to deal with different categories of invasive plants in order to meet the needs of different interest groups (e.g. certain plants with commercial value may be cultivated providing that the landowner accepts responsibility for clearing costs in surrounding areas).

## CONCLUSIONS

South Africa emerged from a 'dark age into an enlightened era'. Working for Water represents a serious attempt by the progressive political leadership of the day to improve the quality of life of the previously disadvantaged sectors of society in a global order increasingly driven by so-called 'neo-liberal' economic forces. Herein lies a threat: WfW is, and remains, essentially a public works programme, funded more by the fiscus through the taxpayer than by demand-driven economic forces, although valiant attempts have been made to justify the expenditure on environmental economic principles and the generation of secondary industries. However, as Marais et al (2000) conclude: 'the net economic effect of the fynbos WfW programme on government revenue is negative'. The threat is that currently fashionable economic paradigms assert that public works programmes are inefficient, non-sustainable approaches to alleviating poverty. Theory holds that Adam Smith's 'invisible hand' of market forces will inevitably result in a 'trickle down' of benefits to the poverty-stricken sectors of society. Others hold that this rarely occurs, that such policies favour the 'haves' at the continued expense of the 'have nots'. The South African government is faced with the dilemma of choosing the 'neo-liberal' or the 'social democratic' approach, with indications that there is vigorous debate between left and right. There may be solace for those who intuitively or intellectually challenge the renewed faith in market forces in the thought that most, if not all, so-called developed nations have faced similar challenges in the past:

> In this nation I see tens of millions of its citizens – a substantial part of its whole population – who at this very moment are denied the greater part of what the very lowest standards of today call the necessities of life. I see millions denied education, recreation and the opportunity to better their lot and the lot of their children. I see millions lacking the means to buy the products of farm and factory and, by their poverty, denying work and productiveness to many other millions. I see one third of a nation ill housed, ill clad, ill nourished. It is not in despair that I paint you that picture. I paint it for you in hope – because the nation, seeing and understanding the injustice in it, proposes to paint it out. The test of our progress is not whether we add more to the abundance of those who have much; it is whether we provide enough for those who have too little.

These are not the words of Luthuli, Sobukwe, Mandela or other heroes of South Africa's struggle. In fact, they are the words of Franklin D. Roosevelt before initiating 'New Deal' public works programmes when confronted with the reality of the 1930s Great Depression in the United States.

## Postscript

The first Working for Water research symposium was held in Cape Town in late August 2003. The event was hosted by WfW's research teams, which, since 1999, have studied issues ranging from operations management to the use of insects in the biological control of invasive alien plants and the cost benefits of ridding South Africa of alien plants. Apart from bringing together researchers from many disciplines, a key aim of the symposium was to develop a database on its research findings that would be accessible to everyone. The research will also be used to develop teaching material for schools in conjunction with Department of Education officials, 'translating science in popular materials and getting it out there'. About 2.5 per cent of the project's annual budget of 400 million rand is spent on research that provides crucial information on managing water and biodiversity and how to effectively add economic value to the cleared plant matter. Research has shown, for example, that more than 60 million cubic metres of water were added to local dams after alien vegetation was cleared from the Sabi Sands catchment area in Mpumulanga Province. Organizers are also concerned about what happens to the workers when they leave the programme or its activities end in an area. Working for Water has created about 20,000 temporary jobs and training opportunities this financial year alone. (synthesis of *Mail & Guardian* article, 1–7 August 2003)

## ENDNOTES

1   Hannah Reid and co-editors are thanked for useful comments, as is Guy Preston, 'driver' of the programme.

## REFERENCES

Asmal, K. (2000) 'Keynote address: Two oceans', *Proceedings of Symposium on Best Management Practices for Preventing and Controlling Invasive Alien Species*, Working for Water Programme, Cape Town

Gore, W. T. (1997) *Feasibility Analysis of Charcoal Production*, Technical Report, Mafisa, Johannesburg

Henderson, L. (1995) *Plant Invaders of Southern Africa*, Plant Protection Research Institute, Handbook No. 5, Agricultural Research Council, Pretoria

Kasrils, R. (2000) 'A water perspective on alien species', *Proceedings of Symposium on Best Management Practices for Preventing and Controlling Invasive Alien Species.* Working for Water Programme, Cape Town

le Maitre, D. C., Versfeld, D. B. and Chapman, R. (2000) *The Impact of Invading Alien Plants on Surface Water Resources in South Africa: A Preliminary Assessment*, CSIR Division of Water, Environment and Forestry Technology, Stellenbosch

Marais, C., Eckert, J. and Green, C. (2000) 'Utilisation of invaders for secondary industries: A preliminary assessment', *Proceedings of Symposium on Best Management Practices for Preventing and Controlling Invasive Alien Species.* Working for Water Programme, Cape Town

van Wilgen, B.W., Marais, C., Magadlela, D., Jezile, N. and Stevens, D. (2002) 'Win-win-win: South Africa's Working for Water Programme', in S. M. Pierce, R. Cowling, T. Sandwith and K. MacKinnon (eds) *Mainstreaming Biodiversity in Development*, World Bank Environment Department, Washington, D.C.

# 9

# People, Perspectives and Reality: Usangu Myths and Other Stories, Tanzania

*Julie Thomas, Geoffrey King, Susan Kayetta*

## INTRODUCTION

Usangu, in southern Tanzania, offers a 'who-dunnit' with a cast of characters whose individual interests coincided to confuse reality and to marginalize issues of poverty and the environment, even while using the environment and poverty as guises for action. Local, national and international actors, through good intent or neglect, oversimplified a complex situation, leading to inappropriate actions that have had, and will continue to have, negative effects on local livelihoods of the most vulnerable and on the environment. However, most local resource users, whose livelihoods and well-being are inextricably linked to Usangu's environment, were effectively excluded from the decision-making processes that have affected those livelihoods.

The lessons learned in Usangu have wide applicability. In a resource-scarce world, we need to recognize that environmental management is about trade-offs. Addressing environment and poverty requires not just a technical approach; instead, power relationships should be addressed through negotiation across the social and political spectrum. Negotiation is essential at all levels – from national to local levels, and with all stakeholders – through representative processes which ensure that the poor and marginalized have a voice. This will inevitably lead to a broad agenda and require trade-offs between different actors. Negotiation will create both winners and losers; protection is required to ensure that the losers are not always, as in Usangu, the poor and marginalized.

Technical facts provide just one strand of knowledge that feeds into the negotiation process. In a Western context, technical information has high value, and tends to underpin decision-making; however, valuation processes may be different in an African context, even amongst technically trained people. Local understanding and perceptions may be critical in finding – or obstructing – solutions; Western technocratic evaluations may not be 'politically right' in local circumstances. The Usangu case demonstrates this dilemma well. Similarly, protectionism, or other singularly focused agendas, can rarely provide effective and sustainable solutions as the interests of groups key to overall success are almost inevitably excluded. Environmental linkages may also be distant and obscure; environmental impacts may be felt far from the root cause of the problem. The impact of international trade is but one example.

This chapter describes the scene, the actors and the different acts in the play that was acted out between the early 1990s and 2002. Lessons are drawn which can guide future actions in similar circumstances. The play ends with no 'guilty' parties; in a sense, we are all culprits, limited by our beliefs and interests.

## PROLOGUE: THE STAGE IS SET, THE ACTORS ANNOUNCED

The Usangu catchment lies in southern Tanzania. An area rich in natural resources, it supports a diversity of livelihoods and ecosystems of local, national and international importance. Locally, some 500,000 people in approximately 350 communities depend upon Usangu's resources for irrigated rice, dryland maize, pasture and domestic uses. Nationally, it is an important producer and exporter of both rice and livestock. Internationally, its wetland is known for its birdlife and meets the criteria of the international Ramsar Convention, while downstream the vast Ruaha National Park comprises miombo and riverine ecosystems, and attracts increasing numbers of international tourists.

Usangu is formed from a circle of hills that drain into a large plain containing an immense wetland; rivers from the surrounding hills meet here to form the Great Ruaha River. The hills form part of the southern highlands and have long been settled, with gentler sloping areas cleared for cultivation. By contrast, the plain remained largely a wilderness area until about 1940, except for some livestock keeping by the indigenous Sangu, who were few in number. Irrigation changed this situation, providing a magnet for immigrants. Irrigated rice production was introduced by Baluchi immigrants (see Box 9.1). With plentiful land and water on the edge of the plain, many others from all over Tanzania have

*Source:* Sustainable Management of the Usangu Wetland and its Catchment (SMUWC) project

**Figure 9.1** *Irrigation in Usangu; a view from the air*

*Source:* Sustainable Management of the Usangu Wetland and its Catchment (SMUWC) project

**Figure 9.2** *Irrigation in Usangu*

migrated to Usangu to improve their livelihoods, relying upon irrigated rice as a main cash crop. National policies and international interventions (e.g. by the World Bank; the Canadian International Development Agency; the United Nations Food and Agriculture Organization (FAO); the United Nations Development Programme (UNDP); and the African Development Bank Group) have promoted and supported these developments. Irrigation continues to attract people, and the irrigated area is still expanding and will likely continue to do so until all water is used, fuelled by national pro-poor policies that promote irrigation as a means for livelihood security. However, each new irrigation farmer also requires land for rain-fed maize production, for livestock and for housing; land-use conversion for non-irrigated uses far exceeds that for irrigation. Plentiful grass and water in the seasonally flooded wetland also attracted pastoralists and their livestock, beginning in the 1950s and peaking during the 1970s.

---

## BOX 9.1 THE BALUCHIS, TANZANIA

Baluchi immigrants are said to have first come to Tanzania as guards to the sultan of Zanzibar. Successful businessmen, they have moved throughout the country, engaged in farming, hunting and commerce. It is probably hunting which first brought them to Usangu, where they continue to retain a hunting concession. Once there, they probably quickly recognized the potential for irrigated farming, using skills transported from Baluchistan.

---

The people of Usangu are almost entirely dependent upon their environment. Most people are farmers, and while land is plentiful, water to make that land productive – from rain and rivers – is in short supply. The environment also provides, directly, most other essentials of life – water for domestic uses and for livestock; grazing and browse (most people keep livestock); fuel (from the abundant woodlands); building materials (wood, thatch, mud and brick materials); medicinal plants; fish and wildlife; minerals (artisanal gold mining occurs locally within Usangu); and other minor environmental products. Wild resources (e.g. fruits, fish and wild meat, wood and thatch for resale, etc.) also provide an important safety net for the most vulnerable in times of hardship. The Usangu wetland also has spiritual value for the indigenous Sangu.

Downstream from Usangu the Great Ruaha River flows through the Ruaha National Park, and then on to feed the Mtera hydropower reservoir before joining the Rufiji River – one of East Africa's most significant freshwater sources – which flows to the sea. Few people live in these areas; but the Usangu wetland and Ruaha National Park and ecosystem are of particular interest to national and international environmental non-governmental organizations (NGOs) and tourist lobbies. These ecosystems are almost entirely dependent upon the river inflows from upstream.

## ACT 1: THE PLAYERS REVEAL THEIR AGENDAS; INTERNATIONAL, NATIONAL AND LOCAL STAGES ARE REVEALED

The plot starts with water shortages and national electricity rationing. During the early to mid 1990s, the national electricity company, TANESCO, faced water supply problems at its main generating facility at Mtera. This threatened national economic development, as Mtera at that time supplied some 80 per cent of national electrical power. Simultaneously, the Great Ruaha River, which feeds Mtera, started to dry up seasonally in the Ruaha National Park, beginning in 1993, although there is evidence of reduced dry season flows since the 1970s. This threatened wildlife and tourism. The 'obvious' conclusion was drawn between these two events, and the finger of blame was pointed upstream at Usangu and, in particular, at irrigation that had developed over the previous 50 years (Box 9.2), partially by indigenous people but more recently from policy decisions and physical support.

National and international support for irrigation in Usangu reflected the prevailing wisdom of the time. Food security was to be obtained through agricultural development, built on the Western technological model of mechanization, irrigation and high inputs. Even until recently, international donors and national departments were supporting irrigation developments in Usangu based on these technical assumptions, and with little impact monitoring. Evidence of negative impacts was rejected; in the absence of absolutes, and bolstered by a view of irrigation as 'good', it was easy to declare evidence as 'inconclusive'. For the Ministry of Water (supported by international donors), overall water supply and management was the focus, with 'improved' water-use efficiency assumed to be achievable through engineering solutions, thereby securing livelihoods and releasing more water for use downstream. For the partner organization, the Ministry of Agriculture, food production was the objective and irrigation was part of the solution, not a problem. Its focus was on technical systems management for farmers within the irrigation system. This department resisted – and still resists

– the notion that irrigation is responsible for the river problems. The other major national player, the Ministry of Natural Resources and Tourism, saw the issue only in terms of biodiversity and protected areas – the national park and surrounding game reserves, as well as the Usangu wetland.

---

## BOX 9.2 IRRIGATION IN USANGU

The first irrigation farm was developed as an experimental farm by the United Nations Food and Agriculture Organization (FAO) during the early 1960s. It expanded to a commercial state farm known as Mbarali, which opened in 1972.

This was followed by the Kapunga state farm, which was opened in 1992, and the Madibira farm, established in 2000. Both of these were financed by the African Development Bank Group. By the time that Madibira opened, the failure of 'state' farming had been recognized and the farm was developed as a smallholder enterprise (although designed and built as a state farm).

Meanwhile, smallholder irrigation systems developed apace. Many of the larger systems have been subject to 'improvements' supported by international donors. Improvements generally involve replacing traditional weirs of sticks and stones (inherently porous and impermanent) with concrete weirs. Traditional structures could raise the river water level to that of the canal intake only over limited time periods. However, impermeable structures raise the water level throughout the year. This increases the security of the water supply, but also increases the amount of water that can be taken at any one time and the time period over which it can be taken. This, as well as concrete intake structures, straitened canals, system design changes and drainage to return wastewater to the river, all offer 'water management' advantages. However, in the absence of effective management structures, they encourage excess consumption, an increased period of consumption and overall increased water use.

One particular aspect of this is that large price incentives for the early crop encourage 'top-enders' to take advantage of their position within the system and to plant their rice earlier and earlier, back into the period of lowest river flows at the tail end of the dry season. This has a knock-on effect of increasing water availability downstream later in the season – encouraging more people to irrigate.

Elsewhere, often downstream of the schemes, individuals take water as they can. Downstream, rivers rarely have enough height to allow water abstraction. However, tail (waste) water from the schemes being returned to the rivers in canals often has enough height. System improvements therefore increase opportunities for 'tail-enders' to abstract water, increasing overall water use.

On the whole, the absence of a holistic systems perspective and a disregard for the cumulative effect of improvements have increased water abstraction, both in total and over time, and have led to the seasonal drying of the river.

---

There was no holistic vision or integrated approach. This fitted with a sectoral approach to national resource management, in which the 'environment' was an 'add-on' to sectoral management, and ignored the social and human dimensions. In doing so, it made water availability in the river worse, not better. However, it fitted donor interests, with their short-term funding cycles and internal desires for definable and visible responses and solutions; few careers have been built on supporting long-term locally led processes!

Local people had a different perspective. To them, water equated with livelihoods, and the infrastructure 'improvements' offered new opportunities for exploiting available water to improve their lives, especially for the 'tail-enders' (those towards the end of the water supply system) who were outside the formal systems and, therefore, outside the ambit of interests of both the ministries of water and of agriculture. 'Wastewater' from the schemes was available and accessible (at an elevation to allow abstraction), and offered opportunities other than seeing it return to the river. Without any attempt to achieve a meeting of minds on objectives, and in the absence of effective systems of regulation and enforcement, local interests (e.g. livelihoods and profit) prevailed over the potential regional and national value of the engineering 'improvements'.

Meanwhile, in Usangu itself conflicts were arising over access to resources, especially water and grazing – both between and among irrigators and pastoralists. There was also increasing concern expressed over environmental issues. Population expansion and unmanaged exploitation now leave many without water for parts of the year, and have led to deterioration of water quality, reduced pasture area and quality, and reduced fish catches. They have also nearly eliminated large wildlife and led to overexploitation of some woodlands, and reduced availability of other environmental resources. Secondary impacts include loss of woodland and wetland habitat, and reduced dry season flows, leading to deterioration of riverine habitat and economic impacts. Environmental changes are also occurring within the plain, including the seasonal drying of rivers, the non-flooding of large parts of the wetland, and the resulting subtle yet real degradation of wetland soils and vegetation (including changes in grass species towards less palatable species, and bush encroachment).

Political power and the impact of these changes depend upon one's position along the watercourses. On the Usangu plain, those closest to the sources of water in the hills (top-enders) see fewest impacts and also tend to be those with greatest political power, allowing them to protect their interests. Impacts become increasingly pronounced as one moves downstream (see Box 9.3). Political power declines in the same direction: impacts have been greatest on the most vulnerable and/or marginalized who are least able to compete for resources. Such impacts include increased insecurity of livelihoods; declining health (e.g. water quality and reduced food production); increased distances to resources (e.g. water, wood and thatch), increasing the burden on women and children; declining wealth (especially fewer livestock, as well as reduced food production for some); and pressure on children to provide labour rather than go to school. Traditional water users (especially the Sangu in downstream villages), tail-end irrigators, pastoralists and fishermen have suffered the most.

---

## BOX 9.3 WINNERS AND LOSERS IN USANGU

Irrigation has been good to the people of Usangu. It has offered livelihood support, security and even prosperity to tens of thousands of farm families and to a supporting network of merchants:

> To be fair, for me, my farming is very helpful to my livelihood. I have a decent life, eat well and raise my children well. I have enough money to pay for health services and my children are in school. (Carlos Mtove, irrigator, Madibira)

But the gains have not been evenly spread. Top-enders have gained the most. Ability to control the water, especially access to early season water for an early crop at premium price, has brought great prosperity. Those further from the source have also benefited, but to lesser extent. Harvesting closer to peak harvest time, prices are much reduced and the absence of local storage and marketing structures leaves them at the mercy of traders. The tail-enders depend upon 'left-over' water from those higher up the water system. In good rainfall years they benefit; but in poor years they may not even plant:

> Very little water reaches this area. Sometimes a year can pass without any cultivation. Last year, for example, I did not cultivate at all. (Boas Mtewuve, tail-end irrigator, Mfumbi)

But for those downstream of the irrigation systems, irrigation has been a disaster as wet season water for cropping and fishing, and dry season water for domestic uses and cattle, has been redirected into the irrigation systems. For these people, and for the wetland environment, the success of irrigation in Usangu has come at a cost:

> In the past, water was free. It didn't do any work and it spilled out all over the place. Now that irrigation has started water availability is a problem. (Mzee Komizambili, Sangu farmer from a downstream community)

# ACT 2: A CIRCLE OF BLAME IN USANGU BENEFITS A COLLUSION OF INTERESTS

> We do not know whether these experts ever thought how we would be affected by their decisions. (Sultani Matinda, pastoralist, Usangu)

The scene changes to Usangu where three state farms (all internationally funded) and 30,000 farm families are abstracting water for irrigation. Two of the state farms were developed without any environmental impact assessment (EIA) and the third had an EIA limited to the locality without consideration of larger cumulative and downstream issues. Other donor activity supported smallholder irrigation. Although irrigation had initially been cited by TANESCO as the cause of the river drying up, the political and economic importance of irrigation is such that this cause was downplayed and alternate causes were sought. The donor and national agency agendas were pro-irrigation. And within Usangu, the irrigation farmers and the supporting political structure saw no problem with irrigation. Such interests also coincided with national and local prejudices to transfer 'blame' from irrigation onto pastoralists and fishermen, both of whom were politically and socially marginalized and had little voice in local decision-making.

An 'invasion' of pastoralists since the 1950s, seeking livelihood opportunities, was seen as causing wetland degradation and increasing direct water use through seemingly increasing livestock numbers. Evidence cited included highly visible tree and bush clearing around stock *kraals* (especially by the Sukuma pastoralists, who are commonly said to have deforested and destroyed their own homeland), and bush encroachment onto the grassland. Although accurate data on livestock numbers and pasture resources was almost entirely absent, 'huge' numbers of livestock were thought to far exceed available feed resources. This was depriving Usangu 'residents' of access to water and land, causing inter-communal conflict and resulting in degradation, which, through ill-defined processes, was leading to the drying of the Great Ruaha River. The parallel 'invasion' of cultivators into Usangu was conveniently ignored.

Another common view blamed the drying of the river on reduced flows in tributary rivers flowing from the highlands. Forest clearing and generalized degradation in the highlands were seen as causal. Support for this view came from visible reductions in dry season flows in traditionally perennial rivers passing through populated areas on the plain; the presence of upstream irrigation off-takes was not taken into consideration.

Often, these 'causes' were combined. Generalized degradation – in the highlands from deforestation and in the lowlands by pastoralists – was alleged to be destroying the environment, leading to the drying of the river. One internationally supported project referred to 'damage, deforestation, degradation, depletion and impending catastrophe'. However, despite the absence of hard data or clear processes, such extreme sentiments rang no alarm bells; the prevailing prejudice satisfied all actors.

With this set of strongly held beliefs in place, and catalysed by perceived threats to economic development from electrical shortages, the scene was set for action. International pressures also supported acceptance of restoration of flows in the Great Ruaha River as 'the thing to do'; but this was never critically examined. The pressure was to 'do something' – to take action. For example, one environmental film gained an international audience for prevailing prejudices, but failed to critically examine the issues. Environmental NGOs, national and international, also raised concerns over Usangu, gaining national political support for protection within the area. One international environmental NGO influenced government to the extent that it declared the restoration of flows in the Great Ruaha River by 2010 as a national target. National and local players rallied around this NGO, using it to provide credibility to their own protectionist agendas. The circle of blame also offered opportunities for new national actors to enter the scene. For example, prior politics had produced two national agencies with responsibilities for the Ruaha. Events, over time, had marginalized one of these; but the developing water crisis created an opportunity for it to re-establish its position by latching onto the issue and promoting more extreme positions.

However, those most affected had very limited involvement in the debate. Many players, from the local to the international, were making independent decisions on the management and development of Usangu. Policy-makers in Dar es Salaam and tourists from afar had a greater impact on the policies of organizations working in the country than did local people affected by those policies. For example, the major international donor supporting irrigation only re-examined the evidence (and changed its view on the impact of irrigation) following international pressure from individuals and groups, and the threat of environmental embarrassment caused by a focus on economic development. Such organizations worked at a national level, with national policy-makers who were equally removed from the realities of life in Usangu.

Decisions about and for Usangu were made by people distant from Usangu, based on very limited information and understanding; local people were essentially not involved in the decision-making process. Decisions were driven by national and international interests in the need for a 'right' (and preferably simple) answer to the problem. But who was the answer to be 'right' for? At the time there was no coherent framework, at any level, for environmental management or cross-sectoral thinking – except for traditional management, which was largely neglected by the major players. And traditional management of the shared resources was under increasing stress as resource scarcity increased. For example, groups of traditional irrigation water users and agreements for water sharing were breaking down under the pressure of ever-increasing competition for water, occasioned by new users outside of these groups. What was missing was a reasoned evaluation of the assumptions behind the 'crisis'; the crisis itself satisfied the agendas of all players except the most vulnerable.

With national and international environmental NGO support, the wetland was declared a nationally protected area. One of the rationales for this was based on an unproven hypothesis that the wetland stored water for release during the dry season, and that degradation was reducing this storage and release. The concurrence of interests allowed this hypothesis to stand without examination and to dictate action. However, this hypothesis simply ignored the effects of upstream irrigation on the source of the water, satisfying the irrigation lobby and its international donors. Superficially, the protected area allowed protection of biodiversity, a priority of international and national NGOs. Poorly advised by local agents, they did not take into account the environmental system as a whole (the wetland cannot be considered independent from its catchment) and the fact that biodiversity was threatened more by loss of inflows than by anything happening in the wetland. The tourist lobby was satisfied by the (unrealized) promise of more water in the river and the declaration also suited those who were anti-pastoralist. National protected-area policy within Tanzania promotes total exclusion; thus, previous users – notably pastoralists and fishermen – were excluded from the area.

Meanwhile, irrigation had continued to expand, both in area and through an extended season. Irrigation was seen as 'good', and received donor and national government support under the precepts of supporting livelihoods and national economic development. This precluded a critical evaluation of irrigation under local circumstances. Conversely, pastoralism was still seen by many as a 'backward' system of resource management, and one that runs contrary to government desires to provide services to its population. Nobody challenged these underlying assumptions. Indeed, as described above, the powerful actors in this story were happy with the actions being taken.

The net effect was to encourage increased water use (see Box 9.2). When some enforcement was finally introduced, and the improved structures were used (as intended) to manage flows and increase returns to the river, it was at the expense of the tail-enders, who are also the poor. In normal to low rainfall years, they saw a loss of water for both irrigation and domestic uses, which critically affected their livelihoods. Even for domestic uses, alternative water sources were scarce and generally unsanitary. Not only do these people feel that they have a 'right' to water, such livelihood effects run counter to government and donor policies geared towards poverty reduction and helping the poorest of the poor. Moreover, the tail-enders were not involved in the decision-making process to manage water availability, and there were no mitigation measures to support the 'losers'. Where consultation did occur, it was with irrigator associations within the formal schemes, membership of which was often limited to 'landowners'. Tail-enders, renters and women – who are the majority of users – tended to be excluded. Water managers were interested in increasing water in the rivers and took little note of the wider implications of their decisions.

# ACT 3: MISLEADING ANSWERS IN A CLIMATE OF SELF-INTEREST

## Act 3, scene 1: Power and the perils of information

Enter stage right the internationally funded Sustainable Management of the Usangu Wetland and its Catchment (SMUWC) project. This project was predicated on assumptions arising from beliefs as described above, notably that there was a causal link between water shortages at Mtera and activities in Usangu, and that improved land and water management in Usangu would solve the problem. Improved scientific knowledge (to be provided by the project) was seen as key to this. Existing knowledge was somehow absent from the debate (see Box 9.4).

The SMUWC project provides an interesting perspective on donor funding. It arose from the need to address problems created in substantial part by donor interventions. A holistic and proactive approach with effective prior analysis could have avoided such problems. However, funding is generally available only to address specific issues; if there is no 'problem', then there is no funding. The 'problem' that SMUWC was designed to address was, of course, determined by national and international players, and was couched in their terms. Internationally funded projects also generally eschew politics; yet, politics in Usangu were key to addressing the issues that the SMUWC project was formulated to solve.

---

## BOX 9.4 NEW KNOWLEDGE OR THE 'RIGHT' KNOWLEDGE?

Many of the findings of the Sustainable Management of the Usangu Wetland and its Catchment (SMUWC) project were, in fact, not new, but confirmed previous studies. Critically, at least two previous studies had found that water shortages at Mtera were unrelated to water use in Usangu. Earlier studies on irrigation had cited water shortages as the limiting factor on irrigation expansion; the current area far exceeds that originally envisaged. Agricultural statistics, admittedly dated and suspect, showed no evidence of the vast cattle herds claimed.

Why did national and international actors ignore these studies? Was it that they failed to provide them with the 'right' answers? How many projects have been funded where adequate knowledge already exists? Even now, in Usangu, some actors are still calling for more information!

---

Here the story takes an unexpected twist, as improved knowledge failed to support the prevailing beliefs. First, hydrological information showed that water shortages at Mtera were not primarily due to activities in Usangu. Despite increased water use *within* Usangu, annual water flows *from* Usangu had only been marginally affected. Dry season flows were reduced; but these, while critical to the Ruaha National Park, never contributed significantly to water volumes at Mtera, which was designed as a storage reservoir, almost entirely dependent upon wet season inflows. The wetland was largely absorbing the effect of increased local water use; water holding within the wetland (the wetland maximum area) was being reduced; but wet season flows downstream were being maintained. Meanwhile, the national urgency to act has been reduced by new electrical developments that reduce the importance of Mtera as an electrical source (to 37–50 per cent of the national supply, depending upon the season).

Second, neither pastoralism nor upland degradation were found to primarily cause water shortages, and many of the underlying 'facts' about livestock numbers and livestock-feed balances (carrying capacity) were found to be inaccurate (see Box 9.6). Livestock numbers were found to have been wildly exaggerated and were, in fact, stable and probably decreasing, while evidence of the 'prevalent' degradation in both the highlands and the plain was hard to find. Rather, it became clear that water abstraction for irrigation was overwhelmingly the primary cause of the drying of the river and the wetland (see Box 9.5).

---

# BOX 9.5 THE WETLAND ECOSYSTEM

The Usangu wetland is a product of water inflows from upstream. While no scientific studies have been undertaken, it seems probable that the grasslands were produced by a combination of prolonged seasonal flooding and saturation, followed by intense fires that records show used to sweep the plain from end to end.

With upstream abstraction of water for irrigation, there is less flooding (in both area and duration). The western half of the wetland no longer floods regularly. With less water, there is less grass growth, and most grass growth is now removed by cattle. This means that there is less fuel for fires, which are now less extensive and of lower intensity. 'Degradation' of the grassland has resulted, demonstrated by the invasion of woody species and changes in grass species.

---

The 'invasion' of pastoralists was also recognized as inaccurate and a reflection of prevailing attitudes. Most people in Usangu are immigrants, not just the pastoralists, and pastoralism was the original dominant human land use of the area. While pastoralist numbers have increased greatly, there has been a parallel 'invasion' by cultivators into areas previously used by pastoralists. Increasing cultivation has not only taken land from pastoralism, but also cut across traditional cattle watering routes and reduced water flows to remaining pastoralist areas. This could be described as an 'invasion' of pastoralist rights to water. Moreover, there are few true pastoralists in Usangu; most are now agro-pastoralists who participate in irrigation, although generally as tail-enders and outside the formal irrigation structures.

---

# BOX 9.6 THE CATTLE MYTH

The issue of cattle in Usangu provides a good example of how myths are created and perpetuated when they feed the agendas of powerful parties.

Prior to the Sustainable Management of the Usangu Wetland and its Catchment (SMUWC) project, the last agricultural estimates were for 1987. These showed total cattle numbers of 458,000 for *the region* containing Usangu. In the absence of further data, interested parties multiplied this figure by an assumed factor of 10 per cent per year to arrive at a figure of 2 million cattle in Usangu by the end of the 1980s.

At the same time, pasture resources *within* the wetland were calculated from carrying capacity data based on the regional climate, as expressed in an old management text. Two factors were missing in this analysis. The annual flooding of the plain invalidated the climate-based carrying capacity data. Second, livestock do not only use the wetland but all of the plain – a much larger area. Furthermore, livestock movement is central to grazing management, allowing forage use at its most nutritive time and then later use of re-growth, thereby maximizing carrying capacity.

SMUWC carried out five aerial surveys of livestock numbers over three years. All gave results within about 10 per cent of an estimated average figure of approximately 300,000 cattle, with almost no seasonal variation. A parallel range survey provided an average carrying capacity of around 500,000 cattle (with wide variations depending upon the year). Despite the reliability and consistency of this data, people are still arguing over cattle numbers and range resources.

International support for finding solutions in Usangu must address the cultural differences in approaches to information, and recognize and support those who ultimately make decisions. Improved scientific information helped to define cause and effect – something that was not previously fully understood. However, it did not meet generalized acceptance, as was originally expected. Instead, it confronted personal experiences and beliefs, as well as existing power structures and economic interests. A lack of understanding of scientific processes and information further undermined the credibility of the information. The project's revelations were not always well received and there was, and remains, enormous resistance to the 'scientific facts' produced (see Box 9.7). The technical complexity of the situation and its revelation by 'outsiders' (the SMUWC project) undermined the project's credibility and acceptability; this demonstrates the need in such circumstances for local 'champions' to deliver the message. There was a lack of understanding of the way in which the information was collected. Local people were not directly involved in deciding what data to collect, or in the data gathering and analysis, and local information was not taken into account effectively. Information was also generally presented by external agents rather than by locally respected leaders, further undermining its perceived validity to local people. The information often challenged what local people saw (although cause and effect were often misinterpreted), and contradictions were not adequately explained at local levels. It also contradicted national messages on Usangu and on the environment in general (e.g. on planting trees, degradation and deforestation). Resistance may also be partially attributed to simple inertia: individual and institutional reluctance or incapacity to take on new information and adapt accordingly.

Nevertheless, acceptance was greater amongst local marginalized groups, such as pastoralists and fishermen, to whom the information provided power. Other local people were also often able to understand, when matters were explained, and to rationalize the differences between their observations and the information presented. However, resistance increased further up the power structure, with various parties intent upon protecting their own agendas, often involving individual power or livelihoods. Empowering people with knowledge often led to conflict with local officials unused to being challenged. Although decentralization is national policy, and natural resource management policies emphasize public participation, administrations often have yet to come to terms with such changed power relationships. This is often due to the fear of losing economic benefits derived from rent-seeking opportunities from natural resources. Challenges to local administrations were often met with persecution to the extent that several deaths resulted from clashes between government and local resource users. Poor knowledge of rights, limited access to judicial processes and a weak judicial system limited redress and the effectiveness of local empowerment.

---

## BOX 9.7 CONFRONTING LOCAL BELIEFS

There are firmly held beliefs in Tanzania, entrenched by national campaigns, concerning trees and water.

Trees are believed to bring rain, and planting trees is a national agenda. When the Sustainable Management of the Usangu Wetland and its Catchment (SMUWC) project pointed out that trees use water and, therefore, are not always beneficial for catchment management, it was pilloried in the national press.

A similar story applies to burning, which is seen as a major source of degradation of miombo woodlands. Again, there is a national campaign against burning. However, these woodlands depend upon fire for their existence.

---

Local players, for whom prior blaming had proved politically profitable, ignored the information – and even belittled it – and continued as before. At a workshop to present preliminary SMUWC findings, the project was accused of 'voodoo science' and ridiculed in the media, which relied on information from local leaders. Project information challenged the water rationale for the wetland protected area, with both local and national implications and, therefore, opposition. TANESCO, the national energy agency, publicly rejected the information since it implied that management, rather than inflows, was the cause of problems at Mtera. TANESCO pays a large water user fee and may therefore assume a 'right' to water. It was able to use this leverage to continue the cycle of blame. International agencies were no better. The information challenged donor activities, which were predicated on engineering solutions aimed at 'improved' water management. But these activities had assumed their own momentum and were difficult to revise. One major donor flatly rejected the information (although it subsequently came to accept it). And the major NGO simply overlooked the information in early planning for its intervention (although, again, it eventually embraced the information).

The demand by major players for information and action was also too fast for local capacity. When the major international donor finally accepted that irrigation 'improvements' were part of the problem, it responded initially by requesting 'quick fixes' – and was financially ready to support those fixes – despite the evidence that sustainable solutions rested with building local capacity and commitment, and addressing local political and other interests. That donor now recognizes this and is supporting the development of local institutions and processes for negotiating water rights amongst different users.

Overall, the potential for sustainable solutions has been reduced by political processes which focus on visible outputs, and on institutional and personal agendas, rather than underlying causes. The SMUWC project was assumed to contribute by improving information. However, when it successfully did so, it found it lacked an audience due to wider political interests. Core issues – declining water flows, threats to the national park, the Ruaha ecosystem and the Usangu wetland, and conflicts within Usangu – became marginalized by the momentum and political interests of the main external players.

The SMUWC project was not, however, an innocent bystander or victim of these political winds. There was a fundamental failure to recognize the intensely political nature of the project. The project was late in understanding that science alone would not dispel the myths about Usangu; it failed to understand the politics and vested interests behind the myths. It made no effort to understand how decisions were made and never attempted to become a credible source of information within that system. It passively accepted the view that the information would speak for itself. This was convenient for those who challenged the information; the information was always presented and seen as 'project knowledge'.

The project also needed to support individual and institutional change so that the information generated could be used effectively. It needed to create systems to facilitate access to, and efficiently use, the massive amounts of information generated. In the absence of such systems, it has been easy for national and donor actors to commission new studies based on 'insufficient information', rather than use the information available. Such studies are employed to delay difficult decisions on how resources should be utilized in Usangu (and/or to support decisions that have short-term political support). Nevertheless, the project was constrained by the mandate which it was given and donor pressure for results.

There is a lesson here for donors and project designers. The project was designed to operate outside the system; it was not located within any specific organization, with established counterpart staff and reporting structures. Its mandate was to provide information, not to facilitate local organizations to generate the relevant information needed to answer the nation's questions. This would have implied a very different approach and a longer commitment; conversely, the approach taken did provide high-quality information in a short space of time. However, the pace of information generation exceeded the capacity of local institutions to absorb and use it. Another important factor was the difficulty of translating scientific subtleties into the local language. Scientific information is generally presented in written format, and Tanzania's non-reading culture inhibited communication.

## Act 3, scene 2: Completing the picture

The macro-picture offered above is but the 'tip of the iceberg'; the situation is complex and cannot be reduced to simple cause-and-effect statements. While irrigation was the proximate cause, the real causes lay within the socio-political situation. There are not just one or a few large water users, but some 30,000 irrigation families. Even the large state farms are now primarily operated as smallholder schemes. The issue is more than just water and, thus, techno-engineering solutions are insufficient. Whole solutions will not only involve developing skills in land and water management, but addressing issues of governance and civil society – of how local people have a voice in making decisions about the future of Usangu. It requires opening up the process of decision-making; improving transparency; developing 'system'-level understanding (upstream-downstream linkages) that was previously missing; addressing power imbalances through bringing the community and marginalized groups 'to the table' and empowering them with knowledge; and generally improving local access to, and management of, the environment.

The solution requires looking beyond the proximate causes and addressing the underlying causes of water abstraction:

- An expanding population within Usangu was also driven by poverty and lack of livelihood alternatives within Tanzania.
- Techno-physical improvements to 'improve' water use efficiency increased both the amount that could be abstracted at any one time and the time over which water could be used over the year. This, in turn, encouraged irrigation expansion and greatly increased total and seasonal water use.
- Price incentives encouraged people to irrigate earlier and earlier, pushing water demands back into the end of the dry season, when river flows were minimal, and directly leading to the seasonal drying of the Great Ruaha River.
- The absence of effective grain storage and marketing systems encouraged early high-value plantings and expanded acreage, thus increasing water use.
- Family socio-economic circumstances (e.g. availability of labour or cash, health concerns such as HIV, etc.) determined cultivation timing and made it difficult for farmers to coordinate planting within an irrigation block. This creates a 'mosaic' of fields, from just planted to harvested, so that there is an extended time demand for water within an irrigation block and reduced water-use efficiency.
- A low input-output system created problems. Few inputs are used in rice farming by tail-enders, so there is little cost in 'having a go', even if yields may be low or a crop failure possible.
- Institutional structures for water management were not representative of many water users.
- There was an inadequate policy for water resource management prior to the water policy of 2002 and, subsequently, the lack of capacity and resources to implement a sustainable water resource management policy.
- There was an absence or inadequacy of local fora (e.g. community-based organizations, NGOs, etc.) for voicing concerns and negotiating solutions.
- Capacity shortages for effective enforcement were prevalent.
- Economic incentives to use water more efficiently were ineffective.

No solution is possible without addressing these (and other) issues. In fact, the situation could deteriorate. Technical solutions focusing on 'improved water management' may provide short-term relief but will fail in the long term and may, by increasing the potential to abstract, exacerbate the situation.

Irrigation, as currently managed, has exceeded a threshold, and the Great Ruaha River, the wetland and the environment, in general, are

*Source:* Sustainable Management of Usangu Wetland and its Catchment (SMUWC) project

**Figure 9.3** *The Ruaha River, which has dried up seasonally since the early 1990s*

paying the physical price. But indigenous Sangu communities, pastoralists and fishermen have paid the economic and political price. Payments are still to be made. The action of 'closing' the wetland, as a protected area, will increase physical and social pressures on the remainder of the Usangu plain, increasing competition over resources in which the poorest will certainly be the greatest losers and be forced to exploit their environment further. District revenues, substantially dependent upon livestock, will also be dramatically reduced, with subsequent impacts on district service delivery to its people (or the alternative of increased taxes).

Irrigation has been an economic boon to Usangu, drawing in the population, creating new livelihood opportunities, reducing dependence upon rain-fed farming, and generally underpinning the economy of the area. However, it has come at a cost to marginalized groups and to the environment, which need not have been the case. Understanding the dynamics of water use and careful management of irrigation could allow for more equitable benefits from Usangu's water: an irrigated production nearly equivalent to current production, continued resources for pastoralists and fishermen, and maintenance of the Usangu wetland and of downstream ecosystems.

216

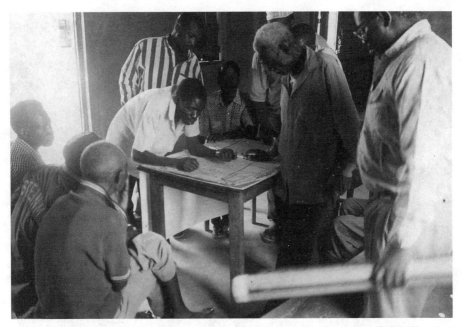

*Source:* Sustainable Management of Usangu Wetland and its Catchment (SMUWC) project

**Figure 9.4** *Supporting communities to have greater involvement in decision making in Usangu*

Improved knowledge has given some concerned actors increased confidence, while decentralization has increased the potential for greater local involvement in decision-making over Usangu. Local communities and marginalized groups have been particularly empowered, both by the information provided, by an improved understanding of their environmental rights and by fora established for engagement between stakeholders. Increased opportunities for them to be heard served as an incentive to understand and accept information provided. Communities working closely with the project were empowered to start taking responsibility for their own development, tackling such things as building schools, organizing transportation, demanding services from the district and so on. Pastoralists and fishermen formed groups and represented themselves to government and in workshops and other fora. Irrigators, once understanding that they are part of a bigger system, were willing to look for solutions. Through self-learning and evaluation of the situation, they realized that they do have the knowledge and understanding to reach sensible solutions, but need support from districts and other responsible bodies, including development of appropriate policies and recognition of their rights and responsibilities.

At the national level, the Ministry of Water came to see the matter as a livelihoods issue, rather than simply a water issue. It strongly

*Source:* Sustainable Management of Usangu Wetland and its Catchment (SMUWC) project

**Figure 9.5** *Activities to increase community involvement in decision making*

presented this case in public fora and further emphasised it in the new national water policy (July 2002). The Rufiji Basin Water Office (RBWO) also embraced a more inclusive and locally sensitive approach to water management (see Box 9.8). International donors and the major environmental NGO also came, eventually, to accept the information and locally driven solutions as the 'way forward'.

The intermediate level, however, was not sufficiently engaged, and personal and political agendas at this key level stalled the process. In particular, the 'threat' of improved understanding built on perceived threats arising from decentralization – threats that were perceived, in very real terms, as threats to power and income. Advances were made; the local district established a multi-sectoral planning team which developed a community-led planning process. Through this process relations between communities and the district generally improved and village priorities are now better reflected in district plans. However, not everyone has embraced the new roles required by decentralization: districts as facilitators of change and of management, with power increasingly assumed by local communities and individuals. Increasing knowledge and power within communities is still seen by many as a threat and even as a personal affront to their position and authority.

Although politics needs to be engaged with at all levels, from the community to the national level, this is a difficult thing to achieve within a 'project' environment.

The processes in Usangu both support, and are supported by, broader developments in Tanzania, such as the process of decentralization. With decentralization, local people, communities and institutions are gaining authority over their own lives. The work in Usangu has supported that process, providing local people with knowledge, and helping them to use that knowledge to protect their own interests. However, such support for openness and transparency can come at a price, and local people who stood up to authority became targets for that authority. In addition, 'rights' can be promoted without an understanding of the accompanying responsibilities. However, people can only be expected to take on responsibilities if they have a say in the decision-making process.

---

## BOX 9.8 THE RUFIJI BASIN WATER OFFICE, TANZANIA

The Rufiji Basin Water Office (RBWO) is charged with responsibility for water management in the Rufiji Basin, including Usangu and the Ruaha. Set up as a traditional water management authority, it has responsibility for implementing the new water policy (July 2002), which aspires to 'put in place fair and equal procedures in access to and allocation of water resources so that all social and economic activities are able to maximize their activities'.

The RBWO has recognized that implementing this requires looking at water management in a more integrated fashion and effecting water management through the water users, rather than through external impositions. It has begun to support water user groups, strengthening those which already exist and facilitating the formation of new groups. It is also working to facilitate collaboration between user groups in order to negotiate and agree upon water rights along common water sources. Key water managers within Usangu have also been brought together to agree on action.

In its first year it was effective in increasing flows; but this was done without consultation with tail-enders and downstream communities, causing severe local hardship and much resentment. This lesson has been learned and affected communities have now been brought into the decision-making process and measures have been put in place to protect the losers. For example, boreholes have been installed for tail-enders' domestic needs.

The RBWO has also established, and acts as secretariat for, a Ruaha planning group. This is a multi-stakeholder group which addresses resource management in Usangu as a whole, integrating national and local interests.

---

# FINALE

Despite gains made in Usangu, politics is still inhibiting the realization of solutions. Despite increased general understanding of cause and effect, problems remain in separating significant from minor causes. Issues of livestock numbers and degradation are still being debated. Individual agendas – irrigation, conservation and tourism – are still acting as 'flagships' for international and national support, without necessarily addressing the system and its inter-linkages as a whole. Issues of poverty, and broader issues of the environment, continue to be lost in decisions made for political reasons. Support (through SMUWC) has been withdrawn due to the internal politics of the donor agency. Meanwhile, increases in the flows of the river (assuredly temporary) are being trumpeted by that same agency as proof of the effectiveness of the project. This is contrary to all that the project learned and ignores the negative impacts on the poor. Selection of the first three Tanzanian Ramsar sites, supported by another donor, by-passed Usangu despite the mountain of supporting information available. Usangu thus became a victim of inter-agency competition (Usangu has since been declared a Ramsar site and is now in line to receive significant financial support from that donor). Interest has also come from other (NGO) donors, notably a large international NGO which is promoting an integrated approach. However, its country partners had, at least until recently, a narrow 'protect and preserve' agenda, involving barriers and exclusions, and international partners cannot simply impose their own agendas and values. Moreover, in an age of instant gratification and fleeting interests, such narrow agendas offer 'quick fixes' to an international donor base that may lack the 'staying power' to support sustainable processes.

Decisions in Usangu have been based on politics rather than on poverty and the environment. They have not always been 'information based'; science can support decision-making but decisions are, in the end, always political. Usangu demonstrates that poverty and the environment cannot be disengaged from the political arena. Sustainably addressing poverty and the environment requires engaging with the political agenda. It is essential to understand the context within which one is working – to recognize (and use) the driving forces behind those making decisions, and the interests of those without a voice.

From international to local levels, the common link was the need to address poverty and the environment. But all actors had additional agendas and often acted independently, tending to work on specific issues rather than addressing the system as a whole. This led to the imposition of 'technical' solutions to underlying social problems which were presented as environmental problems. It also allowed identification of minor players (pastoralists and fishermen) as 'causal', when their primary crime was simply political weakness.

This is not the end of the story. Pointing 'blame' at specific groups does not lead to solutions. In a sense, we are all culprits – whether we are users of the resources, government or other individuals or groups with specific agendas, or 'independent' researchers with science-based belief systems and a lack of sensitivity to local norms. Solutions will emerge from seeking areas of commonality in beliefs and interests, within a holistic framework of understanding and action.

## LESSONS LEARNED

While information is critical to effective and sustainable decision-making, information alone may not provide acceptable solutions. Decision-making – and providing effective solutions – involves a political process that may be more or less independent of scientific information. The question must be asked whether an externally funded project can or should engage in political processes – and whether it can be effective if it fails to do so.

Information is only useful if it is credible to potential users. In Tanzania, credibility may have less to do with scientifically valid processes than with its perceived source. Identifying 'champions' and involving them in framing the questions, collecting the information, and presenting the results may be as important as the analytical process itself.

Furthermore, information value is reduced if it is inaccessible, or if the potential users lack the capacity to use it. Projects such as SMUWC, which are designed to focus on information generation, may thus have limited impact and sustainability.

Environmental management and sustainability is a negotiated political process. It is impossible to take politics out of poverty and the environment. We need to understand and address power imbalances over access to natural resources and acknowledge that there will be winners and losers. The agenda is often established by external agencies, and the debate is moderated by these or other external parties. Often, the voices of the losers are not at the negotiating table, undermining the sustainability of agreed 'solutions'. For solutions to be sustainable, negotiations must be inclusive, while recognizing that it is never possible to get everyone to the table. Win-win opportunities are few and far between and, in reality, there will be losers; usually the losers will be the poor and/or marginalized and vulnerable. Understanding belief systems and motivations for improving environmental management in Usangu is an important component of negotiation and process transparency.

Environmental management requires a holistic and integrated approach. However, the more holistic the approach, the more complicated it is, the more people are involved and the more political the process. As a result, it may be more difficult to find points of engagement.

Environmental management is also not seen as an entry point for achieving outcomes in other sectors such as good governance and social policy. It may, therefore, be difficult to engender support from these sectors, although such support is essential for effective and sustainable environmental management. Again, a holistic understanding of development is essential to provide mutual benefits across sectors.

Tackling these sorts of issues cannot be done at distinct levels – local solutions alone, national policies alone and technical interventions alone. There is a need to see and address all aspects of the system as a whole.

There is also a need to understand real causes and effects, and how these really impact upon poverty, the poor and the environment. Over-generalization is dangerous. In Usangu, stakeholders were generalizing about the environment and about approaches to poverty, and failed to take into account locally specific issues. Yet, it is these issues which will, in the long term, offer opportunities for sustainable solutions – or undermine 'solutions' imposed from the outside.

# 10

# Community-designed, built and managed Toilet Blocks in Indian Cities

*Sundar Burra, Sheela Patel and Thomas Kerr*

## INTRODUCTION

This chapter describes the involvement of an alliance of three Indian organizations in community-designed, built and managed toilet blocks that now serve more than half a million low-income urban dwellers in eight cities in India. These three organizations are: the Society for the Promotion of Area Resource Centres (SPARC), the National Slum Dwellers Federation (NSDF) and *Mahila Milan*. SPARC is an Indian non-governmental organization (NGO) established in Mumbai in 1984 that began working with women pavement dwellers. The NSDF links together and represents organizations and federations of slum dwellers throughout India; by March 2002, it was operating in 52 cities and nine states with over 750,000 members. The largest membership is in Mumbai where 250,000 households are members. *Mahila Milan* (meaning 'women together') are cooperatives formed by women slum and pavement dwellers that work very closely with the NSDF. These community toilet blocks are part of a larger programme of work in which the alliance of SPARC-NSDF-*Mahila Milan*[1] is involved. It includes community-managed resettlement programmes (see Patel et al, 2002), 'slum' rehabilitation programmes (for instance, the construction of apartment blocks in Dharavi, Mumbai's largest and perhaps most dense 'slum' to allow housing improvements without displacing any inhabitants) and housing programmes (for pavement and slum dwellers) (Patel and Mitlin, 2001).

# THE INADEQUACIES IN PROVIDING SANITATION

During recent decades, few city governments in India have invested much in extending provision for sanitation to the 'slums.' It is common for between a quarter and half of the population in Indian cities to have inadequate or no provision for sanitation, with most of those lacking adequate provision living in 'slums' (see UN-Habitat, 2003). Lack of funds may be an explanation for the lack of attention to sanitation in many cities; but this is not so for cities such as Mumbai and Pune where, until recently, municipal authorities did not spend the funds that were available for improving sanitation. The inadequacies in water and sanitation provision in cities such as Bangalore also cannot be explained by lack of funding since very large investments have been made in infrastructure there; here, it is political choices regarding what infrastructure to prioritize and what to ignore that explain the large inadequacies in provision, despite the city's economic success (UN-Habitat, 2003; see also Sinclair Knight Merz and Egis Consulting Australia, 2002; Benjamin, 2000).

In Indian cities, what little investment has been made in sanitation in low-income areas has generally been through local bodies (slum boards, housing authorities, development authorities and municipal corporations) building public toilet blocks; these bodies are also meant to maintain them. But the number of toilet blocks built in any year does not seem to be based on an assessment either of need (in relation to the population) or of available budgetary resources (as noted already, resources allocated to sanitation often remain under-utilized).

For the public toilet blocks that are built, the traditional method of doing so has been for the municipal government to estimate the cost of construction according to a government-prepared schedule of rates and then call for tenders from contractors. Generally, this is managed by the engineering wings of local bodies and rarely has there been any discussion with the community where the toilet block is to be located – for instance, regarding the location, design, construction and provision for maintenance. In addition, the agencies responsible for construction and maintenance have little accountability to the communities in which they build. There is no sense of ownership among the inhabitants or their organizations of the new toilet blocks. The quality of toilet construction (undertaken by contractors) is often poor and the design often is inappropriate – for instance, with limited water supplies (so the toilets get blocked and dirty).

Municipal corporations have conservancy departments whose duty it is to clean and maintain public toilet blocks, as well as to maintain drains and streets. But the staff of such departments usually fail to clean and maintain the public toilet blocks in slums and the local population has no control over them. Communities often have to pay the municipal staff extra money to do the job for which they are already being paid. Municipal bureaucracies are also large and cumbersome, making the job of supervisory staff difficult, and attempts to impose discipline among the staff invariably fail. The local government bodies that build the public toilet blocks see these as their property and make no effort to involve communities in their maintenance.

The public toilet blocks are often in serious disrepair within three months of being constructed. Thus, in most cities, there are few operational toilet blocks for large sections of the population and people have little or no alternative but to defecate in the open. The space around the public toilets often becomes heavily used for open defecation. Communities often have no waste collection, so the toilet block also becomes a place where household wastes are dumped. Women suffer most from having no accessible and safe toilet. They often wait until nightfall to defecate to protect their modesty – but this need to wait until dark also causes widespread gastric disorders. Widespread open defecation, in turn, produces a very large health burden and contributes to high infant and child death rates.

Various other organizations such as charitable trusts, NGOs, international agencies and local business associations (such as rotary clubs) have had some involvement in 'toilets for the poor' projects. These projects often build 'pay-and-use' toilets. In many cities, there are agencies that function as contractors, construct sanitation facilities and appoint caretakers whose job it is to keep the facilities clean. User charges help to pay the salaries of caretakers and cleaners and provide materials and cover maintenance. These public toilets work well in large concourses such as railway stations and bus stops; but it is not a workable solution in slums because of the high prices charged: usually 1 rupee per person for each time the toilet is used. A family of five would have to spend 150 rupees a month to allow each member to use these toilet blocks just once a day, and this is not affordable for the majority of the urban poor. As in the government-built toilet blocks, the question of community participation in designing, constructing and maintaining these 'pay-and-use' toilets does not arise. Thus, neither the government toilet blocks nor the private or charity toilet blocks serve slum inhabitants: the corporation model, led by engineers and built by contractors, results in early deterioration and disuse; the 'pay-and-use' approach produces toilets that are too expensive for low-income households to use.

# THE POLITICS OF SANITATION

One critical question is, thus, when and under what circumstances do city authorities develop some sensitivity to issues of sanitation for the poor? When does investment in extending sanitation to the 'slums' and informal settlements begin to figure in municipal budgets? For the city of Mumbai (formerly Bombay), India's financial capital, the first investment in a comprehensive drainage system for parts of the city was spurred by external pressure. At a conference in 1867 on cholera, the French and Egyptian representatives referred to Bombay as a 'cholera nest'. Then, in 1876, the Egyptian Board of Health imposed a quarantine on ships carrying pilgrims which had departed from Bombay. Arthur Crawford, the municipal commissioner, argued that in order to maintain Bombay's role as an important port within the British Empire and to overcome the fear of exporting cholera, financial assistance was required to improve the city's sanitation. Here, as in many other cities at that time (including New York and London), the fact that cholera epidemics were threatening the city's economic future helped to overcome the reluctance of governments and of middle- and upper-income groups for large public investments in water and sanitation (Rosenberg, 1962; Chaplin, 1999).

More than a century later, pressure for more attention regarding sanitation came mainly from civil society. The city of Mumbai had sought funding from the World Bank to expand its sewer system and received a US$167 million non-concessional loan and a US$25 million concessional loan;[2] but the original project focused on setting up marine outfalls and sewage treatment plants. The loans were approved and the project was initiated. But the city government had to be reminded by NGOs that half of Mumbai's population lives in slums and informal settlements where the priority was for installing toilets and sewers, rather than the construction of sewer outfalls and sewage treatment. The municipal corporation responded by offering to provide some minimum sanitation for approximately 1 million people, using a small part of the available funding to do so.

Various reasons help to explain the lack of attention to sanitation in Mumbai over the years. One is the fact that the diseases and very large health burdens associated with inadequate sanitation no longer affect most middle- and upper-income groups as their homes and neighbourhoods receive piped water and connection to the sewer system (Chaplin, 1999). Another is the inaccurate stereotypes about the poor held by most middle- and upper-income groups, who judge the poor to be 'freeloaders' who apparently get access to free amenities. But the reality for most of the urban poor is that they do not get free amenities and they often end up paying far more than middle- and upper-income groups for water. Meanwhile, the only toilets they have access to are ones for which they have to queue and they usually have to pay 1 rupee for each use. Middle- and upper-income groups also see 'the poor' as irrational people who moved from 'nice' villages attracted by the bright lights of the city, despite the wealth of evidence over the last 30 years that migration patterns are logical responses by individuals and households to changing economic opportunities. Many in government feel that if municipalities improved conditions in the 'slums', including providing water and sanitation, it would encourage more poor people to migrate there. Even where more progressive attitudes towards urban poor groups become evident in government policies, as in support for 'slum rehabilitation' or recognizing the need to provide alternative accommodation to those displaced by large infrastructure projects, it is generally only those who can prove that they arrived in the city some years previously who are eligible.

In Mumbai (and many other cities), three further reasons help to explain the lack of attention to sanitation. The first is the concentration of many 'slums' and informal settlements on land belonging to national government institutions such as the railways authority, the port authority or the airport authorities. These national government agencies will not permit municipal corporations to provide sanitation or other amenities to the population settled on their land, fearing that this would legitimate these settlements so that the inhabitants could negotiate the right to stay there. The second is the reluctance of international funding agencies to see public toilets or community toilets as an appropriate solution. Although ensuring provision for toilets in each house might seem preferable, this would be far more expensive; it is also particularly difficult in many 'slum' settlements because of their high density, with so many people living in each small shelter and with only small and winding alleyways between houses where pipes could be installed. There are also the uncertainties regarding who owns each unit; improving the unit may simply help the owner raise the rent for tenants. Public or community toilets have the advantage of serving both tenants and owners.

The third reason is the political opposition to developing new models of provision for sanitation which have a more realistic chance of ensuring large-scale improvements for low-income groups. Although this chapter describes the growth of large-scale programmes for community-managed toilets in Mumbai and Pune, and smaller programmes in other cities, this faced many political obstacles. Many politicians and bureaucrats have opposed these community-managed processes. For politicians, it removes from their control a key part of the patron-client relationships with 'slum populations' through which they sustain their political careers. Many politicians in Mumbai and Pune opposed the alliance's schemes for community toilets because they feel that they are the true 'elected' representatives of 'the poor' in their constituency, and when NGOs deliver solutions and show how it should be done, they feel threatened. As will be described in more detail later, politicians have also tried to disrupt the management of community-toilets by saying that no one should pay to use them. Many municipal councillors actively opposed the community toilets because these provided councillors with no 'cut' or because they represented the contractors' lobby; as the community toilet programme gathered momentum, contractors objected to their loss of contracts. Community management also went against the long and dishonourable tradition of contractors, engineers and councillors getting a cut from each project, often through inflating the cost estimates. Government staff responsible for developing public toilet blocks also did not like working with the women's committees who now had key roles in designing and managing the construction of the toilet blocks because they found it difficult to approach them for bribes.

However, over time, the alliance has tried to involve politicians and civil servants in the community toilets and to demonstrate to them that they benefit from supporting community-driven processes. Some councillors were supporters from the outset, while many others became supporters when they saw the results and the popularity of the community toilet blocks. Some politicians up for election have recognized the benefit of associating themselves with community-managed toilets within their constituency. In February 2002, several politicians standing for office even advertised in a Mumbai newspaper that, if elected, they would follow the SPARC model, without ever having asked SPARC or contacted SPARC.

Two other factors helped to change the policies and attitudes of government to sanitation for slums. The first is a recognition that as India's major cities seek to be globally competitive, they are being assessed on the overall quality of life for their inhabitants. Poor sanitation is clearly an indicator of a very poor physical environment. Like the city's wealthier groups, global capital investment wants to protect itself from violence, disease and conflict. This has made the allocation of some funding to sanitation for the poor less contentious. But the second factor is the demonstration by the organizations of the urban poor of their capacity to design, build and manage their own toilet blocks in ways that provide a much better quality service and that cost the city authorities less than the toilet blocks they formerly paid contractors to construct.

## WHAT PEOPLE WANTED AND WHAT THEY COULD DO THEMSELVES

In 1985, as the women pavement dwellers in central Mumbai began to discuss with SPARC what their needs and priorities were (including what kind of house they wanted), the subjects of access to water and toilets was one of the most common themes. The pavement dwellers had no place to defecate and no legal access to water. Many of the women worked as servants in nearby houses and therefore used the toilet facilities of their employers, or they defecated in the open or into newspaper and threw it away. As noted earlier, women often waited until nightfall to do so.

Not surprisingly, good provision for water and sanitation was a high priority for the pavement dwellers; but there was a recognition that even if toilets in each home was preferable, if you had less than 20 square metres for a family, it was difficult to fit in a toilet. The toilet would also have to be next to the 'wet area' in a small house where washing, laundry and cooking took place – and the women knew that water supplies were likely to be irregular, so it would be difficult to keep the toilet clean. It was also recognized that community toilets were much cheaper per household served (and that community toilets could also include large tanks to ensure regular water supplies). In addition, there were government subsidies available to support the construction of community toilets. Discussions with slum dwellers produced comparable conclusions about the need for community toilets.

The women pavement dwellers went to visit communities who had community or public toilets, and they saw the poor management and the fact that the area around them was often used for open defecation. They saw the queues early in the morning as most people rushed to defecate before going to work – and how children were simply pushed out of the queues. Also, early in the morning, women are often cooking food for the family or getting ready to go to work, so they do not have time to accompany the children to the toilets, and instead let them defecate outside their house.

When women's groups suggested improvements to municipalities, they were laughed at. When they suggested that community processes could build better-quality, better-designed community toilets than the municipality at a lower unit cost, they were ignored. Few engineers would concede that low-income communities could do this. When international donors were approached for support, they did not have mechanisms to allow them to fund something as cheap as this and community organizations did not fit into their project cycles and procurement procedures.

However, the alliance decided to build some toilet blocks, drawing funding from the UK charity Homeless International, as well as other donors. This followed the alliance's long-established practice of supporting urban-poor community organizations who want to try out new ways of addressing their problems, of learning from these experiences and, over time, of developing precedents and practices that work. These precedents then serve to show municipalities and donors what community organizations can do and demonstrate to international donors that community toilets are a solution. This is never easy, especially for official donors, in part because the projects are so simple and cheap (official donors prefer expensive projects because these reduce administrative burdens and staff costs per pound or dollar spent). A ten-seat toilet block that can serve a community of 500 persons can cost as little as UK£500 or US$800, especially if there is piped water and sewers to connect to. This is less than the daily cost of most foreign experts.[3]

The following sub-sections describe some of the earliest experiences with community toilet blocks in Mumbai, Kanpur and Bangalore that were built between 1988 and 1996; community toilets were also being built during these years in Hyderabad and Lucknow (see NSDF et al, 1997). The construction of these toilet blocks was usually preceded by community-managed slum surveys to demonstrate the need and the inadequacy of public provision.

## Initial work in Mumbai

A *Mahila Milan*/NSDF survey of 151 settlements in Mumbai with 1 million people found that there were 3433 seats provided by toilets built by the municipality (one for every 1488 individuals) and 80 per cent were not working. Most toilets had broken doors and many had overflowing septic tanks, latrines clogged with excrement and sites covered with waste.

The alliance's early experiences with community-designed and managed toilets in Mumbai showed the difficulties in developing a new model. For instance, one toilet block faced problems when the authorities refused to provide a water connection, and the children's

**Figure 10.1** *Aundh toilet block built by the community in Bangalore*

toilets within it suddenly disappeared as someone extended their house. Another toilet block faced difficulties because of official opposition to its connection to nearby sewer mains that had to cross a road.

With World Bank funding for sanitation in Mumbai approved, there was a recognition that some of this had to be used to improve sanitation in low-income areas. The municipal corporation was keen that the alliance should construct community toilets – even if this was not in the original loan agreement. SPARC was invited by the additional municipal commissioner to participate in a programme to construct 5000 toilet blocks. By now, SPARC had experience of community-built toilet blocks in five cities and was already in discussion with government officials on how to support community-driven and managed sanitation. What the alliance suggested was simple: the city should pay for the capital cost of toilet construction (and the community-managed process would cost no more than the contractor-built toilets that the municipality was used to funding), and the communities would manage and maintain the toilets themselves (and generate the funds to do so). But the World Bank team wanted the inhabitants of 'slums' to get organized and bid against each other to get the funds to build the toilet blocks.

231

The Bank also wanted NGOs and contractors to bid for these tenders at three stages:

1  NGOs and contractors would publicize the scheme among slum dwellers and then organize these communities so that they could bid for the construction contracts.
2  NGOs and contractors, with the help and approval of community groups, would design toilets and collect funds to allow for toilet maintenance.
3  NGOs and contractors would build the toilets.

Each of these stages was seen as being independent of each other – and the rule was that if an agency applied for one of these stages, it was not allowed to take up work in another stage. The alliance felt that this was completely inappropriate as it failed to recognize how community-driven processes should link the three stages and it did not agree to take part.

## Work in Kanpur

A survey in 1993 by the Kanpur Slum Dwellers Federation found that 471,156 people were living in 228 'slums' of which 66 per cent had no toilets and 21 per cent had inadequate toilets. With the help of federation members from Mumbai, a ten-seat toilet was designed and built with maintenance and running costs covered through a pay-as-you-use system – 10 rupees a month per family for those in the community, 1 rupee a day per use by outsiders. This made it possible to employ a full time worker to clean the stalls, keep the water tank filled and collect fees from outsiders. The Kanpur Slum Dwellers Federation and *Mahila Milan* also built a small two-seat public toilet in one of Kanpur's railway slums; but the railway authorities demolished it. They then built a ten-seat block on municipal land at the end of the settlement. Another toilet block was built in a slum on the edge of Kanpur; after a long negotiation, the community's 600 strong *Mahila Milan* collective was able to get enough land for a ten-seat toilet with room for a *Mahila Milan* office, a caretaker's room and a courtyard for outdoor meetings. The toilet block was built within the compound of an overhead water tank on land owned by the Kanpur Water Authority. The same pay-and-use system generated funds for maintenance and to pay the women who looked after the toilets and filled the water tank. The women who managed the construction recognized that the toilet had to have a constant water supply in order to ensure that it could be kept clean, so water was drawn from three sources: a municipal tap (with water a few hours a day); a hand pump (as a supplementary source when needed for washing, bathing and toilets); and a large internal water storage tank

## Work in Bangalore

Despite the fact that Bangalore is one of India's most prosperous cities, half of the city's population live in slums and most have no piped water, toilets or drains (Rosenberg, 1962; Chaplin, 1999). Bangalore's out-skirts are dotted with enormous resettlement colonies, set up by the slum clearance board over the past 20 years as tens of thousands of poor families evicted from different parts of the city were dumped there. Conditions are often far worse than in the older and more crowded slums towards the centre of the city. Large areas of the city have no sewers and most sewage and wastewater drains into open drains. This also makes it more difficult and expensive to build community toilets because there is no connection to sewers and often no water mains to draw on.

The first community-built toilet block was in Doddigunte, with work beginning in 1994. This is a large and fairly recent settlement of 375 houses at the city limits. It is a 'declared slum' and most people have identity cards from the slum clearance board. Only a few hand pumps serve the 2000 inhabitants and, though a sewer line runs along one side of the settlement, there were no toilets. People were defecating in nearby fields; but as development in surrounding areas was intensifying, it was getting increasingly difficult to do so, especially for women as they sought private places to squat.

With 20,000 rupees start-up money from SPARC, a group of residents began building a communal toilet. However, as soon as digging began, the landowner complained, which forced the work to stop. A year later, with help from the Karnataka Slum Dwellers Federation (Bangalore is in the state of Karnataka), work began again; but this time there was opposition from neighbours across the street who did not like the idea of slum dwellers getting toilets. The police were called and worked stopped again. The team then went to the city's Deputy Commission of Development, who granted them a 'no objection' certificate.[4] Work resumed, but the toilet ran into trouble because there was insufficient downward slope in the long connection to the sewer line. The laying of this pipe had to be redone. The toilet block cost 40,000 rupees: 20,000 rupees for building the foundation, walls, doors and roof, 12,000 rupees for pipes, sewer connections and the construction of chambers, and

8000 rupees for redoing the pipe to the correct level. But this still represents the equivalent of around UK£53 or US$85 per seat. A second smaller community-built toilet was built serving 30 houses, with much lower unit costs. The four pour-flush latrines drained into a small brick-lined soak pit and then into a drain, as there were no sewers to which to connect. The toilets were entirely community built, with the enthusiastic involvement of women who dug, mixed concrete and carried bricks. The construction took ten days and cost 3000 rupees (at current exchange rates, UK£10 or US$18 per toilet).

# THE COMMUNITY TOILET PROGRAMME IN PUNE

In Pune, a partnership between the municipal government, NGOs and community-based organizations built more than 400 community toilet blocks between 1999 and 2001. These have greatly improved sanitation for more than half a million people. They have also demonstrated the potential of municipal-community partnerships to improve conditions for low-income groups. Pune has 2.8 million inhabitants, two-fifths of whom live in over 500 'slums'. Various local government bodies, such as slum boards, housing authorities, development authorities and municipal corporations, are meant to provide and maintain public toilets in these settlements. But provision is far below what is needed and for much of the 1990s, the city authorities failed to use much of the budget allocated for public toilets.

In 1999, the municipal commissioner in Pune, Ratnakar Gaikwad, sought to greatly increase the scale of public toilet construction and to ensure that more appropriate toilets were built. Advertisements were placed in newspapers, inviting NGOs to make bids for toilet construction. Between 1992 and 1999, only 22 toilet blocks had been constructed, while the new programme planned to build 220 blocks during 1999/2000 and another 220 during 2000/2001. The contracts were not only for building toilets, but also for maintenance. In awarding contracts, priority was given to settlements with more than 500 inhabitants and no toilet facilities and, after these, to areas where facilities were so dilapidated that they needed replacement.

NGOs were expected to quote at less than the cost estimated by the corporation. The 15 per cent implementation fees that had been charged by the agency during the past were not permitted. Bids from eight NGOs were accepted after a review of their track record. SPARC was one of the NGOs that received contracts, working with the NSDF and *Mahila Milan*. The alliance of these three institutions had been working in Pune for five years prior to this, supporting a vibrant savings and credit movement among women slum dwellers which had included experiments with community toilets. Now this alliance became one of the principal contractors and constructed 114 toilet blocks (with more than 2000 toilet seats and 500 children's toilet seats). The alliance designed and costed the project, the city provided the capital and the communities developed the capacity for management and maintenance.

Between 1999 and 2001, more toilets were constructed and more money was spent on this than during the previous 30 years. More than 400 toilet blocks were built with over 10,000 seats at a cost of around 400 million rupees (approximately UK£5.3 million or UK£53.30 per toilet seat). Assuming that each toilet seat was used by 50 individuals each day, more than 500,000 people benefited at a capital cost of UK£10.70 per person served. This programme also helped to recon-figure the relationships between the city government and civil society as NGOs and communities were not 'clients' or 'supplicants', but partners. The city government recognized the capacity of community organiz-ations to develop their own solutions, supported by local NGOs. The division of roles was also clear; city authorities changed their role from being a toilet provider to setting standards, funding the capital cost of construction and providing water and electricity. The NGOs and community organizations designed, built and maintained the toilet blocks. This programme was also unusual for India in its transparency and accountability; there were no deals struck behind closed doors. There was constant communication between senior government officials and community leaders. Weekly meetings brought all stakeholders together to review progress and identify problems that needed to be addressed. All aspects of costing and financing were publicly available. And the access that community organizers had to senior officials also kept in check the petty corruption that characterizes so many commu-nities' relationships with local government agencies as more junior government staff and local politicians demand illegal payments.

One factor that did constrain community participation was the municipal commissioner's desire to complete the programme while he was still in office. In addition, some NGOs that obtained contracts were actually thinly disguised fronts for contractors, and their poor perform-ance, in part, undermined the legitimacy of genuine organizations. Some NGOs also struggled to develop more participatory engagements with community organizations and lacked roots that were firmly based in the urban poor communities. Despite these limitations, in many places, the inhabitants had the central role in the design and construction of these toilets. Some women community leaders took on contracts themselves and managed the whole construction process, supported by engineers and architects from SPARC. It took time for the (usually) illiterate women in each community to develop the confidence that they could manage this process. As one leader, Savita Sonawane, noted: 'In the beginning, we did not know what a drawing or a plinth was. We did not understand what a foundation was or how to do the plastering. But as we went along, we learned more and more, and now we can built toilets with our eyes closed.'

Over time, these women's groups learned how to deal with local government bureaucracies and this gave them the confidence to deal with other government officials. These groups also kept a close watch on costs. But there were many prejudices against community management that had to be overcome. For instance, when a group of women began to negotiate with shopkeepers for materials to build the toilets, seeking the lowest price, they found that they were not taken seriously and had to bring their husbands. Some government staff did not want to work with organized women's groups because they felt unable to ask these groups for the bribes they usually received from contractors. In the programme's first phase, about half of the toilet blocks were built by slum communities; in the second phase, this rose to three-quarters.

## NEW OPPORTUNITIES FOR COMMUNITY TOILETS IN MUMBAI

In November 1998, the World Bank and the municipal corporation in Mumbai invited the alliance back because the approach the former had originally suggested was not working. Part of the reason for their change was the evidence from Pune that the new models suggested by the alliance were possible. One of the additional commissioners in Mumbai had visited Pune in early 1998. The alliance suggested that a toilet block should be built in order to develop tools and procedures for a larger programme. A toilet block was constructed at Chickalwadi – and using this as a demonstration, the World Bank and the municipal corporation designed a tendering strategy that would give NGOs equal status with contractors. This also meant that the World Bank had to change its regulation that NGOs could only be involved in projects that cost less than US$10,000. In 2000, SPARC won the tender to build 320 toilet blocks with 6400 seats in 20 wards.

SPARC set up a project management unit which was supervised by Nirman, a new non-profit company that the alliance set up to undertake

*Source:* Homeless International

**Figure 10.2** *The community-designed Chikhalwadi toilet block in Mumbai under construction*

projects, in part because of the much greater scale of the alliance's involvement in development projects. On behalf of Nirman, UTI Bank provided the municipal corporation with the performance guarantee that was needed to sign this contract, and the project began soon after. The target was to complete the 320 toilet blocks by March 2003. When it became apparent that this deadline could not be met, the World Bank initially argued against any extension. However, the alliance argued that for a project that had taken eight years to design, it was surely overly ambitious to expect it to be completed in two years! Moreover, it was a project that was demonstrating a new way of providing sanitation to very low-income city dwellers. Eventually, the deadline was extended to December 2003. As of July 2003, 180 toilet blocks are completed and another 110 are underway.

There were various difficulties working with the municipal corporation that needed to be addressed, in large part because it was not used

to working with NGOs. There were constant delays in getting per-
missions to build toilets and this, in turn, meant that the actual building
took much longer. Managing the paperwork, regulations and bills for
this project proved extremely complicated, and the alliance has had
serious delays in receiving payments (which inevitably slows down or
disrupts construction schedules). SPARC had to provide much of the
funding up front because of the delays in receiving funding from the
municipality. Many toilet blocks also took longer to construct than
anticipated because they used the same site as old and abandoned
toilets, which meant that these old structures had to be removed.

## INNOVATIONS IN COMMUNITY TOILETS

The alliance developed various innovations in the design, construction
and management of toilet blocks, learning from the experience of the
blocks constructed between 1994 and 1998. Unlike the previous
municipal models, they were bright and well ventilated (usually with
grilles placed high up on the wall between the back-to-back stalls and
gaps at the top of the doors and side walls so that ventilation occurred
on all four sides), with better quality construction (which also made
cleaning and maintenance easier). They had large water storage tanks to
ensure that there was enough water for users to wash after defecation
and to keep the toilets clean (unlike many of the earlier public toilets
that had irregular and inadequate water supplies, which made personal
hygiene and toilet cleaning difficult or impossible). Each of the new
toilet blocks had separate entrances and facilities for men and women,
which gave women more privacy and was much preferred by women to
the previous model, where men's and women's toilets faced each other
and often resulted in lack of privacy and harassment.

Another innovation was special provision for children's toilets, in part
because children always lose out to adults when there are queues for a
toilet, and in part because many young children are frightened to use
conventional latrines (which are dark and often smelly, and many have
large pits which children fear that they will fall into). Mothers are also
frightened that children will fall into toilets and often encourage them
to defecate in the open, so it becomes a common sight to see two to four
children sitting together, defecating in front of a toilet. Children under
seven years of age comprise a significant proportion of the slum
population – often one in four. The children's toilets were specially
designed for children's use – including smaller squat plates, handles that
the children can hold (to prevent overbalancing when squatting) and no

**Figure 10.3** *Community-designed children's toilets in Byanapalli settlement, Bangalore*

large pit openings (they defecate into a shallow trench that is flushed regularly). In many toilet blocks, toilets were also designed for easier use by the elderly and the disabled.

Toilet blocks also included a room where the caretaker and their family could live, which meant lower costs for management and maintenance (as the caretaker's accommodation formed part of the payment). Despite all of the attempts within India to liberate scavenging castes from the jobs of cleaning toilets, the reality is that these jobs are still done by *dalits* or specific communities within such caste groupings. By creating a space within the toilet blocks for their homes, and giving them a minimum wage, the toilets are maintained and the households have a secure home and a livelihood.

In some toilet blocks, where there was sufficient space, a community hall was built; in others, a meeting space was created in a terrace on top of the toilet structure. Small fees charged for the use of these meeting places helps to cover maintenance costs. Furthermore, having a community hall on top of the toilets brings pressure on the caretaker to keep the complex clean. Despite these innovations, the actual cost of the toilet blocks was 5 per cent less than the municipal corporation's costing. The whole toilet block programme was also celebrated as each toilet block was opened with a toilet festival at which the contribution of all those who had helped in the programme could be acknowledged – including people from government agencies and from communities.

Toilet blocks were also deliberately built in central locations that were community gathering points, not in isolated peripheral locations. This helps to ensure that the toilets and the sites around them are kept clean and informally monitored. While outsiders may see this linking together of community toilets and meeting spaces (including community halls) as an aberration, such a space serves many ends. In dense settlements the only space for people to gather is often around the water taps and toilets, so it makes sense to create such a communal space within or around the community toilets. The creation of such communal spaces also begins to transform the manner in which people relate to the toilet structure as it becomes a space for social interaction. This also generates a desire to keep it clean. The committees that manage the toilet blocks gradually formalize the maintenance and management process, which, in turn, helps to develop formal structures within the community. Since these committees have to deal with both their community and with government agencies, their confidence and net-working skills increase. The establishment of these new relationships with city governments can also demonstrate to the community leaders how their community structures could change if they were able to access the government resources that are available to invest in housing.

Among the other innovations introduced in many toilet blocks were the following:

- Toilet blocks were designed and built for heavy use (e.g. with better provision for queuing). In conventional toilet blocks, men and women are in the same queue and there is much acrimonious jostling; men often push their way past women. In the federation blocks, there are separate queues for men and women and space for people to wait outside each toilet stall.
- Doors swing both ways, making it much easier to enter when carrying a bucket of water; the conventional government models have inward-swinging doors that force the user to press against the (often) dirty inside walls to open the door and get out.
- Outside walls are clean, with no plumbing as the toilets are inside an enclosure. This cuts the cost of the compound walls and keeps the exterior walls clean (rather than being the dirty backsides of toilets

stalls with often rusty leaking plumbing) so that the toilet block has a clean public face. It also means more privacy for the users.

- In many designs, back-to-back toilets feed directly into a single central pipe with a single inspection chamber, which cuts costs.
- No middle men are involved in their construction, so no contractor profits have to be paid.
- Pour-flush toilets are used, where half a bucket of water is thrown in the pan to clean it. Each toilet has a water seal which keeps smells down but does not require costly venting or flushing hardware and needs only small volumes of water for flushing and cleaning (dirty/poor-quality water can be used for this, as well).

## Big pipes and little pipes

Most toilet blocks have connections to the city's piped water supplies and sewers and having such connections cuts unit costs as no pumps are needed to tap groundwater and no septic tanks are needed to accommodate the sewage. This also makes evident the division of tasks between 'big pipes' and 'little pipes'. City-wide infrastructure includes big pipes (trunk mains, main sewers and drains) that carry and treat water and sewage; generally, only the city authorities can manage these since they involve 'big' politics and 'big' budgets (although they may contract out the construction and/or management to private companies). But toilets and drainage lines within settlements need small pipes and communities can easily design, build and manage these themselves. The National Slum Dwellers Federation's suggestion to city governments is that they stop wasting money and effort on the little pipe items, which communities can handle for themselves, and concentrate on the big-pipe items, which communities cannot manage. If the city can deliver sewers and water supply to settlements, communities can take over from there, working on the internal small pipes.

## Funding maintenance

With regard to funding management and maintenance, there has been considerable debate about how best to do this. In many districts, people are not used to paying for toilets – and some politicians sought to gain political capital by opposing new toilet blocks that charged any payment (even if it is impossible to envisage how the toilet blocks can be kept clean and maintained without such payment). The alliance promoted a system where each family pays for a pass costing 20 rupees a month. This is much cheaper than the 1 rupee per use charge used by other public toilets (which, for a family of five, would cost 150 rupees a month even if each household member only used the toilet once a day). However, the fact that some elected municipal council members have been demanding that there should be no payments has depressed collection rates in some toilet blocks.

## WHY DID THE ALLIANCE TAKE ON COMMUNITY TOILET BLOCKS?

*To bring communities together.* Toilets can bring communities together; everyone will use them and will also have opinions about them. A toilet building project is small enough to be planned and built within a small budget and time frame, but big enough to start many things happening, including allowing women to get involved in the project, and allowing people to learn how to understand their problems, to work together, to tap skills within the community, to manage money and, finally, to enjoy not having to defecate in the open. If you squat along an open drain all your life, it is very hard to imagine toilets not being dirty places. But if they are clean and well cared for, they become points of congregation. The next step is the realization that slums do not have to be dirty places, but can be beautiful communities in which to live.

*To test new pro-poor policies.* Given the lack of provision for sanitation in cities, it is important to advocate and test new pro-poor policies.

*To expand livelihood options.* This was the first time that many poor communities were involved on this scale of construction. Although the poor always engage in petty construction activities informally, there is never space and resources for their formal participation. The construction and management of the toilet blocks expanded their livelihood options and developed their skills.

*To expand the federation.* Most of the slums in which the toilets were built were non-federated, and working in these areas greatly expanded the base of the federation and trained them to work in many different settlements.

*To strengthen the relationship with the municipal authorities.* Municipal authorities have learned much about developing minimum sanitation standards from the community toilet blocks. The large-scale programmes in Pune and Mumbai encouraged staff and politicians from other municipalities to visit and to learn how to initiate and manage such a process. These programmes also encouraged federations in other cities to negotiate with their municipal authorities to work on this issue.

In Mumbai and Pune, the subject of sanitation for the slums entered the public domain with municipal commissioners and other dignitaries being invited to inaugurate new toilet blocks. This also created a chance for dialogue over other issues such as water, electricity, paved roads and secure tenure. The traditional relationship of politicians as patrons and voters as clients also underwent a transformation. Whereas previously a toilet block was the 'gift' of a local councillor, a member of the legislative assembly or a member of parliament, citizens now saw toilet blocks as their right. Their involvement in developing toilet blocks also built their strength and confidence to negotiate with local municipal officials on many other issues. As pressures build from below, the administrative and political processes are compelled to respond. The culture of silence and subservience begins to give way to a more substantively democratic process.

*To change national policies.* The alliance also sought to change attitudes and policies at the level of the national government. The alliance worked with the United Nations Human Settlements Programme in launching a good governance campaign in 2000 and the NSDF demanded that sanitation be seen as an indicator of good governance, especially women and children's access to it, rather than seeing good governance only in terms of good management of finances and transparency. Good governance is also about the ways in which choices are made regarding investment priorities. At this point, the government of India introduced a new programme – the Nirmal Bharat Abhiyan – where a 50 per cent subsidy for the construction of community toilets is available to local bodies and public authorities. This new programme was influenced by the community toilets built in Pune and Mumbai.

## THE ART OF GENTLE NEGOTIATION

A necessary step in building these kinds of sanitation partnerships is convincing reluctant, and often suspicious, government agencies to stop seeing poor communities as problems, and to start seeing them as contributors to good solutions to city-wide problems. This means negotiation. The increasingly confident negotiating skills of slum dwellers' federations and *Mahila Milan* in Mumbai, Kanpur, Bangalore and Lucknow have obtained commitments to sanitation in slum settlements from many officials in the municipal corporations and state governments. Here are a few of their negotiating strategies.

*Start small and keep pressing. Mahila Milan* in Kanpur and Bangalore started small – negotiating for the corporations to provide hand pumps and water taps in slums. Through these negotiations they gradually gained the confidence, persistence and visibility to press for the next level: community toilets. Starting with small initiatives can show both government and communities that change is possible. Convince the officials that they can use their limited powers to make a small change. First, they might only give limited consent; but later, when they see things change, even in small ways, that consent might become support. Support is the first step in creating a genuine partnership.

*Paint beautiful pictures.* Sometimes, grassroots activism involves a great deal of scolding and finger-pointing: 'Isn't this awful!' 'Isn't that shameful!'. If you are serious about exploring new ways of bringing the poor and the state together to solve the city's problems, this kind of approach has limited utility. People in power are more likely to retreat into their bureaucratic shells when you start pelting them with 'awful' and 'shameful'. A better approach is to kindle their imaginations by describing possibilities in ways that make clear how they can contribute.

*Know more than they do.* When community organizations come into negotiations prepared, with enumeration reports that feature data on all households in the settlement, with toilet construction costs worked out and tested, with knowledge of city infrastructure grids, and with examples of community-state partnerships in other cities, it becomes much harder for government officials to argue against the proposals that you are making.

*Cut an attractive deal.* The slum dwellers federations/*Mahila Milan* around India have developed skills of persuasion in showing local governments that entering into an unconventional toilet-building partnership with a well-organized community organization is a realistic, even attractive proposition for solving big problems that stymie municipalities up and down the subcontinent. A sharp city administrator would have difficulty passing up these features:

- Sharing costs with a community reduces the city's sanitation cost burden.
- When communities build toilets, the city's construction burden is eliminated.
- When communities maintain the toilets, the city's maintenance costs are eliminated.
- Community-built toilets often cost less than those the city builds, so a city's infrastructure budgets can be spread further, increasing service delivery.

# COMMUNITY TOILETS ADD TO THE POOR'S REPERTOIRE

A large community toilet block-building programme encourages communities to undertake projects and to create an environment that makes room for experimentation. Externally supported interventions such as this do not set new standards, but alter and influence the circumstances, which allow communities to develop standards of their own.

*Enable communities to learn by experimenting and by making mistakes.* Solutions to complicated problems do not happen quickly and generally come from trial and error. Learning for any individual generally means having to do something more than once and making mistakes before finally getting it right. This is also true for poor communities, where solutions are much more complicated. To those mistrustful of community involvement in urban improvement, mistakes only confirm entrenched attitudes towards poor people as being ignorant or lazy. An 'only one chance' clause is frequently built into many community participation programmes, which does not allow the learning and training capital produced by mistakes to be reinvested in new processes. Instead, it stops participation at the first sign of error. Poor communities are unable to experiment because they have no margin within their limited resources to absorb mistakes. This is one of the crises of poverty, and this is why these toilet projects make room for, and even encourage, mistakes. The toilets are not theoretical ideas on paper, but real buildings, built in real slum settlements. They are all visited, discussed and analysed within the federation/*Mahila Milan* network and outside of it. Their mistakes and successes are widely discussed and considered and catalyse the projects that follow. The people who built them take their experiences to other settlements and other cities, and become trainers themselves. In this way, the evolution and refinement of ideas occur in practice, in different situations.

*People on the move: train others and break isolation.* People in communities who have built their own toilets are the best teachers for others interested in doing the same. Whether or not their project was successful, their experience can give a head start to other communities, who do not have to start from scratch every time. In order for skills to be refined and spread around, it is important that as many people as possible visit the toilets, participate in their building and return to their own settlements stocked with new ideas. In this way, the learning potential of these experiences is maximized, and their successes and failures are discussed and digested by many others.

*Each new toilet that is built is better than the last one.* With the widespread dissemination of experiences, each project becomes easier, the 'circle of preparation' shrinks and the number of people able and willing to get things done grows considerably. Each time a toilet block is built, it is also cause for a festival to celebrate its opening and each festival draws a larger crowd. It is the ability of the federation/*Mahila Milan* network to link people together and to help them control these processes that make projects possible. It is not true to suggest that all toilet constructions emerged entirely and spontaneously from the communities in which they were built. The lack of toilets is one of the most frequent and urgently articulated problems of slum dwellers; but it is important to understand all of these projects as involving a potent, external intervention – somebody coming in from outside of these particular communities, shaking things up, asking questions, posing challenges, and intentionally pushing forward the steps required for communities to plan and carry out solutions to their own sanitation problems. In this case, the outside group is the NSDF-*Mahila Milan*-SPARC alliance.

*No two toilet blocks are alike.* The toilet projects all work along the lines of some of the federations' fundamental ideas about building the capacities of communities (see Box 10.1); but all toilet blocks are different as they represent tailor-made responses to particular local needs and realities. The different toilet projects reflect different political climates, different negotiating strategies, different degrees of official support, different materials markets, different skill levels, different site realities, different access to sewer and water mains, and different community dynamics.

---

# BOX 10.1 THE TOOLS THAT BUILD COMMUNITY CAPACITY

### Daily savings

Community-managed savings and credit groups in which each member saves each day underpin the whole slum dwellers' federation/*Mahila Milan* structure. These groups are seen as the glue that holds the federation together. There is no minimum amount that the savers have to contribute each day. Women are particularly attracted to savings groups, as these provide crisis credit and can develop into savings accounts that help to fund housing improvement or new housing and loan facilities for income generation. The daily contact between each saver and the community representative collecting the savings also acts as a constant source of information on what people's difficulties are and how they can be addressed. When people want access to credit, the savings collector has personal knowledge of family circumstances and can vouch for them. The savings are usually managed at local 'area resource centres', which also serve as key focuses for community discussion and for planning and managing community initiatives. Savings groups often work together to develop their plans for new housing or other initiatives.

## Surveys and maps

Community-managed household, settlement and city surveys are important in helping communities to become self-sufficient, to strengthen their organization and to create a capacity to articulate their knowledge of themselves to government agencies and others with whom they interact. The National Slum Dwellers Federation (NSDF)-*Mahila Milan*-Society for the Promotion of Area Resource Centres (SPARC) alliance helps communities to undertake surveys at various levels, including the listing of all settlements, household enumeration and intra-household surveys. The alliance also builds their skills in mapping services, settlements, resources and problems so that they get a visual representation of how their present physical situation relates to them. These maps are also particularly useful in developing plans for improvements with external agencies. The information-gathering process often begins with hut counting as a community is visited for the first time, and many men and women from the federation and *Mahila Milan* hold meetings with residents and talk about their work and why they have come. Questionnaires and other survey methodologies are discussed with communities and modified as necessary, and all data are returned to them to be checked and, where needed, to be modified. Detailed hut counts, with each hut given a number and marked on detailed maps, have proved particularly important in managing resettlement. The repeated interaction with a community through hut counts, household surveys and settlement profiles also establishes a rapport with them and creates a knowledge base that the community owns and controls.

## Pilot projects

Pilot projects are universally accepted as experimental learning tools that can be used to test possible solutions, strategies and management systems. Pilot projects start when a particular community wants to address one of its problems. Once completed, the experience can be reviewed and the community and others (including government agencies) calculate what it would cost to scale it up. Pilot projects also help to set precedents that are used to promote changes in policies, practices or standards.

## Exchanges

Since 1988, there has been a constant process of exchanges between communities. Community members, beginning with the pavement dwellers, travelled first to other settlements in their own city and later to other cities in India to visit other communities. They shared their knowledge, finding people interested in acquiring their skills and understanding. Although most exchanges are within cities or between cities, there have also been many international exchanges, with community organizers from India visiting many other countries (including South Africa, Thailand, Cambodia, Laos, Uganda, Zimbabwe and Kenya) and community organizers from these countries visiting India.

*Don't waste time waiting for ideal conditions.* None of these toilet blocks are perfect. Most were built under circumstances that could be considered impossible. But what every toilet block represents is a vital investment in learning and human capacity. These are the building blocks of large-scale change, much more than perfect designs or innovative engineering. One of the NSDF's principles is that you should never allow your work to be held up while you wait for something else to be ready, or some other condition to be put in place. You have to start, since conditions will never be perfect, no matter how long you wait.

Sagira, one of the senior members of the Byculla *Mahila Milan* and veteran trainer of dozens of community toilet and house construction projects all over India, makes an analogy with the process of making salt from seawater. You stir and stir and stir and stir, until you are so tired of stirring. Just when you think nothing will happen, and there is no use carrying on with this stirring, the salt crystals begin to form. They will not form without all that stirring. In the same way, solutions to complex problems do not happen overnight, but need the same sustained, faithful nurturing and pushing

*Start with sanitation rather than land tenure.* The alliance originally developed to fight against the insecurity that poor communities face. Since local governments will not allocate land to the poor, their houses and neighbourhoods encroach on lands that are either publicly or privately owned and designated for other uses, such as parks, railway lines or airport perimeters. When communities live on land to which they have no acknowledged right, they become perpetual supplicants who have to comply with the demands of the landowners. The informality of their settlements means that they cannot demand the same rights as legal landowners and house owners from city administrations – including provision for water, sanitation and electricity. Instead, these communities have to resort to informal feudal linkages for 'protection' and, as noted earlier, often pay more for services than 'formal' citizens. They also face the indirect costs from the health problems and healthcare and medicine bills that come from a lack of a safe water supply and inadequate sanitation.

For organizations of the poor, the demand for sanitation is strategic because the city government and other parts of civil society can easily see the relationship between the poor and their sanitation needs and their own heath and well-being. The demand for sanitation is also less threatening than any demand for land tenure. Of all the basic services that the poor have begun to demand, during recent years, sanitation has begun to be less contested than others. This is especially so when the sensibilities of upwardly mobile middle-class citizens are affected by seeing people defecate in the open. It takes much longer to draw the connection between housing and the sense of security that the poor in cities need for their well-being and the quality of life.

*Why the poor make good sanitation partners.* In the projects described here, there was a fundamental change in roles as urban poor communities in different cities took part in designing, building and managing their own toilets and then invited the city to inspect what they had built. The poor no longer have to beg the city administration for basic services. They own the process and are the ones telling the city how they would like it to progress. Behind this dramatic transformation are some clear ideas.

Communities can make good decisions about sanitation systems that match their capabilities, budget and settlement realities. The job of providing basic services to any large city is a vast field of shared responsibility and involves many people: officials who set priorities, engineers who draft plans, contractors who perform civil work, water and sewage departments that oversee maintenance, and special interests that seek some advantage within the process. At the edge of this field of decisions are the people who need water taps and toilets. It has been assumed that these people, particularly the poor, cannot be involved in infrastructure decisions because they lack the required technical expertise. But the poor can be involved, and the technicalities of toilets, water supply and sewerage are not beyond them. Poor people can analyse their own sanitation needs, and can plan, construct and maintain their own toilets.

*Make a distinction between public toilets and community toilets.* This distinction is important because building a toilet in an informal settlement, like any amenity, changes people's perceptions about their own settlement. Public toilets are built to serve the needs of whoever happens to be passing, whether a local or a stranger. To build a community toilet is to acknowledge that a community exists, and that inside that community live women, men and children who have legitimate needs. A community toilet is an asset that belongs to, and is controlled by, a community – not the city or the government, and certainly not passing strangers. Within the murky politics of land and tenure in Indian cities, the construction of a community toilet can be a powerful manoeuvre, especially if it is built by the community itself.

*Develop standards that are realistic for poor communities.* When city governments build toilet blocks in slums, they use the same standard designs – expensive, difficult to maintain and mostly destined to fail. Despite their poor track record, the standard models are constantly repeated, partly because nobody has a better idea of how to do it. Fresh, workable standards for community improvements are badly needed. But can only emerge from a reality which poor people understand better than bureaucrats, and can only be developed through practice. These toilet projects are a search for better standards: standards for financing, designing, constructing and maintaining toilets that are replicable, and which work within the realities of poor communities. Some ideas they test catch on; others do not. It is from this fertile process of experimentation that new standards emerge.

*Why build community toilets rather than individual toilets?* Community toilets can provide everyone, even the poorest, with sanitation, and the costs of ensuring provision for everyone can be afforded. Those who are better off can, and will, gradually bring in individual facilities for themselves for which they can afford to pay. This way the pressure on community toilets will probably reduce over time; but everyone will continue to have access.

*Why feature community managed and controlled toilets?* Toilet blocks produce a possibility of change that helps to develop new leaders, new relationships within communities and new relationships with external agencies. Communities usually get together and community organizations emerge to address negative issues: to fight eviction and demolition, and to cope with extortion. This produces leadership that brokers relationships with those with power, including 'patrons' and those who informally need to be bribed or given favours. Many of the community leaders have similar relationships with the community as their links to the political and administrative wings of government and these are often negative and exploit themselves and their communities. For real change to occur there needs to be different leadership, and different relationships within the community and with the outside world. Yet, unless there is some need and the possibility for change exists, it is extremely difficult to motivate the poor and their nascent leadership to explore this path. A federation structure shows that there are possibilities for communities to conceptualize, design and manage assets that the community holds as vital; this, in turn, raises the possibility of the poor, and women in particular, being able to participate in exploring new roles with their communities.

*Why insist on community construction?* The construction of toilet blocks is something that, with some assistance, anyone can do. When communities get involved in design and construction and its supervision, this provides an insight into what the communities need to do to maintain such a facility. When it is explained to community leaders what must be done to ensure quality (such as the basic materials mixing of concrete, plumbing, etc.), they will supervise the construction that leads to a better-quality toilet. But the most important aspect is to do with linking livelihoods and producing entrepreneurial behaviour among the poor. Most slum people have worked on construction at some time; but they continually face barriers to getting better-paid jobs. By taking the opportunity to become contractors (sometimes as individuals and sometimes as collectives), they develop new skills and enhance their possibilities of getting better jobs in the future. The upgrading of slums will continue into the future; therefore, it is vital that some investment is made to build the capacity and skills of the poor to not only be the builders, but also the managers of such projects.

*Why use flush toilets that are linked to city sewers?* Many sanitation 'experts' claim that flush toilets are unsustainable solutions because of their demand for water and their production of large volumes of sewage. Yet, most slum dwellers seek this solution accompanied by seeking access to sewers because it is familiar and works. Until other methods are shown to work for entire communities, the urban poor have neither the resources nor the patience to explore other options. Any alternative will have to demonstrate its viability to city governments through extensive pilot projects. It should also be noted that the pour-flush toilets used by the alliance use much less water than conventional flush toilets – and often use dirty water.

# CONCLUSIONS

*Exposure is the key.* Urban poor communities can and must be centrally involved in improving their own lives and the general conditions of the city in which they live. There are communities that have taken steps to transform their own lives and settlements in various ways, and they provide powerful examples from which other communities can learn. They become the best catalysts for other larger transformations. They can also change the attitudes of city administrators and the strategies of how services and amenities are delivered to the poor. Exposure to work of this kind is the first step in breaking down the disabling belief that poor people are too marginalized to change things themselves.

*Show how things can be done better.* The community toilet blocks are one among various kinds of initiatives supported by the alliance around India. Different groups undertake different processes in different cities or city neighbourhoods, focusing on developing new housing or upgrading existing housing or community-managed resettlement or sanitation. All are underpinned by representative local organizations, including community-managed savings and credit schemes. The NSDF helps each group to carry its initiatives through to a conclusion. Once a solution has been developed and its relevance to other locations becomes apparent, the group who implemented it becomes a training resource in the slum dwellers' federations and can begin to assist other groups. The community toilet blocks demonstrated to local governments that improved sanitation was possible at costs that they could afford.

*Accept different degrees of involvement from government.* Bringing sanitation to all poor communities in Indian cities is a job that poor people cannot do alone. The toilet projects all represent, to varying degrees, partnerships that begin to break the conventional approach to service delivery. They also bring communities and governments together to work in new ways. The Bangalore municipal corporation, for example, has been a tentative partner, only going so far as to allow the toilets to be built, while the Kanpur municipal government went three steps further: providing land and water connections and helping to pay for one of the toilets.

*Women are at the centre of changing settlements.* While the lack of sanitation affects everyone – men, women and children – it is women who suffer the worst consequences of not having sanitation (and the harassment when they have to defecate in the open), and it is usually women who take responsibility for supervising sanitation for children. By creating ways for women to be drawn into the development of toilet blocks from the outset, the alliance seeks to create the space and opportunity for women to participate in the design, management and maintenance, and to become the trustees of the resources that it creates within communities. If women in poor communities understand how toilets are constructed, and are able to participate in the construction, their ability to manage and maintain them will be enhanced. Eventually, these women can go out and train others, which means that, gradually, it will be possible for all settlements to build their own low-cost toilets where they are needed. These settlements will also be able to manage and maintain these toilets. The community construction of toilets also enables women to develop skills in masonry, material production, project management and maintenance skills, which they can use later in their communities' house-building projects or as they manage other toilet building.

*People are the best experts.* One long-established myth is that experts are needed to plan improvements in slums. But the realities of life in India's slums are something that slum dwellers themselves understand best. This sounds obvious, but those who make decisions about slum improvement programmes operate on the assumption that they (or their experts) know best, although people living in slum communities can do it better. If experts had a better track record, their expertise might have more credibility.

The slums in India are the homes for most of those who actually build cities: masons, pipe layers, cement mixers, brick carriers, shuttering designers, stone cutters, trench diggers and metal fabricators. The poor, as they construct their own homes and neighbourhoods, are also already the designers and implementers of India's most far-reaching systems of housing and service delivery. The systems that they use to do so are not ideal, are largely 'illegal' and are often inequitable; but they reach down to the poorest groups and cover far more ground and affect far more lives than any government programme could ever achieve. Officials, with their rules and procedures, are apt to view the informal processes through which the poor create their own homes as misbehaviour, and to seek ways of controlling or punishing what is actually a reasonable and ordered response to urgent needs, where no 'legal' alternatives exist.

## ENDNOTES

1   Termed 'the alliance' in the rest of this chapter.
2   Most loans from the World Bank are provided at interest rates that fully recover the costs for the Bank – so-called 'non-concessional' loans. The Bank also has a soft loan facility – the International Development Association – which provides loans with a very low interest rate, although these are only available to low-income nations.
3   Foreign consultants often charge UK£500 to £1000, or US$800 to $1600, a day and receive an additional daily allowance that covers their living expenses in top-class hotels.
4   A 'no objection' certificate is generally the easiest way to get official recognition that what you are doing or planning to do is not illegal. It requires the least commitment by the government, makes no change in the status quo and costs the government no money. But it can represent a vital first step towards official approval for community-driven solutions.

## REFERENCES

Benjamin, S. (2000) 'Governance, economic settings and poverty in Bangalore', *Environment and Urbanization*, vol. 12, no. 1, pp35–56
Chaplin, S. E. (1999) 'Social exclusion and the politics of sanitation in urban India', *Environment and Urbanization*, vol. 11, no. 1, April, pp145–158
NSDF, *Mahila Milan* and SPARC (1997) *Toilet Talk*, SPARC, Mumbai

Patel, S., d'Cruz, C. and Burra, S. (2002) 'Beyond evictions in a global city; people-managed resettlement in Mumbai', *Environment and Urbanization*, vol. 14, no. 1, pp159–172

Patel, S. and Mitlin, D. (2001) *The Work of SPARC and Its Partners Mahila Milan and the National Slum Dwellers Federation in India*, IIED Working Paper 5 on Urban Poverty Reduction, IIED, London

Rosenberg, C. E. (1962) *The Cholera Years*, University of Chicago Press, Chicago

Sinclair Knight Merz and Egis Consulting Australia, in association with Brisbane City Enterprises and Feedback HSSI – STUP Consultants – Taru Leading Edge (2002) *Bangalore Water Supply and Environmental Sanitation Masterplan Project; Overview Report on Services to Urban Poor Stage 2*, AusAid, March

UN-Habitat (2003), *Water and Sanitation in the World's Cities: Local Action for Global Goals*, Earthscan Publications, London

# 11

# 'Concertación' (Reaching Agreement) and Planning for Sustainable Development in Ilo, Peru

*Julio Díaz Palacios and Liliana Miranda Sara*

## INTRODUCTION

Ilo is a port city in southern Peru, close to the Bolivian and Chilean borders, with around 70,000 inhabitants. Over the last 20 years, the quality of its environment has been much improved despite being an industrial town with rapid population growth and very limited external support. Progress includes much improved provision for water, sanitation, solid waste collection, electricity and public space (including the reclamation of beaches and the seafront for the population), reduced air pollution and extensive tree-planting and street paving programmes. A municipal programme has also ensured that land is available for housing that even low-income households can afford, and this has avoided problems of illegal settlements. Most of the public works were financed and executed through partnerships between municipal government and community-level management committees.

This chapter reviews this two decades' long experience with 'environmental governance', focusing on the politics that allowed the development of a coherent, long-term programme for sustainable development. After outlining what has been achieved, the chapter describes the process that the city and its citizens experienced as environmental and development issues were integrated within the city's planning and management. The process demonstrates the strength of local social actors who developed and implemented, via participatory budgeting processes, the plan for sustainable development within a national legislative framework. These active engaged citizens proved to be powerful instruments which favour continuity in implementing development processes, despite changes in local officials. The chapter also summarizes recent changes in this planning process and describes how progress is now being challenged because of a recent change in municipal government.

## THE BIRTH OF THE EXPERIENCE

In 1980, Ilo was a crowded industrial and fishing town with its employment base and economy dominated by a copper refinery and one of the world's largest copper smelters, owned by the Southern Peru Copper Corporation. It had very serious environmental problems, in large part because of the air pollution and wastes generated by this corporation, but also because of pollution from fishmeal industries and because of the lack of investment within the city in basic infrastructure and services.

During the beginning of the 1980s, the *Movimiento Político de Izquierda UNI* (UNI Leftist Political Movement) was elected to the municipal government in the province and became involved in three key processes:

1 Identify and respond to Ilo's economic, social and environmental problems.
2 Understand and manage development problems in the private and public spheres.
3 Get Ilo residents to imagine how the city felt and thought, as if the city was a living being (e.g. 'I am affected by many changes that make me into a sick city and I would like to be a very different city').

By degrees, these three processes created new ways of thinking about development, with the following ideas becoming central:

- Development is a right that every person has, but it must be won.
- Problems can become opportunities in certain contexts.
- Multi-sector and cross-cutting approaches are needed to address the serious environmental problems.
- Integrated visions of what is wanted must be developed, connecting all parts of reality and linking them to concrete actions.
- Economic development can occur in harmony with the environment.

- Cities do not just happen, they are created; they are products of social production.
- Without planning, decentralization and democracy, there will be no development.
- We only love what we know and only protect what we love.

In large measure, the citizens of Ilo forged the city's identity and engaged in the process of collectively creating the city through a confrontation with the state and with the Southern Peru Copper Corporation. The conflict with this mining company centred on the very serious contamination problems that this company generated from 1960 onwards. The copper refinery located 7km north of Ilo and the copper smelter, 17km north, process 60 per cent of Peru's copper and generate an enormous volume of sulphur dioxide, producing sulphur dioxide concentrations in Ilo many times higher than World Health Organization (WHO) recommended standards (Boon et al, 2001). There are also serious problems with suspended particular matter, and a WHO mission expressed concern about the health risks to Ilo's population from respiratory diseases, asthma, chronic bronchitis and additional total mortality; there was special concern for children. The technology exists to control this air pollution and is used in many copper refineries and smelters; but this was not used in Ilo (Boon et al, 2001). In 1988, Peru's largest mobilization in defence of the environment was held in Ilo, leading to the city's plan for environmental recuperation. Speaking at this forum, Ernesto Herrera, Ilo's mayor between 1990 and 2001, stated:

> . . . what was most important in the development process in Ilo was the environmental theme and how the community mobilized to demand an end to contamination created by the washings, wastes and sulphurous smoke from Southern Peru. The largest mobilizations were organized; local and international lawsuits were brought in the US and Europe [against the Southern Peru Copper Corporation]; laws were enacted and multi-sector proposals were offered. No form of building agreement or exerting pressure was ignored. The great mobilizations in Ilo in favour of the environment took place several years before the Rio [Earth Summit] conference, at a time when the environment was still a marginal theme in Latin America. (Díaz Palacios, 2000)

This grave social and environmental conflict, after a very intense phase of accusation, mobilization and social pressure, passed to another phase of solutions developed through direct negotiation. This produced a plan for environmental recuperation that has guided the principal decisions on environmental investment, both at the mining company and in local government. Much has been accomplished, though much important work remains to be done.

# THE ACHIEVEMENTS, 1980–2003

In Ilo, the initial feelings of alarm over what was happening to the city and the early innovative ideas gradually grew into support for a way of going forward based on reaching agreement, trying to create 'the city I want to be . . . an integrated city . . . not just a factory and bedroom city but one that can recover its history so that nobody should ever feel that he or she is in some place with no roots; a city with efficient ways of meeting needs. I want to be a humanistic city' (Díaz Palacios, 2000). With regard to the future, unlike those who merely let things happen or who just wonder at what happens, the people of Ilo placed their bets on 'making things happen.' Table 11.1 summarizes the improvements achieved between 1981 and 1998 in various environmental indicators; although there is no data available for events after 1998, it is likely that conditions continued to improve from 1998 to 2003.

## Community management committees

One of the most important actors in Ilo's development over the last 20 years has been the community management committees set up by residents who join forces to carry out projects that directly benefit their neighbourhood. To date, 160 streets have been paved, 8000 trees planted, 5180 dwellings improved, green areas much expanded and water and sanitation systems improved through the system of active participation of management committees.

Management committees are established at meetings of neighbourhood committees; once established, they request formal recognition from the municipal government. This recognition is then formally acknowledged through a municipal resolution. Their aim is the joint management and financing of projects that are developed and implemented with other institutions, including an active role for the municipal government, the federation of settlements and the local non-governmental organization (NGO), Labor. The residents who serve on the management committees have various ways of funding and executing the works. These include direct contributions from the

**Table 11.1** *Changes in Ilo's key environmental indicators, 1981–1998*

| Environmental indicators | 1981 | 1998 |
|---|---|---|
| Illegal land uses for housing | 35% | 0% |
| Drinking water supply with home connections | 40%* | 85%* |
| Capacity reduction in the home drinking water system | 60% | 30% |
| Wastewater treatment | 0% | 95%** |
| Solid waste collection | 58% | 93% |
| Solid waste treatment | 0% | 93% |
| Paved streets in the city centre | 35% | 80% |
| Paved streets in outlying neighbourhoods | 0% | 60% |
| Disposal of mining industry slag on the seacoast | 100% | 0% |
| Existing green areas | 2ha | 30ha |
| Emission of sulphurous gases from the copper foundry | 100% | 85% |
| Boron content of Ilo's drinking water | 10.7mg per litre | 4mg per litre |
| Arsenic content of Ilo's drinking water | 0.13mg per litre | 0.05mg per litre |
| Morbidity rate resulting from respiratory conditions | 31% | 30% |

*Notes:* *In 1981, drinking water was available for an average of two hours per week. In 1998, the average was six hours per day.
** Treatment in tertiary bio-stabilization ponds (oxidation ponds suitable for irrigation).

residents, group funding-raising activities such as raffles and food sales and support from municipal government. They can also draw on cement provided on credit and on Banco de Materiales (the Materials Bank), sometimes with additional support from grants or donations.

## Water, sanitation, solid waste and energy

Ilo has adequate provision for its water and electricity needs already guaranteed for the next 25 years – although in 1980, it had a serious water shortage. Its location in an arid, rocky desert area has meant that water has always been in short supply. Water comes from three sources: the Locumba River Basin, 90km away; its own Osmore River Basin, which had been dry for many years and has now been stabilized through the Pasto Grande Project; and wells that have been reopened in the small Ilo Valley (an area of 400ha).

Ilo's current and future power supply comes from a number of different sources: the Aricota and Charcani hydroelectric plants; thermoelectric sources, including a coal and gas plant; and an existing 5 megawatt thermal power station as a backup. Since Ilo is an industrial city, it has a relatively high consumption of electricity.

Ninety-five per cent of Ilo's wastewater, equivalent to 240 litres per second, is treated in a wastewater treatment pond and two small recycling modules known as bio-filters. Twenty-five tonnes per day of solid waste is collected and disposed of in a sanitary landfill run by a micro-enterprise. As Table 11.1 shows, the proportion of the population receiving solid waste collection services has greatly increased. Surveys indicate that public opinion considers Ilo to be a clean city.

## Housing and urban expansion plans and programmes

Despite the city's rapid population growth – its population increased fivefold between 1960 and 2000 – there have been no land invasions or illegal land occupation by low-income groups seeking land for housing. A government programme of providing land for housing has managed to meet the land requirements of low-income households. All new settlements have been developed within municipal and housing association programmes, in which housing plots are gradually serviced, while they are also undergoing legal and physical reorganization. This is a process that is jointly managed and self-financed by the community. Through these efforts, 6000 lots have been serviced for housing purposes in the urban expansion area known as *Pampa Inalámbrica*.

The city of Ilo is situated on a sloped coastal fringe, with an average width of 2km. Urban occupation has gradually taken over the seaside areas, next to industrial uses. To accommodate Ilo's demographic growth, higher ground (500m above sea level) was designated as an urban expansion area owing to its flat surface and capacity to house more than 60,000 residents. Ilo's municipal authorities acquired this urban expansion area under a provision in the 1984 Urban Development Master Plan. The municipality subdivided the urban land into lots earmarked for three different groups: private housing associations; government housing programmes (ENACE and FONAVI); and the Municipal Housing Programme run by the provincial municipality of Ilo. This acquisition of land in advance of need and its subdivision made it possible to meet housing demand for different sectors of the population – and enabled the municipality to establish various different procedures that allow a range of lots to be developed so that they can be afforded by all social groups.

The lowest-income households acquire their lots within the Municipal Housing Programme's three-step process:

1   The municipality receives applications, assesses them jointly with resident leaders (to verify social need and rule out those who already own a house or site) and selects eligible candidates. The eligible candidates are then ranked, a process that includes rating their participation as local residents. Land sites are then allocated. This initial period is the 'gradual urban servicing period', with residents helping to clear and prepare the site and undertake the survey. Streets and plots are laid out and the site plan is made, with different areas given their designated use and public water taps and septic tanks constructed, with active support from the municipal drinking water and sanitation company. This stage ends when the selected households occupy their lots.

2   The programme checks to ensure that the social organizations and the beneficiary population meet the following parameters: occupation of the plot by the beneficiary family; the preparation of plans for electrification, water and sanitation; road-grading levels; and execution of works such as tree-planting arrangements, street grading and marking, earthworks, identification of tree-planting points and construction of community and/or individual latrines. This stage ends with the execution of the adjudication documents.

3   Further physical and administrative reorganization occurs. The social organization is required to begin the servicing of the lots, as planned during the previous phase. The beneficiaries must complete at least one basic service during this step, and, at a minimum, financing must be approved for the other two. This step ends with the delivery to each plot occupant of the definitive title to the property.

The beneficiaries themselves pay the costs of this urban servicing process, and of the assigned lots, to a cost not exceeding the equivalent of US$60. The work is jointly managed and self-financed. Through the various management committees, the beneficiary population coordinates support from a number of public and private institutions, such as NGOs, private enterprises and national programmes set up to address extreme poverty. The servicing process takes from one to three years; the speed with which it is done depends upon the beneficiary population's management capacity. Similar strategies support self-help house construction.

Thus, through a creative and sustained policy on finance, credit and community service, people who have very low incomes now own their own house plot and have their own house, made from proper materials, through mutual assistance and cooperation.

## The city re-establishes its connection to the sea

Over the last 15 years, there has been a long-term programme to recover the seafront for use by the population. More than ten enterprises and settlements that had established themselves on the seafront were relocated to allow the construction of the Port Pier. This pier has transformed the urban coastline, making it a space much used and enjoyed by the inhabitants. This also connected city life with the sea.

Along the steeply sloped, grey rocky land that characterizes the city's urban surface, different community organizations have built plazas and stairways. They have greened these areas, using plants that do not require fertile soil or much water, and have planted trees that provide shade. The pier now occupies an area of 3km and marks the city's intersection with the ocean. This change allowed the urban buildings in this area to reorient their frontage to the coast. The pier begins with the old customs wharf (*muelle fiscal*), which is over a century old and is a square. Tree-lined walkways lead to an open-air amphitheatre that can accommodate 3000 people. Garden paths adjoining the plaza with water fountains lead to a seaside playground complex. To the north, a paved road leads to Boca del Río ('river mouth') Beach, with space designated for high-density housing, administrative buildings (such as the city hall) and cultural and tourism buildings.

## Integration with the road system

Another of Ilo's accomplishments is to have developed its international and regional road connection. There is now a paved road from Ilo to the capital of Bolivia, La Paz, with a journey time of five hours. There are plans to extend the paved road that now reaches Tacna up the coast to the national capital, Lima. Since the 1992 signing of the agreement between Peru and Bolivia, Ilo has had a strategic role as the headquarters for Latin American integration with the Pacific Basin. This agreement allowed Bolivia (a landlocked country) access to beaches, the port and the shore. With a view to developing Ilo as a bio-oceanic port, during the past five years investments have been made in highways, water projects, an airport and industrial infrastructure.

## Development and environmental conflict with Empresa Southern

Empresa Southern (Southern Peru Copper Corporation), Peru's largest copper company, established copper refining and smelting in Ilo approximately 40 years ago. Only a small fraction of the hundreds of millions of dollars that this company and five fishmeal companies in Ilo generate remains in Ilo in the form of capital, and there is little processing within Ilo of the raw materials extracted. Ironically, for a city with good environmental management, environmental contamination is still very serious because of the 1800 tonnes of sulphur dioxide emitted each day by Empresa Southern's four smoke stacks. Five sulphur dioxide sampling stations were set up in 1997. These showed an air pollution level in one location that was 14 times the limit recommended by WHO. Even in the more distant Pampa Inalámbrica, the concentration of sulphur dioxide was found to be more than three times the WHO permitted standard. An analysis of hospital records shows that a much higher proportion of in-patients come for the treatment of respiratory ailments than is normally the case in Peru.

For many years, Ilo was considered a place where money could be made from mining and fishing jobs, but not a city in which to live. Many families moved away from Ilo because their children were suffering from asthma. Many families from Ilo invested their earnings in businesses or housing in other cities to 'get away some day' from this contaminated city. An estimated US$12 million to $15 million flows out of the city, each year, for this reason.

The fact that the WHO considers Ilo to be one of the most polluted areas in Peru has meant that the leaders in Ilo have long feared that this would deter external investment and frighten tourists away. While urban environmental management has been unable to solve this problem of atmospheric contamination, the Southern Peru Copper Corporation has been persuaded to invest US$200 million in other environmental projects, such as the rewashing facility that ended pollution in Ite Bay and the civil works to prevent slag from destroying the beaches in the northern part of the city.

By law, the air pollution must be reduced to permissible levels by 2006. Southern Peru Copper Corporation has indicated that the production of sulphuric acid using the sulphur dioxide formerly discharged into the air is a good investment, and that it would collect the sulphur dioxide to make sulphuric acid until emissions were reduced to 5 per cent of their current levels. Although this was good news, when copper prices fell as the result of the Asian crisis, the company lost its

263

initial conviction. Ilo's inhabitants will continue to fight to ensure that they can breathe clean air. Although the main problem remains to be solved, the unifying and creative impulse of joint environmental action has been indirectly responsible for many of the city's accomplishments.

Today, Ilo's citizens are endowed with well-developed environmental awareness. There have been important achievements in environmental management, such as the clean-up of the bay through a system of oxidation pools for wastewater, a solid waste management programme, larger green and reforested areas for the urban community, a computer-driven system for monitoring air quality and an environmental education programme.

## THE COORDINATING AGENCY AND STAGES IN THE PROCESS

The agenda for change promoted by the elected municipal government in Ilo went through five different stages:

1 1981–1983: Unity and popular organization for the struggle were affirmed: *'el pueblo unido, jamás será vencido'* ('the people, united, will never be vanquished').
2 1984–1987: There was a struggle for environmental quality – *'agua sí, humo no'* ('water, yes; smoke, no') – and human rights, fighting *'por el pan y la belleza'* ('for bread and beauty').
3 1988–1992: Gains were consolidated and identity was affirmed: *'construir una ciudad habitable donde todos puedan y quieran vivir'* ('building a habitable city where all can and want, and would love, to live); the focus was also on accelerating the passage *'de una ciudad de paso a una ciudad para vivir'* ('from a transient city to a city in which to live').
4 1993–1998: An international position was promoted: *'Ilo, puerto ecológico, biooceánico y primer balneario turístico del sur'* ('Ilo, an ecological, bio-oceanic port and the south's premier seaside resort').
5 1999 onwards: The focus has been on searching for sustainable development and relaunching coordination with its surrounding region (the southern Macro region).

The first stage emphasized the environmental axis, although rooted in local problems; later this was complemented with promoting economic and social development. In other words, environmental concern led to understanding and taking on board the sustainability and development approaches. The thematic emphases are reflected in various versions of the integrated plans, with the latest being the Plan for Agenda 21 Sustainable Development to 2015, the most integrated agenda proposal in Peru to date.

## The Ilo XXI Sustainable Development Plan

The Ilo XXI Sustainable Development Plan, which sets out a plan for local development for the next 15 years, was formulated though a process of dialogue and consultation involving local officials, the public sector and civil society organizations. It accords with Agenda 21, as approved at the 1992 Earth Summit and ratified in Rio + 10.

This sustainable development plan was possible because of the conviction and will of municipal officials, leaders and institutions in Ilo and its citizens; close to 2500 individuals participated during the latter part of 1999 and through 2000, making this one of Ilo's peak periods of participation in recent decades. This energized the city's social fabric, heightening its capacity to evaluate, reflect upon and design proposals, build consensus and provide impetus to decentralization in decision-making.

Objectives that were achieved comprised the following:

- provide Ilo with a shared vision of the future;
- agree upon a new version of the current integrated development plan;
- develop and strengthen local institutions;
- improve efficiency and effectiveness of the municipality;
- promote public and private investment (large, medium and small enterprises).

Results that were obtained included:

- the Ilo XXI Sustainable Development Plan;
- guidelines for a new version of the Territorial Planning and Development Plan (*Plan de Acondicionamiento Territorial*);
- the Urban Master Plan (*Plan Director Urbano*) – finished and approved;
- guidelines for a new version of the Environmental Management Plan (*Plan de Gestión Ambiental*);
- proposal for creating Ilo's Provincial Development Council (*Concejo de Desarrollo Provincial*);

- the Plan for the Institutional Development of the Provincial Municipality (*Plan de Desarrollo de la Municipalidad Provincial*);
- approved regulations and standards;
- the monitoring and evaluation system.

The process involved the actors in a number of stages and processes. While the planning process was continuous, there were five principal stages:

1 creating awareness and motivation and organizing;
2 analysis, diagnosis and organization;
3 drafting proposals and consultation;
4 presentation of the plan; and
5 dissemination and setting up the plan for execution.

A further stage is future monitoring and evaluation of compliance with the plan and new versions of it. However, for reasons explained below, full compliance with this process has not yet been achieved.

In parallel, there were four organizational processes:

1 technical: corresponding to work with consultants and officials;
2 participatory: involving social actors and organizations;
3 political: corresponding to the intentions and political projects of the mayor, the municipality and local actors; and
4 dissemination and communication.

The first stage was made up of activities to disseminate, mobilize, create awareness and gather people, organized by the municipality and the institutions of the city of Ilo.

The second diagnostic stage consisted of organizing the consultants' group (of seven individuals), as follows: a project director; a general assistant in charge of the Ilo plan; and individuals responsible for macro-regional and international coordination, economic development, urban development, environmental management and municipal institutional development.

Within the city's institutions, three thematic groups were installed:

1 macro-region and economic development;
2 social development, with four sub-committees on education regarding family violence, health, institutions and social organizations; and

**Table 11.2** *The process for developing the sustainable development plan*

| | Stage 1 | Stage 2 | Stage 3 | Stage 4 | Stage 5 |
|---|---|---|---|---|---|
| | Creating awareness and motivation and organizing (June–July 1999) | Analysis, diagnosis and organization (July–September 1999) | Drafting proposals and consultation (October–December 1999) | Presentation of Ilo XXI Sustainable Development Plan (December 1999) | Dissemination and setting up the plan for execution (January–December 2000) |
| Technical process | Definition and approval: terms of reference for Ilo XXI | Surveys, interviews and focus groups. First version of municipal reports. First version of thematic groups' reports. Visits to Ilo from Porto Alegre for presentation and discussion of experience in participatory budgeting | Second version of technical reports per thematic group. Workshop on strategic planning of Ilo XXI. First version of Ilo XXI Sustainable Development Plan. Visits from external experts | Evaluation and contribution from local actors. Second version of Ilo XXI | Design of action plans for competitiveness. Encourage macro-regional coordination. Human resources development plan |
| Participatory process | Seminar on 'The Southern Macro-region and the Role of Cities' | Organization of working groups, workshops and thematic groups. Actors' workshops (youth, women, seniors) | Meeting with officials, municipal employees and workers. Workshops to propose thematic groups. Competition on 'Ilo: the City We Want' | Leaders' workshop for consultation and revision of Ilo XXI | Setting up management promotion committees for the participatory budget. Consult with citizens, approve Ilo XXI. January 2001 (third version) |
| Political process | Municipal agreement on the plan. Establishment of the promotion committee | Constitute political and technical committees | Workshops on 'Municipal Policies and Mission' | Will of municipality and local actors is ratified to implement Ilo XXI and create the Council for Provincial Development | Allocation of budget to execute the plan by the municipality |
| Dissemination process | Presentation in an Agenda 21 seminar by the Cities for Life forum (Lima) | Broadly based call to constitute groups and permanent dissemination | Presentation at the Agenda 21 seminar organized by the Cities for Life forum. Session of the Information Council | Gathering together all of the information on Ilo XXI | Intensive dissemination of the Ilo XXI Sustainable Development Plan |

3  urban environmental development, with the support and participation of the Masters students in urban environmental management at the Universidad Nacional San Agustín in Arequipa.

Each group evaluated the situation and the proposals; in parallel, the consultants conducted surveys, interviews and focus groups for institutions, actors and the general population.

Based on these activities, a first report was drafted: a diagnosis of Ilo. This report was also the basis for the thematic workshops on socialization and developing proposals on economic development, social development and the urban environment. The principal products of this stage are the final reports of the consultants on their respective topics, reports on workshops held by the actors and the documents presented by the winners of the writing and drawing contests, 'Ilo: the City We Want'.

In a third stage, the proposal for the Ilo XXI Sustainable Development Plan was formulated, based principally on consulting with the working groups. Workshops covering the following topics were held: the strategic plan for sustainable development; leaders in development; negotiation; design of municipal policies; and operational planning.

The fourth stage consisted of presenting and debating the second version of the plan and approving it in principle, as well as ratifying the political and social will to implement it, and, lastly, creating the Development Council to this effect.

It is worth noting that in the fifth stage, after the second version of the plan was presented in December 1999, the local provincial government led an intense participatory process during 2000 to broadcast the aims and the scope of the plan, making it possible for leaders and citizens to shape the new initiative and to take ownership of it. This prepared the terrain and set the stage for the first key goals that had to be met in local development and in regional coordination. Other important tasks included selecting priority projects; drafting an action plan for competitiveness; setting up the management committees as the building blocks of the Development Council; formulating the human resources development plan; promoting the participatory municipal budget; and writing the technical guidelines for dividing the city's most important expansion area into districts. All of this work was done before the plan was formally approved (see Diagram 11.1).

Looking back at this process, it was pioneering in many ways. As one urban specialist commented:

> Building a city of the future is a task that involves us all. But there is no creation without a project, and the project must be

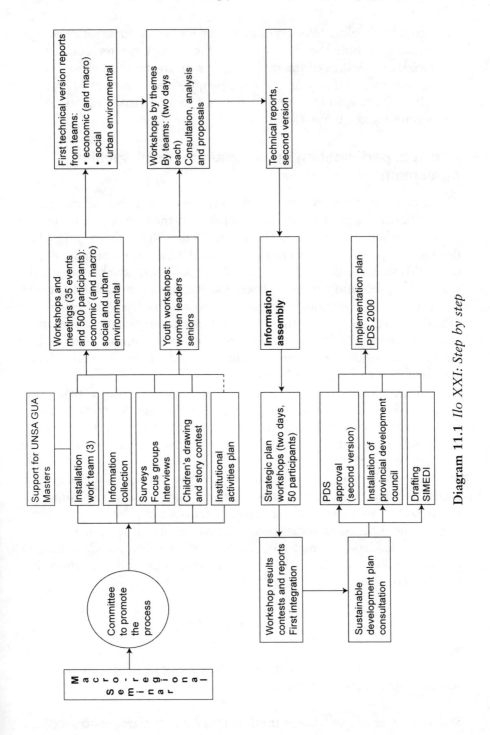

**Diagram 11.1** *Ilo XXI: Step by step*

integrated, global; our political imperative is to create and make accessible the means so that the project can include the needs and desires of the majority. The means must be adjusted to the cultural mechanisms of the people. The citizens exist; yet often those who monopolize power and knowledge prefer to ignore them. (Borja 1995)

## Principal participating actors and modes of seeking agreement

The provincial municipality was the principal actor; but it worked in close alliance with local actors, a number of them permanent such as NGOs, Labor and Ilo CEOP. Other actors have been important depending upon the circumstances, as was the case, for example, during the 1980s with the defence front (*frente de defensa*), which included the political parties, and neighbourhood and women's organizations. Later, when these organizations declined due to the institutional crisis that affected Peru so profoundly, the habitat management committees (*comités de gestión del hábitat*) began taking on a significant role; their strength stemmed from their commitment to improving the living standard in their neighbourhood.

In time, the social and small business organizations that were reactivated became decisive actors through the 'development management committees' organized around a particular theme. Today, these are effective operators of the sustainable development plan and the participatory budget. For each specific area of agreement, the actors involved are different. For example, in environmental management issues, we see NGOs and environmental committees, including the health sector; in issues relating to public works and pilot projects, there are neighbourhood associations; in sustainable development plans, provincial leaders and mid-level leaders take the lead; and, finally, in decision-making we have the local officials, with the education and health sectors playing key roles.

## TANGIBLE RESULTS

Among the results derived from the experience of development based on reaching agreements, are the following:

- The conversion of 'claimant inhabitants' into 'citizens who propose,' with increased environmental and civic awareness, and with a democratic culture in politics and development; these citizens now amount to a substantial social capital.

- A shift from 'unsolved environmental problems, held to be irreversible' to the solution of these problems. For example, the agreements with the copper company and the Peru Energy Ministry should mean that, by 2007, air pollution will finally be controlled.
- The transformation of the old mining-fishing camp into an integrated city, equipped to a significant degree and with an urban aesthetic. Today, this is one of its high points and a source of collective self-esteem; Ilo is considered the best-planned and equipped city on the Peruvian coast.
- The evolution of the precarious municipality of the 1980s into the present effective local government, with initiatives of its own. For example, this municipal government participated in creating the mining code and the customs code during the 1980s and 1990s. For the last five years, Ilo has been considered an example in sustainable development planning and environmental management; more recently, it has become well known for its habitat committees and participatory budgeting process.
- Passage from the inefficient use of resources to the more recent practice where a 15-year strategic plan furnishes guidelines and the mode of 'participatory budgeting' influences resource allocation, overseen by participatory budgeting 'watch committees' (*comités de vigilancia*).
- Significant improvements in the living standard of citizens, with growing coverage and quality in public services (see Table 11.1).
- A municipality that has, and is applying, an institutional development plan to adjust to the new challenges of sustainable development. It is the only municipality in Peru that has invested more than US$60,000 in its sustainable development plan and its Urban Master Plan.

The experience of reaching agreement in Ilo may have contributed a basic methodological sequence that has been used in other locations, both within Peru and abroad: identify the problem and/or opportunity; identify the actors involved; make the decision to hold a dialogue and organize for this purpose; negotiate and reach agreements; execute agreed actions; follow up and evaluate results. Ilo has become a point of reference and a training site for officials and leaders in certain local development topics; the city is also part of a number of networks, among which are Foro Ciudades para la Vida (Cities for Life Forum), a Peru-wide network of local governments, NGOs, enterprises and

271

universities committed to sustainable development (Miranda and Hordijk, 1998), and Red Perú de Iniciativas para la Concertación (Peruvian Network for Agreement-based Initiatives). Furthermore, the experience in Ilo has contributed to public life in Peru by helping to promote environmental policies and standards, introducing conflict resolution methods, showing how a city can be governed democratically and creating a culture of development.

The development of a local identity has been and continues to be a decisive factor. Designing and building important mental spaces in a participatory way has contributed to Ilo's identity. A youth meeting concluded, for example, that:

> Ilo has been changing from a transient city to a city to live in, with a tradition in organization and democracy, with intense participation. There are new sea-breaks with walks, and squares and streets, all of which beautify and integrate the city transversally. The most important achievement is strengthening democratic participation; this generates identity and the feeling of belonging in the population, and builds a positive vision of the future for the city, with a good and healthy environment and integrated sustainable development. (Youth meeting, 1999)

This identity is slowly becoming a catalyst for the production of social capital, expressed in the degree of participation and organization, in growing credibility and cooperation, in the development of a work ethic, solidarity, complementation and creativity, and in the quality of institutions and the entrepreneurial attitude, all of which also makes for synergies in the process of meeting development goals.

## THE CURRENT SITUATION

After seven consecutive terms of office with democratic management and with mayors who were committed to, and guided by, a strategic vision, there was a dramatic change for Ilo. On 1 January 2003, the city found itself under the leadership of a new mayor, whose background has been to radically oppose all previous administrations.

A month before the municipal elections in November 2002, this new mayor seemed to have no chance of being elected, since he was in fourth place in the polls. Even so, he won. How can this be explained?

- No candidate with any chance of being elected agreed to present themselves as a person who would represent or carry forward the political ideas and projects of the seven previous administrations. After many years, that local group's power had eroded. The situation was further affected by events surrounding the previous mayor, who had resigned to take up a seat in congress, leaving as a substitute a weak person with unimpressive leadership and representation skills.
- Less than a month before the election, the candidates most likely to win, those positioned at the centre or progressives, fell into a vicious political fight marked by excesses and verbal violence, which alienated the electorate who, ultimately, rejected all of them.
- The eventual winner offered tax relief, including relief for interest and overdue payments. This generated mass support, especially in light of the recession and underlying persistent poverty (over 60 per cent of the population is poor). This was the factor that carried the most weight, while in other respects the winning candidate's platform was similar to the one that has guided Ilo's development for the past two decades. Amongst all of this confusion and opportunistic offers, the present mayor was elected with only 40 per cent of the votes.

This leads us to the following conclusions:

- With weak and fragmented political parties and a crisis in the institutions of democracy after a decade of corrupt and centralist government (under former President Fujimori), to be elected and serve as mayor is one of the few remaining ways of gaining experience in leadership. In this sense, the fact that between 1981 and 2001 Ilo had only two mayors (each elected for several terms of office) ultimately had grave consequences because this inhibited the process of developing leaders in institutions, politics and society at large – people who could have then maintained the processes that were under way. Thus, the alternating re-election of just two leaders turned out to be a political feature that took its toll on the city's political life.
- Processes of change (involving approaches to development, new forms of interaction between the state and civil society, governing styles, the war on poverty and a range of environmental concerns) do not follow a linear evolution and can suffer periods of inaction. The fact that the exercise of power may fall to different parties and groups is a good thing, though not if this leads to extreme policy

swings. What is required is a deepening of positive processes, searching for new paths without losing sight of the fact that development is a cumulative process and is multidimensional. In any case, if we are to build continuity into the political process, a new political culture must be nurtured, with new attitudes on the part of citizens and new approaches to winning and exercising political power from government without stimulating civic irresponsibility.

- All of this depends on the behaviour of civil society as much as on the behaviour of political actors. Key areas are the development of citizenship through organizations, and an awareness of rights and duties, with new features such as the planning cycle, reaching agreement on key governance issues and new ways of operating institutions democratically. Civil society thus becomes a counter-weight to government (that is always in danger of excess or serious distortion in the exercise of power) and is also a factor in local government.

- There is no doubt that devising and approving a new, shared vision of the future, with development plans that reflect it, are important steps. But these are insufficient to ensure continuity in development, especially when it must necessarily be based on deep-seated changes. Nonetheless, a vision and a plan constitute the initial steps of the lengthy and complex process of development. The experience of Ilo and elsewhere in Peru demonstrate that vision and plan must be reflected and complemented in a 'collective process,' where a broad range of interests are cohesive, and citizens develop their awareness and acquire an identity and some sense of belonging, thus becoming the active dynamic subjects of development. As a result, public opinion expresses itself in participation and the process of reaching agreement.

Practical verification of these points is demonstrated in two recent events. During the 2002 electoral campaign, the new mayor offered to respect the participatory budget (i.e. the organized community's right to influence the allocation of resources from the municipal budget). However, upon taking office, he declared that he would ignore the participatory budget model. But the community's representative organizations reacted, demanding that the rights that they had won should be respected. This compelled the mayor to go back to respecting participatory budgeting. In this conflict, Ilo's civic society ensured that 80 per cent of the investment from the municipal budget came into the participatory budgeting discussions (a total equivalent to approximately US$2.5 million).

To a great extent, the Ilo community forged its identity and became closely involved with the city's process of collective creation through the 20-year face-off with the state and with the Southern Peru Copper Corporation. One of the most important advances in this struggle was the approval, in 1989, of an environmental recovery plan, which included the industrial re-conversion of the copper foundry by the end of the century. The mining company did not comply with its commitment and did what it had always done: delay, and then delay some more. It put pressure on the national government's mining ministry to postpone, until 2007, the investment required to reduce sulphur emissions to permitted levels. Contradicting the firm stance in favour of environmental decontamination that previous municipal administrations had taken, the new mayor favoured the mining company. This upset many people. Citizens were quick to react, energetically questioning the mayor's subordination to the multinational; as a result, he was compelled to change his position.

In these two episodes, we see that it has been the organized community who ensured a continuity of actions and processes capable of organizing the city in a better way. This is, after all, a city in its fifth year of participatory budgeting, with a coherent citizenry whose identity was forged in the heat of social and environmental conflict – a city whose people have understood that, among other things, they have the right to enjoy a clean and safe environment, and a city that acted quickly through public opinion so that two of its most important political and social rights would be respected.

Even so, the organized community has new challenges to face. The new mayor has declared his opposition to the work and contributions of civil society organizations, including participation in the Cities for Life forum itself, where the Ilo municipality holds the vice-presidency. The mayor is also attempting to disregard the development management committees that were set up after the Ilo XXI Sustainable Development Plan. He does not promote participation, and avoids or evades social mobilization, trying to calm or neutralize it by offering unattainable prizes. He disregarded and fired the municipal executive teams, which had been trained for several years, substituting them with personnel with no training or experience. He will not coordinate or respect the autonomy of the social organizations. He maintains a discordant relationship with regional officials and with the media. Some civil society organizations in Ilo are initiating a legal process to request their right for new elections in order to oust this mayor.

Ilo's experience – with its creative contributions to public administration through building bridges between local government and the citizens, along with other local experiences and national networks such as the Cities for Life forum – contributed to transforming important national issues into legal mandates and local public policies, as noted below.

The first set of contributions involves promoting sustainable development – making it obligatory for local officials to promote participation in the government budget according to the agreed development plan and in other aspects of public administration; guaranteeing access to information; and, finally, creating and maintaining political features such as coordination, consultation, reaching agreement, evaluation and control, reporting and civilian oversight.

A second contribution is that the local government now has the authority to formulate plans for developing institutions and training personnel (including officials, employees and civil society leaders) to enable them to carry out their duties more efficiently, based on the principle of co-responsibility. What was optional has thus been transformed into a mandatory feature of public life, showing that decentralizing and modernizing the state can also be accomplished from the base or 'the bottom up'.

In this light, the essentials of the process unfolding in Ilo have been guaranteed. The current mayor will prove to be no more than an aberration. However, close study of these events should provide important lessons that will help to avoid future errors. This unique Ilo process, then, might be slowed down; but it cannot be stopped.

## FACTORS THAT FAVOUR THE PROCESS OF REACHING AGREEMENT

Seen as a whole, the political experience in Ilo, from the initial action to the process of reaching agreement, produced a wealth of knowledge. We learned about reality in depth; found innovative ideas and principles; experienced how organizations can play leading roles; witnessed how local government can operate based on the democratic exercise of power; and gained self-esteem. We saw citizens discover their potential in their growing capacity to understand and express communal problems and solutions (with communal work, as a basic expression of solidarity, comprising a feature of traditional Andean culture), and understood the limits of local development and the opportunities that it offers. All of this proved to be a strong stimulant for planning as a way of expressing the will of the people. Thus, a new tradition has been born.

These moving forces found expression in a variety of ways, as research has shown:

- In the political will of local authorities to assume the cost (and the benefit) of reaching agreement, in order to make management democratic and express the will of the people. This allowed the private sector and NGOs and community-based organizations (CBOs) to contribute with their own budgets to investing in the implementation of their sustainable development plan. It also underpinned the increasing allocation of the municipal investment budget to the participatory budgeting process – from 15 per cent in 2000, to 40 per cent in 2001, 60 per cent in 2002 and 80 per cent in 2003. In 2004, it is expected to be 100 per cent.
- In the shared vision of the future, respecting differences but producing goals and priorities expressed in plans. This process builds trust and cooperation.
- Leadership in the process of reaching agreement, in public and private organizations, with leaders who were able to gather people around. Their transparent and positive work also had an educational effect.
- Priority goals and actions materialized; projects were concluded with success.
- Channels for participation and reaching agreement were flexible and changed according to evolving circumstances.
- Management capacity evolved; this is also the basis for even greater future skills.
- Participation and the process of reaching agreement were institutionalized, with formal municipal norms and procedures, including access to public information.
- Exogenous parties played a dynamic role (e.g. a private initiative, a particular NGO, etc.).
- Local identity has developed apace; people increasingly feel that they belong to the society and the city of Ilo. For instance, seven out of ten Ilo citizens expressed their will to continue living in Ilo, compared to the 1980s, when most did not want to stay.

These factors have not been unconnected. Indeed, certain threads show that they are, in a general strategic way, part of a whole:

- the flexible construction of social issues, encouraging popular participation and organization, information and communication, with shared objectives;

- the construction of a local society which seeks to ensure that the production of local wealth benefits the city's population through fiscal policies and the reinvestment of company surpluses, and through instilling certain traits in the people of Ilo, such as hard work, solidarity, the capacity to make proposals and be proud, and the ability to have a shared collective project;
- the creation of local government, converting the precarious municipal authority that existed 20 years ago into an effective organ of local government, in close collaboration with community organizations.

## LIMITATIONS OF THE EXPERIENCE

Limitations included:

- the negative impact, on a number of levels, of the centralized state, which generates dependency and the petitioner mentality among local governments, hampering the possibility of independent administration (at present, the national government transfers less than 5 per cent of the national budget to the 2000 plus local governments);
- the municipality's initial lack of preparation in the political and administrative spheres with regard to participation and reaching agreement;
- the low status and unequal educational backgrounds of local actors, and the risk of personalizing processes;
- the precarious nature of economic resources to fund projects, along with the risk of disappointment when priority projects could not be paid for, and the slow pace of the initial improvements;
- the institutional weakness of the actors involved, and a certain dependency of social actors on strong groups because of their capacity to propose and fund projects;
- the self-exclusion of certain key actors, such as most people from business, and unevenness in the participation of the remaining actors because of the high social cost of participatory processes;
- the open and covert opposition of certain public-sector groups who take their political cues from national ministries, and political polarization in the run-up to elections; this was quite common during the Fujimori era.

# CONCLUSIONS

Reaching agreement requires a set of approaches and methodologies that enrich democracy and help to make public administration more efficient and effective. This also contributes to making citizens stronger, empowering them in the exercise of their rights and in participating in decision-making. Today, nearly 20 years after the local pioneering experiences, *concertación*, or reaching agreement, has been incorporated within public policy and the dialogue between the government, political parties and civil society. In examining the recent political history of Ilo, the principles, the innovative ideas, the approaches discussed above and, finally, the facts that we have presented must be all be considered.

# REFERENCES

Boon, R. G. J., Alexaki, N. and Becerra, H. (2001) 'The Ilo Clean Air Project: A local response to industrial pollution control in Peru', *Environment and Urbanization*, vol. 13, no. 2, pp215–232

Borja, Jordi (1995) Presentation at a seminar on 'Desarollo Urbano Afortunado: Propuesta de decálogo para uso de los gestores del desarrollo urbano' at el Instituto de Desarrollo Urbano de Bogotá, Colombia.

Díaz Palacios, J. (2000) *Manual de Planificación y Gestión de la Agenda 21 de las Ciudades*, Union Iberoamericana de Municipalistas (UIM), Peru

Díaz, D. B., López Follegatti, J. L. and Hordijk, M. (1996) 'Innovative urban environmental management in Ilo, Peru', *Environment and Urbanization*, vol. 8, no. 1, April, pp21–34

López Follegatti, J. L. (1999) 'Ilo: A city in transformation', *Environment and Urbanization*, vol. 11, no. 2, October, pp181–202

Miranda Sara, L. (1996) *Ciudades para la Vida: Experiencias Exitosas y Propuestas para la Acción (Cities for Living: Innovative Experiences and Proposals for Action)*, IPADEL-IHS-PROA-PGU/Naciones Unidas, Lima

Miranda Sara, L. and Hordijk, M. (1998) 'Let us build cities for life: The National Campaign of Local Agenda 21s in Peru', *Environment and Urbanization*, vol. 10, no. 2, October, pp69–102

# 12

# Conclusions

*Stephen Bass, Hannah Reid, David Satterthwaite and Paul Steele*

---

## CONTEXT: THE POLITICAL UNDERPINNINGS OF POVERTY AND ENVIRONMENTAL DEGRADATION

In this book, Chapters 2 to 11 propose lessons that may be drawn from their respective case studies. These are lessons that relate to their specific location and political and institutional context. For most, they include examples for the international agencies that were involved. But can general patterns also be drawn in order to enable governments, donors and non-governmental organizations (NGOs) to become more effective in their broader aspirations for poverty reduction and environmental management? Can the case studies reveal generic political and governance conditions for moving from the bottom left-hand box in Table 12.1 (poverty and natural resource degradation) to the top right-hand box (reducing poverty and improving natural resource management)?

**Table 12.1** *Different combinations with regard to poverty and environment*

| | |
|---|---|
| Natural resource management improved | Natural resource management improved |
| Poverty/environmental health burdens not reduced | Poverty/environmental health burdens reduced |
| Natural resource degradation | Natural resource degradation |
| Poverty and large environmental health burdens | Poverty/environmental health burdens reduced |

Any search for general lessons risks oversimplifying or misreading the case studies, or subordinating them to a neat but questionable theory of change. For instance, in many of the case studies, government decentralization and more democratic forms of local government were important for poverty reduction. However, in the case study in northern Nigeria (see Chapter 6), decentralization undermined traditional political systems that had served both farmers and pastoralists by guaranteeing local populations access to resources or to tenure. Generalizations may also be used by particular interest groups to provide an exaggerated or false legitimacy for claims or actions that may, in fact, go against poverty reduction or better environmental management (or both). The case studies from Nigeria and Tanzania (see Chapters 6 and 9) illustrate this: particular poor groups (pastoralists) were blamed for environmental degradation that they did not cause in order to justify external interventions. There is also a considerable body of literature stating or claiming causal linkages between poverty and environmental degradation that has been shown to be untrue or exaggerated, as well as a tendency for international agencies to use inaccurate 'crisis narratives' to legitimate their involvement (as discussed in, for instance, Roe, 1995; Leach and Mearns, 1996; McGranahan, 2002). Moreover, these crisis narratives tend to be perpetuated by the media (Leach and Mearns, 1996). There are potential traps here for donor agencies, as they continually seek narratives and other means to legitimate their work to the politicians who oversee them, and to the rich world voters whose support they require.

Nonetheless, with these warnings in mind, some consideration will be given to:

- how poor people were affected (positively and negatively) by the political change processes in the different cases studies,
- how environmental management benefited from pro-poor changes;
- which stakeholders supported pro-environment, pro-poor changes; and
- what tactics can be used to encourage more support for pro-poor environmental outcomes.

## Why it is hard to achieve pro-poor environmental outcomes

The case studies presented in this book illustrate three key issues that make it particularly difficult to achieve pro-poor environmental outcomes. These may be summarized as the costs imposed on poor people by private-sector drivers of growth; fast-changing dynamics of globalization; and government investments aimed at national benefits. We now examine these a little further.

*In most low-income and many middle-income nations, most potential for economic growth is linked to private-sector exploitation of natural resources.* This results in far more pressure on natural resources than in countries with strong and prosperous industrial and service bases, where growth is less dependent on their own natural resources. If there are many profitable opportunities for the private sector outside farming, fisheries, forestry and mineral exploitation, there tends to be less pressure on natural resources. This also means that opportunities for poverty reduction are not confined to natural resources, so the conflict between private sector-driven economic growth and a more equitable distribution of natural resources (for poverty reduction) is also reduced.

*One critical issue is how politics reacts when the environment is under stress.* In many of the case studies, natural resources are under great pressure because they provide the basis for most people's livelihoods, while also providing key opportunities for generating wealth and power. Where natural resources have such importance, there is usually a shift from administrative control to political control. For instance, in the East Africa case study (see Chapter 5), politicians turn natural resources into marketable commodities as a way of paying for political support.

*In most case studies, many key decisions regarding what resources are exploited, by whom and the form of that exploitation are political decisions, which are usually made independently from a concern for poverty reduction or for environmental management.* They are not driven by science in the sense of 'good natural resource management practice', nor are they driven by poorer groups' environmental problems (or interests). In circumstances where natural resources provide most poor groups' livelihoods and represent most available wealth, the need for inclusive and accountable political systems is obvious – to ensure that the poorest and least powerful groups have influence, and to ensure good practice in natural resource management.

*All of this is being increasingly affected by international dynamics.* External pressures are mounting on what might once have been isolated societies, populations, labour forces and governance structures. Such groups are increasingly subject to changes over which they have little or no control. Support from higher levels of government and international agencies for improving local living conditions, or for environmental management, is not guaranteed and can be compromised. The unfair trade policies through which rich nations protect their farmers and other producers may compromise what might once have been comparative advantages. For instance, the population in Laborie (or of Saint Lucia, in general) could not change the low prices on offer in the international market for their bananas. The coffee farmers in and around Manizales have to live with international prices for coffee that often fall to the point where the returns are very low. Level 4 in Diagram 1.1 (see Chapter 1) – international policies and institutions – is, in some ways, becoming a more powerful influence than the levels more proximate to the poor.

*Finally, several case studies show how the poor often bear the costs of investments aimed at (or justified as being for) national benefits.* There are several tensions between local needs and extra-local needs. Political systems need to broker these in ways that do not mean that powerful external groups benefit while local poor groups become marginalized or impoverished. In the northern Nigerian case study (see Chapter 6), the water needs of the residents and businesses in the city of Kano (located outside the case study area) are a legitimate need which deserves to be considered, but not by measures that have such disastrous impacts on the livelihoods of so many people. The need for hydro-electricity to support Tanzania's development is not in doubt (see Chapter 9); but did it require the impoverishment of so many in the case study region? If environmental problems attract political attention, they are not usually the problems that most concern poor groups. For instance in Usangu, it was water shortages that limited the capacity of a hydro-electric dam (leading to national electricity rationing) and threatened a national park (a key part of tourism revenues) to which national politics reacted. The responses reflected the concerns of middle- and upper-income groups, most of whom lived outside Usangu. Developing a stronger and more prosperous economic base for Kenya may well require titanium mining; but as Chapter 5 on East Africa questions, why with so few local benefits? The need for measures to protect wildlife and forests is not in dispute; but do these have to be done in ways that emphasize global bio-quality (e.g. rare species) and that marginalize or impoverish poor groups and their interests in local bio-quality (e.g. provision of diverse foods and 'insurance' against famine)? Central governments (and central government politicians) inevitably want to limit the powers and scope for action of local governments and local citizen bodies to control any activities that the former deem to be in the national interest, even while they decentralize responsibilities to local bodies without the resources and revenue-raising powers to meet them.

## Environment as an avenue for promoting political change

If the case studies show that 'improved governance' can produce better environmental management, can better environmental management be a way to improve governance? In some case studies, 'better environmental governance' helped to push broader improve-ments in local governance and progressive political change (e.g. in Pakistan, Saint Lucia, India, China, Peru and Colombia). The case study in Laborie (see Chapter 7) revealed the value of new forms of local governance, participation and communication channels for involving people in development. Good local governance for the environment was shown to be a key part of empowerment, rights, democracy and participation, as well as being important for practical issues of efficiency and effectiveness in delivering goods and services to people and communities. The stronger local village organizations in the China and Pakistan case studies (see Chapters 4 and 2) are emerging as important players for building formal local governance capacity. In northern Pakistan, members of the legislative council are increasingly sourced from leadership developed through the Aga Khan Rural Support Programme (AKRSP)-supported village organizations – including village forest and livestock specialists. The Pakistan government's first step towards decentralization of power in northern Pakistan is being undertaken with the help of AKRSP.

The rise of environmental rights in the constitutional processes in East Africa has led to many public-interest legal cases that have much wider implications for accountability and transparency of government.

In Pune, India, the involvement of NGOs in toilet construction was conducted in an unusually transparent manner – all aspects of costing and of financing were publicly available – and the access that community organizers had to senior officials also kept in check the petty corruption that characterizes so many communities' relationships with local government agencies (see Chapter 10). Furthermore, it helped to bring about a positive configuration of the relationship between the city government, NGOs and residents. The city government recognized the capacity of community organizations to develop their own solutions when supported by local NGOs. In this way, environmental issues can be said to have opened up space for greater participation and engagement by civil society.

## THE IMPACTS OF POLITICS ON POVERTY AND THE ENVIRONMENT

This section reviews the poverty-reducing and environmental benefits from certain political changes, and if both can be improved together – or if there are trade-offs.

# Benefits gained by poor people from the political change processes

One key justification for the much expanded definition of poverty used in this book is the reminder that it offers of the many different entry points through which poverty can be reduced. Poverty defined and measured only in terms of private income or consumption tends to mean that only measures to increase income or consumption are considered poverty reducing.

Chapter 1 listed eight aspects of poverty (see Box 1.1). Here, we consider which aspects were addressed by the different case studies, grouping them into:

- increasing poorer groups' incomes or asset bases;
- providing or improving infrastructure and services;
- securing safety nets;
- increasing the 'voice' of poor groups; and
- improving benefits for women.

## Increasing income and asset bases

Increasing poorer groups' incomes and/or asset bases provides perhaps the most direct means of poverty reduction, as well as opening up the means by which further aspects of deprivation can be addressed. For instance, higher incomes permit more necessities to be afforded (e.g. food, safe water, medicines, healthcare and keeping children in school). Increased incomes depend largely upon whatever employment is generated by private-sector investment locally and whatever demand exists for goods or services that can be produced locally. Governments and international agencies can aim to reduce poverty by creating new income-earning opportunities. However, except for public works programmes, the scope for doing so is always defined or limited by whether there is comparative advantage for new or expanded private-sector investment. In the Pakistan case study (see Chapter 2), AKRSP emphasized the role of the local private sector in building up comparative advantage for temperate crops, and removing infrastructure and knowledge constraints for growing and marketing these crops.

The South African case study (see Chapter 8) is the only one that centred on a public works programme. In this, government funding was used to tackle an environmental management problem (the removal of invasive plants to improve water management). It was organized in such a way that it provided incomes for low-income groups. The programme

285

reveals the potential of combining an interest in better natural resource management with job creation in order to bring immediate local benefits for poorer groups and large, economy-wide benefits for South Africa. However, such programmes will always be limited by the availability of government funding, and by government preparedness to structure programmes so that employment benefits reach low-income groups. The programme's longer-term impact on poverty will also depend upon whether the employment helps those who took part to develop knowledge, skills or contacts that are useful in enhancing their livelihoods, after income from the public works programme ceases.

The two other obvious ways through which poorer groups' incomes can be increased or their asset bases expanded is through making productive land or new resources available to them or supporting them to make more productive use of the resources to which they already have access. This may require changes in their tenure, or formal recognition of informal resource-using rights. Several case studies (particularly those from Tanzania and Nigeria) show how protecting poorer groups' access to the resources they already use is a critical part of avoiding poverty creation.

There are strong political barriers to increasing poorer groups' access to resources. During the 1950s, land reform or agrarian reform was rightly among the most widely discussed development topics, arising from the observation that most poverty was caused or underpinned by inequitable landowning structures and exploitative landlord-tenant relationships. This remains valid for most of the case study regions. With hindsight, the hopes of international agencies for pro-poor agrarian reform can be seen as naive; how could international agencies work through existing government structures to implement structural reforms that went against the interests of the most powerful political groups? The interest in what international agencies can do to increase poorer groups' access to resources has since moved on to measures that are more politically feasible. These are largely based on enabling wider participation.

The case study in Laborie (Saint Lucia) in Chapter 7 is interesting in this regard. Its poverty-reducing measures depended upon the availability of resources that were not controlled by powerful owners (in this instance, marine resources) and the availability of publicly owned or managed resources that could be used directly by poor people (e.g. beaches, bays and reefs). This suggests an important question that all donor-funded initiatives should ask: what resources or powers do local governments (or other government agencies) have that can contribute to increasing the income-earning asset base of poorer groups? In Ilo, Peru (see Chapter 11), the government contributed to many low-income households' asset bases by providing them with a secure land plot on which they could build their homes.

## Providing or improving infrastructure and services

A key part of pro-poor environmental improvement is ensuring that poorer groups have access to the infrastructure and services which greatly reduce either environmental health risks (e.g. through safe and sufficient water, good provision for sanitation and drainage, and better-quality housing) or the health impact of these risks (e.g. through good healthcare, including disease and injury prevention, emergency services to respond to acute illness or injury, and safety nets to maintain household consumption when coping with sick or injured members). These aspects of pro-poor environmental improvements tend to be overlooked because 'environmental management' is too often equated with natural resource management and not with environmental health improvement – in spite of the long-established recognition that both are central to 'the environment' side of environment and development (WCED, 1987; WHO, 1992).

Environmental health infrastructure tends to get more attention in urban areas. This may be because 'the problem' is more visible and concentrated, affecting powerful groups as well as the poor. Greater possibilities also exist for urban poor groups lacking infrastructure and services to organize themselves and make demands. Large and concentrated populations also provide economies of scale and proximity for improved infrastructure provision. In three of the case studies, all of them urban, local government played a key role in providing improved water and sanitation.

In Manizales, Colombia (see Chapter 3), this took a 'conventional' form, planned and managed by the city government (run by an elected council) and funded by a local tax base. What makes it unconventional in relation to most other urban centres in low- and middle-income nations is that improved water and sanitation provision actually reached most of the population. Manizales is also unusual in the form and extent to which environmental planning and management occurs. The case in Ilo, Peru, was also more 'conventional' in the sense that it was planned and managed by an elected city government. However, it was unusual on two counts: the proportion of the total population reached, and the means by which most were reached (partnerships between city government and neighbourhood resident committees). In Mumbai and the other cities in India where public toilet programmes were implemented, the programmes were only 'conventional' in that municipal councils supported and helped to finance them. Their innovation lay in the fact that these public toilets were designed, constructed and managed by representative organizations formed by the urban poor and supported by a local NGO. The significance of the community toilets case study lies in how the provision of support to urban poor organizations resulted in a much more effective use of public funding. The community-designed, constructed and managed toilet blocks cost less than the earlier blocks that had been designed by the government and constructed by contractors. But they were better designed, had many desirable characteristics and features that the contractor-built toilets lacked (e.g. special provision for children's toilets, better provision for ensuring water availability, more privacy and convenience for women, and community meeting rooms), as well as making provision for good maintenance (both in institutional and in funding terms) and improved skills and employment through close community involvement. It is clear that the approach also brought political benefits to all those who supported them.

Many rural settlements also concentrate people in ways that can lower the unit costs of providing improved infrastructure and services. Indeed, in many nations, the criteria for defining when a settlement becomes 'urban' are set so high that a significant part of the rural population are deemed to live in 'large villages' with several thousand inhabitants, where there are also economies of scale and proximity for many forms of infrastructure and services.[1] Improving infrastructure itself may also offer one of the main means to support expansion and diversification of local economies, including improved access to external markets. The possibilities for improving infrastructure and services in rural areas are also increased where there are village or community organizations which can organize these key activities – as in the case studies in China and Pakistan.

## Securing safety nets

One key dimension of poverty is a lack of assets that can be called upon, if needed, as a 'safety net'. Chapter 1 noted that safety nets ensure that poor individuals or households can maintain basic consumption when income falls or crops fail, and also ensure access to housing, healthcare, schools and other essential services when these can no longer be paid for. Safety nets are accepted as a necessary part of government provision in high-income nations. The need for comparable safety nets in low- and middle-income nations has been recognized for some years (see, for instance, World Bank, 1990), although so, too, are the difficulties in organizing and funding them (government structures are rarely able to organize and manage them effectively). In addition, a tendency remains for donor agencies to see their role as primarily providing capital for 'productive' investment and not funding for the recurrent expenditures of social programmes or safety nets; doing so, however, excludes those very poor people who themselves may be excluded by the economic growth process.

The public works programme in South Africa (Chapter 8) in part functioned as a 'safety net' programme, providing incomes for many very low-income households. The case study from China (Chapter 4) noted the removal or reduction of government safety nets in terms of government-provided social services, unemployment benefits, pensions and the 'iron rice bowl'. Civil society organizations were meant to fill this gap. Improving local governance for environmental management, through support for community-based organizations and associations, can also strengthen local safety nets. In the case study in Pakistan (Chapter 2), this took the form of external support by AKRSP for the formation of village organizations which were built on an old tradition of self-help and cooperation, with every household being fully involved. In the case study from India (Chapter 10), the two community organizations (the cooperatives of women slum and pavement dwellers – *Mahila Milan* – and the National Slum Dwellers Federation) have, at their foundation, community-organized and managed savings groups. These also serve as safety nets by providing emergency credit and support to help particular individuals or households to cope with shocks.[2]

Many poorer groups in several of the case studies relied on being able to access particular natural resources as their safety nets, very often drawing from land, forests or fisheries to which they had no formal rights. For instance, in Usangu (see Chapter 9), wild resources (e.g. fruits, fish and wild meat, and wood and thatch for sale) provide an important safety net for the most vulnerable in times of hardship. The coastal areas of Saint Lucia have provided safety nets for the landless for many years (see Chapter 7). Moves to improve environmental management need to understand how such informal safety nets function; but often they do not do so, as management systems come to be imposed in ways that exclude poorer groups from resources, including those that function as safety nets.

## Increasing 'voice'

Chapter 1 noted the importance for poverty reduction of reducing poorer groups' voicelessness and powerlessness within national political systems and bureaucratic structures. The case studies illustrate this. But they also highlight the critical step of reducing the voicelessness and powerlessness of particular poor groups within their own localities (districts and villages), local governments and community organizations. In some case studies, this was done through representative governance structures. For instance, in Manizales and Ilo, it occurred through elected local authorities, with many measures by local governments to increase their own accountability.

In other cases, community-based organizations played key roles. In China, households created and operated organizations to help them deal with environmental problems. Water users associations promoted pro-poor management and, under the 1987 law, enabled villagers to elect committees as self-governing local organizations and village assemblies. Despite the flaws described in the case study on China, these committees and assemblies actively pursued villagers' interests, undertaking direct action and negotiating with higher levels of government. The Chinese government tried to restrict participation to the instrumental level, channelling the actions of village committees into strictly apolitical developmental areas to ensure that the committees did not concern themselves with sensitive political issues (although, as the case study noted, this may not have been effective). In India, 'voices increased' when representative organizations formed by poor people were permitted to organize themselves, make proposals and secure official support. In Pakistan, external support for the formation of village organizations and the training of village specialists was instrumental in negotiating a range of government, NGO and private-sector support for local development. Indeed, many AKRSP village organization members now form the newly elected politicians in a region to which representative democracy has been introduced – politicians with a strong understanding of poverty-environment links.

In some case studies, the interests of large sections of the poor were not addressed – for instance, in Usangu, Tanzania, and in northern Nigeria. Here, extra-local agencies had the dominant role in determining 'development' paths (each with their own particular set of priorities), and many or most local resource users had little influence. In both case studies, the apparent needs of irrigation and conservation were used to justify external interventions, blaming certain poor groups for environmental degradation that they did not cause. Again, in both, expanding irrigation and water management served external interests, but not those of the pastoralists, farmers and fishers. The realities of poverty within each locality were lost in decisions made by external agencies. Indeed, in northern Nigeria, external interventions not only failed to address poverty, but further impoverished many farmers and pastoralists.

## Improving benefits for women

In some of the case studies, specific measures were taken to increase benefits for women, or to improve the means by which women could influence projects. In the Pakistan case study, the AKRSP created separate women's organizations in order to ensure their needs and priorities were met. These organizations were linked to mainstream development opportunities (to avoid inadvertent marginalization of women). In the Indian case study, the community organizations formed by the poor to set up and manage toilets had a predominance of female members and elected leaders. Here, too, separate women's organiz-ations (such as *Mahila Milan*) had been established to work in partnership with slum dwellers' federations (most of whose members were men).

In the Work for Water Programme in South Africa, the public works programme sought to ensure that women and single-headed households benefited. Fifty-four per cent of the field workers receiving an income were women. Provisions were also made for childcare (without which many women would have been unable to work) and for reproductive healthcare.

In the projects reviewed by Chapter 4 on China, women in project areas continue to be disadvantaged in areas where improvements could have been facilitated through environmental interventions. Women have important roles in, for instance, livestock training, village meetings and project design; but these roles were not recognized by project manage-ment. No one had seriously assessed their needs or enhanced their participation within projects, and the impacts of projects on gender inequality were not monitored in any meaningful way. The case study noted that taking gender issues more seriously would have improved both the efficiency of projects and their reach by increasing the participation of women. It concluded there was a need to:

- fund women's development and capacity-building to enable greater participation in decisions over natural resource management;
- provide micro-credit for women's groups;
- include local branches of the women's federation in projects; and
- promote and establish a leading role for women in project monitor-ing.

## Did the environment benefit from poverty reduction or were there trade-offs?

The two goals – reducing poverty and improving environmental management – are too frequently approached as though they are in opposition to each other. The case studies suggest that any difficulties in achieving complementarities between environmental management and poverty reduction, or in reducing the conflicts between them, are less about technical issues specific to the locality, and more to do with reconciling the different (narrow) agendas of the different actors. This is well illustrated by the Usangu case study in Chapter 9. Here, the problem was not in developing a technical water management system in which multiple uses could be served, but in the difficulty posed by many powerful players having their own very specific agendas and by political systems marginalizing poorer groups' interests. The Ministry of Agriculture focused on food production and irrigation, and did not want to have irrigation identified as one of the reasons for water shortages downstream. The Ministry of Water focused on engineering solutions in order to increase water supply. The international NGO focused on natural resource conservation. And donor agencies wanted 'quick spend' and quick technical solutions. Similarly, in the case study in northern Nigeria (Chapter 6), the conflicts over resources, the unintended and damaging ecological consequences (i.e. invasion of *typha* grass) and the impoverishment of so many local inhabitants do not seem related to any limited quantity of resources, but to the way in which the resources were used or appropriated by certain players.

Although urban development is often seen as contradictory to good environmental management, the case studies from Ilo and Manizales (Chapters 11 and 3) suggest that any contradictions can, at least, be much reduced; the key requirement is good local governance that is both influenced by poorer (rural and urban) groups and informed by environmental limitations.

The South African case study (Chapter 8) highlighted one important point with regard to complementarity: benefits and costs may operate at different scales. Here, it was difficult to reconcile a focus on the locations where the invasive species needed clearing with the locations where poverty reduction was most needed (or where politicians wanted the Working for Water programme to focus). Good governance should accommodate the different scales at which costs and benefits accrue, and ensure that environmental costs are incorporated within cost-benefit analyses and decision-making. It will inevitably fall to governments to ensure that there is a framework for limiting the transfer of projects' environmental costs to the future, or to other ecosystems or people – especially those who lack the voice to oppose this transfer.

Effective local governance systems, in which lower-income groups have adequate influence, are not likely to be 'anti-private sector', where poverty reduction is served by new investments and employment possibilities. However, giving lower-income groups more influence may, in some instances, have 'anti-environment' impacts, where some poorer groups see 'pro-growth' politicians as better serving their interests. The key to getting a good balance is local democratic processes that are better informed about poverty-environment linkages. Good local governance will exercise checks on the private sector's ability to control resources, to externalize costs and to abuse labour.

There is one major, potential trade-off between poverty reduction and environmental management – the fact that many aspects of poverty reduction depend upon increased resource use and consumption (and, perhaps, increased waste flows). However, there is no evidence from any of the case studies that the resource demands required to eliminate poverty would necessarily threaten good environmental management. The case study of Manizales is also interesting in this regard, as all of the pro-poor measures were developed within a local Bioplan for good environmental management. AKRSP reveals that much of the pro-poor development work is associated with the creation of new environmental wealth (e.g. plantations and orchards in previously barren soil), rather than the democratization of environmental destruction that might have been expected by the cynical observer.

# HOW POLITICAL CHANGES HAVE ACHIEVED PRO-POOR ENVIRONMENTAL OUTCOMES

## Individuals were key champions

The case studies tell us about powerful individuals who promoted good policies:

- The South African minister ensured that the Working for Water programme served both environmental management and employment creation.
- The city administrator in Pune, India, helped to open up possibilities for community-managed toilet blocks.
- Various mayors in Manizales, Colombia, promoted and implemented the Bioplan.

- Various mayors in Ilo, Peru, supported the city's 'pro-poor, pro-environment' measures.
- The AKRSP general manager in Pakistan was vital in ensuring progress in local and national political change.

In addition to these authority figures, in several of the cases, certain individuals working in local NGOs or universities (and, in India, in the urban-poor organizations and federations) had key roles. But it is easy to assume that it is outstanding individuals who are a key part of forcing change for the good, when this may underplay the extent to which the broader social or political circumstances allowed (or did not allow) such individuals to become influential. Democratic pressures have been particularly important. In South Africa, establishing the first democratic government allowed real discussions about the government's role in poverty reduction; in Manizales and Ilo, decentralization reforms and the move to elected mayors (underpinned in Colombia by important changes to the constitution) were key; in India, representative and accountable organizations formed by (women and men) 'slum' and pavement dwellers demonstrated their capacity to design and implement toilet blocks, while local governments permitted them to act. Perhaps this is a more important theme – the extent to which appropriate political structures and reforms give rise to innovation and leadership at all levels – to 'champions' and to checks and controls on anti-poor or anti-environment 'leadership'.

## Poor people as champions of environmental management?

It is too easy for governments and international agencies to view poor groups as the object of their initiatives for poverty reduction and/or environmental management. It is more important to understand what poor people can do themselves if provided with the opportunities. Poor people's own knowledge and perspectives often highlight useful entry points for change. Several case studies point to the tremendous innovation that poor individuals, households or groups can mobilize for poverty reduction and/or environmental improvement in low-productivity or disequilibrium environments:

- in Pakistan, the irrigation channels, reforestation and terracing created by local groups, and the store of indigenous technical knowledge that they have in terms of medicinal plants, water harvesting structures, game trails, non-timber forest products and seed selection;

- in China, the many innovations made by village committees, including developing village codes and charters that detail the rights and responsibilities of villagers and their leaders, which were used to settle water and irrigation disputes and curb illegal tree-cutting, as well as the important role of water-user associations;
- in the cities in India, the innovations and cost-efficiency of the public toilets designed, built and managed by community organizations;
- in Ilo and Manizales, the many initiatives undertaken by neighbourhood or community associations, supported by the municipal government.

There is also the issue of whether poverty (or poor groups) causes environmental degradation. Certain poor groups are often highly visible in degraded environments, sometimes because they were forced onto marginal lands with lower environmental capabilities due to aggressive control by richer groups over all other resources. Powerful economic and political interests have long 'blamed the poor' for their poverty since this is a convenient way of diverting attention from their own role in creating or exacerbating poverty. For those with power, it is also a convenient way to legitimate limiting government anti-poverty measures (and, thus, the taxes such measures would need to draw upon), and to ensure that such measures focus on control.

The most extreme manifestations of blaming the poor for their poverty are, perhaps, mostly historical, although this is a trend that still has importance since government bodies and international agencies still see 'the poor' as a relatively passive 'target group' for whom their policies and projects must be planned. Blaming the poor for environmental degradation has a less pronounced history but remains a common (and influential) trend, especially among certain conservation agencies. This has links with Malthusian worries about population growth and the 'tragedy of the commons' theme (Hardin, 1968). Again, this trend is too convenient for powerful groups as it absolves them of responsibility and obscures what is, frequently, their primary role in environmental degradation. Many aspects of environmental degradation are, in fact, directly linked to extreme wealth and opportunity (the opposite of poverty). High-income levels and the consumption patterns that they permit are associated with the most serious waste generation and greenhouse gas emission implications (Redclift, 1996; Hardoy et al, 1992, 2001).

In Laborie, Saint Lucia, poorer groups were falsely blamed for water pollution. In Usangu, Tanzania, the poor were blamed for environmental degradation that they did not cause. Here, the 'diagnosis' of what was wrong was influenced by groups whose vested interests were served by this incorrect diagnosis. As a result, they marginalized issues of poverty and environment even while using them as guises for action. National, local and international actors have often oversimplified complex situations, leading to inappropriate actions that have had, and will continue to have, negative effects on local livelihoods for poorer groups and on the environment.

In global or national terms, it is always nonsense to attribute most natural resource degradation (such as soil erosion, salinization of land from irrigation, deforestation, over-fishing, overuse of freshwater, and pollution of land and water) to 'the poor'. This is because, in most instances and locations, the poor's poverty is the result of having so little access to soil, water, forests and fisheries. How can 'the poor' be responsible for most soil degradation and deforestation in a continent or nation when they only have access to a few per cent of all farming land and are kept out of most forests (Satterthwaite, 1998; IIED et al, 1999). In many locations, the landless are among the poorest people and clearly cannot have much role in soil degradation.[3] This point may seem obvious; but it is one that is constantly overlooked in discourses about poverty and the environment.

The case studies include examples that demonstrate the lack of association between poverty and environmental degradation, and the clearer association with wealth. In the Pakistan case study, it was comparatively wealthy farmers with larger land holdings who had prominent roles in large-scale land clearing, overuse of chemicals and pesticides, or groundwater over-harvesting. It was also pastoralists with large herds who were more likely to overgraze. The AKRSP experience showed that improving poor people's access to, and control over, natural resources upon which they depend provided powerful incentives for them to manage these resources well, as demonstrated by the village conservation committees for the protection of forests and wildlife. In Ilo, Peru, it was the company managing the copper mining and smelting that was the main cause of environmental degradation (high levels of air pollution, and solid and liquid wastes damaging coastal resources), with citizen pressure being the main means by which these problems were addressed. Where there were particular instances of poorer groups overusing resources, it was often because they were worried that their rights to these resources might be revoked. Other authors have shown that confinement to resource-poor areas does not always lead to increased environmental degradation, but may give rise to prudent natural resource management (Leach and Mearns, 1996; see also Tiffen and Mortimore, 1992).

## Local governments and authorities invariably play key roles

Decentralization (allowing government decisions and programmes to be more rooted in local contexts) and strong local democracy (allowing democratic pressure to hold local governments accountable by influencing such decisions and programmes) might well be expected to encourage pro-poor outcomes and pro-environment outcomes with local benefits.[4] Most case studies demonstrate this well, especially in Ilo (Peru), Manizales (Colombia), the cities in India with community sanitation blocks and Laborie (Saint Lucia). In China and Pakistan, the broad scope of the work undertaken by local elected village bodies is, in effect, decentralization outside formal government structures (although, as the Pakistan case shows, this also helped to build the competence and capacity of formal government structures). The cases also illustrate a role in which local authorities have particular potential: seeking better links between the investments and actions of all of the different groups within their jurisdiction. Companies, institutions, groups and individuals all have particular sectoral interests. Local governance structures should encourage investment while ensuring that it does not generate costs for other groups, or pre-empt local resources that other groups may need.

## National governments lay the foundations

While local government is a key driver for pro-poor, pro-environment change, this can be undermined by the actions and policies of higher levels of government – for instance, by macro-economic policies and national-level funding allocations. Local government in Manizales can do nothing to lessen the civil conflicts in Colombia, which have resulted in a large flow of poor migrants into Manizales. The local government in Ilo has long fought to reduce the very high levels of pollution generated by the local copper industry, but with little success because of limited support from national government (which has the power to stop this pollution). The study of the changing roles of environmental management institutions in East Africa reveals the challenges of linking both the poverty and environment agendas and the actors behind them. Among the positive changes noted are:

- acceptance of the human right to a clean and healthy environment;
- the reforms in forestry, tourism, wildlife and fisheries towards better management, recognizing limited government capacity and attempting to involve the private sector in this management;

- poverty reduction strategy papers providing a high-profile means of reviewing the policy framework through a poverty 'lens' and, consequently, making the conventional 'conservation' environmental management institutions think about poverty;
- the reorganization of environmental management institutions to include the apex institutions for improved coordination with other sectors.

Among the negative aspects are:

- little evidence of effective integration of the 'brown' agenda (with its primary concern for environmental health) with the 'green' agenda (with its primary concern for sustainable natural resource management);
- few mechanisms for effective genuine participation (confirmed by the Usangu case study in Chapter 9);
- lack of information for citizens on key decisions (also evident in Usangu);
- lack of legal redress for the poor (also evident in the northern Nigeria case study in Chapter 6).

Several case studies point to inappropriate government policies as a key factor in natural resource degradation. For example, the poorly planned and managed irrigation in northern Nigeria, the concessions that allow indiscriminate logging in East Africa (Chapter 5) and the Pakistani government's acceleration of natural resource degradation by taking over the management of forests and pasture without real management capacity or accountability (Chapter 2).

## The private sector is a powerful engine of growth . . .

In virtually all countries, governments now encourage the role of the 'formal' private sector in investing in, developing and/or managing public resources. Natural resource and environmental management is increasingly in the hands of the private sector, including foreign or multinational companies. This often involves private enterprises taking over farms, plantations, forests or mineral resource exploitation that were previously government managed. For instance, in every one of the 23 countries studied by Landell-Mills and Ford (1999), private sector involvement was on the increase in the forest sector – from owning forests, to managing environmental services. In no country was nationalization taking place. In infrastructure and service provision, too, the private sector often takes over from government entities – for instance, in providing water and sanitation, electricity, public transport or telecommunications.

## ... but strong accountable local and national governance is needed to ensure it operates towards pro-poor ends

Much government management of natural resource exploitation or marketing is characterized by the high costs of inefficiency, corruption and anti-poor orientation. The critical role of private investment is not in doubt – but what several case studies illustrate are the dangers of a pro-private sector orientation for the environment and for the poor, unless the government (at local and national level) acts as it should to safeguard the environment and the needs and rights of its citizens. In most of the case studies, local governments have proved to be too weak or too unrepresentative to act on behalf of those whose livelihoods are threatened by private-sector investments. In addition, national environmental agencies are also too weak in their links to sources of power and in their capacities to act effectively. There is hope that providing greater scope for private-sector investments will increase total investment flows; but this has not happened in all sectors.[5]

In several of the case studies, government systems have not acted effectively, with the result that private-sector enterprises have too much power and the public has too little control over their operations. Chapter 5 on East Africa pointed to three examples:

1 titanium mining in Kenya, where a Canadian company received a concession which is expected to generate US$50 million to $60 million in foreign exchange a year, but at the cost of up to 10,000 peasant farmers' livelihoods;
2 the National Environmental Management Authority in Uganda, which is under strong political pressure to make decisions in favour of investments such as hydropower and vegetable oil production that may undermine both its autonomy and the public's faith in it as an independent regulatory institution;
3 the Butamira forest reserve in Uganda, which is threatened by the Kakira sugar works and a permit to allow the reserve to be used for 'general purposes' – the change of use to a plantation has meant that local inhabitants are denied fuelwood and other products; no environmental impact assessment has been undertaken, and leaders of pressure groups questioning this development have been harassed.

The Ilo case study in Peru (Chapter 11) points to the political and economic power of the internationally owned copper industry, allowing it to generate very high levels of pollution and waste, which local government has been unable to halt. In part, this was because of limited support for such pollution control from national government. This is a reminder that the issue is not necessarily about 'environmental governance' in the sense of having more effective and accountable environmental ministries and agencies, but about broader 'governance' because most of the key decisions concerning the environment – or that impact upon the environment – are made outside of these institutions.

## Local civil society organizations can have influential roles

Local NGOs have had influential roles in too few of the case studies to allow any general commentary – or perhaps in some they had roles that were not highlighted by the case studies. However, it is worth noting the important positive role played by local NGOs in two case studies: Labor in Ilo (whose main role was supporting local government) and the Society for the Promotion of Area Resource Centres (SPARC) in Mumbai (whose main role was working with the organizations formed by the urban poor). SPARC is also notable in that it actively seeks to avoid taking on any roles that community-based organizations formed by urban poor groups can and should do themselves (Patel and Mitlin, 2004).

The case study on East Africa noted the growing importance of public-interest civil society organizations in Kenya, Uganda and Tanzania, which operated with an environmental lens. These have particular significance where government is weak, as they try to fill the accountability vacuum left by the lack of effective and autonomous environmental institutions able to regulate the private sector. Of course, there is a need to ensure that all such NGOs are in dialogue with the groups whose rights they seek to strengthen – something that certainly is not guaranteed – and that their actions, fundraising and funding allocations are accountable to these groups (also not guaranteed).

## External drivers (donor agencies and international NGOs) need local roots

The case studies pointed to different ways in which donor agencies supported, encouraged or permitted local pro-poor orientations within a focus on environmental management, or, alternatively, good environmental practice within a focus on development. For instance, the Aga

Khan Rural Support Programme recognized the need to work with, and through, local representative organizations within villages, and the value of linking up with the World Conservation Union (IUCN) in order to improve the attention given to biodiversity management by and for poor groups.

In some cases, external funders recognized the need to support locally developed initiatives and processes. In others, they did not, and where they did not, this was for a range of reasons: in some instances, a lack of understanding in part due to poor local data; in others, an agenda that was too narrow; in yet others, a set of priorities that went against the needs of local poor groups and/or good environmental management. Since official donor agencies work primarily through national governments, and support projects or interventions largely negotiated with national agencies, there are obvious needs for checks to ensure that such initiatives bring benefits to those living in the localities where they are implemented. It is important to counter the general tendency for donors to base their projects on assumptions about the problem to be addressed and the approach to be taken to address it (Leach and Mearns, 1996). One way to avoid this is by working with and through local institutions that are accountable not only upwards (to those who fund them), but also downwards (to local populations and the different groups within them).

## Tactics for external agencies in influencing political change to promote pro-poor, pro-environment outcomes

The case studies reveal real practical ways of overcoming resistance to pro-poor reforms and of tackling environmental opportunities and threats within those reform processes. While we cannot offer a definitive set of 'principles' from the case studies, we can highlight some actions – or tactics – that seem to have proven effective in promoting pro-poor, pro-environment outcomes. These may serve to reduce the sometimes lengthy lists often advocated for reform and, thus, help to identify elements of 'good-enough governance' (Grindle, 2002). These tactics are recommended for any 'external' agency – whether it is a national government, international donor or NGO – who wants to support change. However, as the case studies have shown, the ability of such external agencies to really bring about change is often constrained – and, at its worst, can undermine local efforts to promote change. Therefore, external interventions should be cautious and not over-ambitious. The tactics have been organized into three categories:

1   promising areas for promoting pro-poor political change;
2   promising tactics and methods in supporting pro-poor political change;
3   important internal changes required within external agencies.

## Promising areas for promoting pro-poor political change

### Institutionalize pro-poor structures

One indication from the case studies is that if local institutions are representative of those in the locality suffering from poverty, and are empowered to act, pro-poor environmental outcomes become more likely. The case studies showed that where governments, donors and NGOs have really helped to address poverty and improve environmental management, this has, in large part, been a result of their working with local institutions which:

- are accountable to, and work with, low-income groups;
- have the capacity to change approaches or priorities as needed;
- ensure that there are local feedback loops that inform them about necessary changes as interventions develop (including those coming from local populations, especially the poorer and less politically powerful groups);
- are legitimate for the majority of their constituents;
- ensure a clear division of responsibilities and can effectively resolve local conflicts in ways that are pro-poor.

In Pakistan, new village structures based on equitable household membership are now being embedded in local government, while in Peru, popular support ensured that such structures continued even with a change of government that supported them less.

### Support governance systems that allow leaders to emerge

Supporting key powerful individuals can make a difference. The influence of key individuals such as the minister of water affairs in South Africa, various mayors in Ilo and Manizales, NGO and community organization staff in India, and the AKRSP general manager in Pakistan, was noted earlier. But overdependence on single drivers carries risks. For example, there are concerns that the Uganda National Environmental Management Authority is overly dependent upon donor support. The key point is not the identification of key 'leaders' and their support, but supporting democratic and participatory governance systems that allow political and civil society leaders to emerge, to be effective and to be accountable. Within this, the importance of ensuring that women can take on leadership roles should be emphasized. This is also relevant for other groups facing discrimination or particularly difficult circumstances. Part of good governance is providing more possibilities for innovation and leadership at all levels.

## Prioritize the empowerment of women

The empowerment of women was critical to both poverty reduction and environmental management in almost all case studies. Clearly, the most effective way of addressing women's issues is to ensure that there is provision for women to articulate their needs and priorities and to get these addressed – as demonstrated in the India and Pakistan case studies. Where women are responsible for many environmental resources, this is doubly relevant. There are also obvious requirements to ensure external interventions understand and address women's practical and strategic needs (Moser, 1993), to ensure women are included in initiatives, and to remove the constraints that discriminate against women's access to resources and assets and other aspects of development. The means by which this is best achieved will be particular to each location and society. However, the recommendations of the China case study in Chapter 4 are of relevance elsewhere:

- Fund women's development and capacity-building to enable greater participation in decisions over natural resource management.
- Provide micro-credit for women's groups, and give them more control over provisions.
- Include local branches of women's federations in projects.
- Promote and establish a leading role for women in project monitoring.

## Invest in good-quality, locally rooted information

The case studies highlight the importance of a good-quality, locally rooted information system that allows better decisions to be made from a technical point of view, ensures that poorer groups' perspectives are represented and makes relevant information available to all stakeholders. In some cases, it is the lack of such an information system that helps to explain anti-poor outcomes (for instance, in Usangu, initially). In others, the environmental information system helped to underpin more pro-poor decisions – for example, in Manizales, where in each district environmental resource centres were located and 'environmental indicators' were reported to the public, thus mapping progress towards better quality environments. Several other case studies point to how false, misleading or incomplete information (or information only held and available to those in government) led to inappropriate diagnoses. They also show how better information changed diagnoses of who was responsible for environmental degradation. The case of Usangu revealed how a new project to promote sustainable management of the wetland and catchment area produced a more accurate diagnosis; but this was not well received because its findings were inconvenient to powerful interests. This diagnosis could also be dismissed since it was conducted by outsiders rather than local organizations. Indeed, the findings were rejected by the national energy agency, ridiculed in the media and initially ignored by the environmental NGO and one major donor.

## Invest in locally rooted monitoring capabilities

Monitoring has too often been designed with a view of providing information for external agencies. More effort is often needed to develop monitoring systems that support local groups by generating information and local discussions that facilitate locally determined course corrections and reports back to local inhabitants on progress. Users' involvement in monitoring and evaluation is a critical part of empowerment. It also facilitates the flexibility and adaptability required to deal with changing dynamics. The review of projects in China noted the lack of relevant and credible monitoring of the poverty-environment relationship. It described how monitoring still focused on combining surveys on environmental issues with findings from surveys of household production, cultivation and incomes. If the latter showed improvement, it was assumed that living standards had improved. No attention was given to vulnerability (and the often key role of informal safety nets and social networks is reducing this) or to inequalities in consumption and access to household resources. As such, it was not possible to establish whether the environmental improvements achieved were promoting poverty reduction.

## Promising tactics and methods in supporting pro-poor change

### Build diverse coalitions and alliances

Alliances across different stakeholders have been vital in making many of the case study successes possible. In Ilo and Manizales, many different groups cooperated to plan and develop each city. This ensured a robust popular base when the process was challenged by local and external events. Many of the case studies have succeeded by combining the energy and skills of different stakeholders, including the poor themselves, government, civil society (e.g. academia, NGOs and religious groups), the private sector and donors. Each provided complementary skills and resources to develop a real momentum for change. Within this falls the need to encourage responsible private-sector involvement, along with civil society scrutiny and government oversight.

## Scale up and multiply successful initiatives

One obvious recommendation is to seek ways of learning from one successful initiative to help support other initiatives. In many instances, the requirement is for supporting a multiplication of successful local initiatives, rather than increasing the scale of one initiative – as in the case study in Pakistan (Chapter 2) and the hundreds of community toilet blocks in India (Chapter 10). In the Indian example, community exchange visits provided the learning and dissemination vehicle as representatives from one community organization came to see how another had organized, planned and built a community toilet, and discussed with them how it was done. In addition, the Indian case study shows the importance of community organizations having the capacity to demonstrate precedents – in this instance, the fact that the community organization had the resources and capacity to begin building toilet blocks independently from government in order to demonstrate to local government what they could do and then negotiate support for a much larger programme.[6] The stress on supporting the development of 'good local governance' is, in itself, a strategy for scaling up as it provides an institutional precondition for more effective action in all localities.

## Locate particular initiatives within broader policy and learning frameworks

It is too easy for initiatives to be supported by government or donors in isolation from the broader processes of change in governance, environmental management and the major dynamics of globalization. Several of the case studies have succeeded by building on broader governance processes, such as national initiatives for decentralization, constitutional change, democratization and popular mobilization. This gives added momentum to the change process and helps to root governance initiatives in the realities of local contexts. For international agencies, there is also the need to feed lessons from locally rooted learning and monitoring into policy and political processes. It is never easy for international agencies to ensure that the learning from their 'field' initiatives moves upwards to influence country assistance strategies and their own agency policies.

## Pay attention to timing and sequencing

Many changes in governance are needed to ensure institutional signals are consistently pro-poor and pro-environment. Such changes cannot all be introduced at once. Timing and sequencing is important. By a careful staged process, both Ilo and Manizales were able to develop a complex participatory planning process. Similar careful sequencing took place in Laborie, Saint Lucia, in order to develop and sustain the planning and management process there.

# Important internal changes required within external agencies

## Encourage poverty, environment and local politics 'lenses' within development agencies

Those who focus on poverty reduction require a greater awareness of resource management and the politics that influence this; those who focus on natural resource management need a greater awareness of the needs, priorities and capacities of poor groups. Both need a greater awareness of environmental health risks.

## Ensure that what poor people prioritize, and what they are doing or can do themselves, are treated as starting points

Many of the case studies reveal the value of starting with what poor people have and building on what they know. This is also the virtue of the 'sustainable livelihoods' approach.

## Allow a long-term view, and expect and plan for slow results

Change must support the slow, often difficult and sometimes discordant processes through which each society develops governance systems that serve the needs and priorities of the poor and provide them with a 'voice', influence and the rule of law – and in so doing, taking good natural resource management and environmental health seriously. Pro-poor political changes often entail movements forming and developing over time, allowing for learning and consolidation. In many instances, pro-poor environmental management is likely to include transfers of power from local governments to local user groups or community groups – as in Pakistan and China. This requires long-term support in order to overcome set-backs and survive what are often difficult conflicts. In many nations, local governments are not used to working with groups of poor people who can organize themselves, make demands and challenge local government decisions. Local governments may react in an authoritarian way to this.

## Ensure the flexibility to take advantage of new dynamics

Expecting slow results (see above) is not the same as being blind to fast-changing circumstances. It is also important to be flexible and opportunistic about taking advantage of change. In many of the case studies, external events precipitated positive changes in institutions (e.g. new legislation in Saint Lucia and East Africa, and new political leadership in Peru).

## In defining environmental strategy, go beyond 'do no harm' towards 'doing good'

This includes treating 'environmental wealth' positively. A safeguard approach to environmental matters can miss many opportunities to use environmental resources for poverty reduction. Worse, it can reinforce a negative status quo that merely locks environmental resources up for the good of a few. Poverty reduction strategies would do well to develop and employ some kind of 'environmental wealth diagnostic' and dialogue process that reveals what resources are doing – and could do – for pro-poor growth. These should include poor people's perceptions of what 'doing good' with environmental resources will entail.

## Policy consistency and coherence by donor countries

A key challenge now is to locate local poverty and environmental problems within the dynamics of globalizing trade, investment, communications and institutions. The very least that is required is to improve the availability of information on global dynamics, and on how they impinge upon local groups and environmental assets in terms of opportunities and threats. Moreover, donor nations wishing to 'lighten' their international footprint on poor people and their environments will need to change damaging policy and market signals, and make these consistent with their international 'development' objectives in order to provide opportunities and to place clear boundaries around the threats.

## CONCLUSIONS: HOW DONORS MUST CHANGE THE WAY THEY DO BUSINESS

The case studies suggest the need for donors to seriously test different ways of achieving two things:

1 working with disadvantaged groups to address directly their poverty and environmental needs in ways that are driven by their priorities and are supported by their knowledge and capacities; and
2 supporting local institutions that enable new forms of pro-poor environmental governance to form over time, thus encouraging scaling up or multiplication of activities.

That donors should do this, as well as support the elements of 'good governance' outlined above, is not controversial. But it does raise difficult issues with regard to current donor structures and aid instruments, which may not be best suited to the challenges ahead. The case studies warn of the extent to which decisions made by external agencies can get things wrong because of pressures to spend allocated funds and complete projects too quickly, because of very limited local data and simplistic understandings of what underpins poverty and environmental degradation, and because of limited capacity to engage with local stakeholders. It is not yet clear that a shift to direct budgetary support and working through poverty reduction strategy processes (or strategies that help to achieve the commitments within the Millennium Development Goals) will necessarily assist donors in meeting the challenges of locally rooted, locally accountable pro-poor environmental management or environmentally sound poverty reduction.

The desire to support viable pro-poor political change within low- and middle-income countries may necessitate donors taking more of a back seat in order to allow national and local change processes and accountability mechanisms to develop between governments and citizens, without donor projects acting as the intermediary. While these processes and accountability mechanisms remain weak, governments may continue to resist pro-poor change. The case studies in this book illuminate a variety of paths out of this dilemma, which lies at the heart of how external agencies support pro-poor political change.

# ENDNOTES

1   A considerable proportion of the rural population of India and China live in large villages, which in many other nations would be classified as small urban centres.
2   See both the case study and Appadurai (2001).
3   Except, perhaps, as sharecroppers.
4   Many aspects of environmental management centre on reducing the transfer of costs to other regions (i.e. outside the jurisdiction of the local authority concerned) or to the future. These are aspects which local democracy and decentralization would not necessarily be expected to improve.
5   See, for instance, the very limited new private-sector investment flows for water and sanitation provision, even where international agencies have increased their support for water and sanitation privatization (Budds and McGrahanan, 2003; UN-Habitat, 2003).
6   See Patel (2004) for a more detailed discussion of precedent setting and other tools and methods used by community organizations to scale up the scope and impact of their work with local authorities.

# REFERENCES

Appadurai, A. (2001) 'Deep democracy: Urban governmentality and the horizon of politics', *Environment and Urbanization*, vol. 13, no. 2, pp23–43
Budds, J. and McGranahan, G. (2003) 'Are the debates on water privatization missing the point? Experiences from Africa, Asia and Latin America', *Environment and Urbanization*, vol. 15, no. 2, pp87–114
Grindle, M. S. (2002) *Good Enough Governance: Poverty Reduction And Reform In Developing Countries*, Paper prepared for the World bank Poverty Reduction Group, Kennedy School of Government, Harvard University, Harvard
Hardin, G. (1968) 'The tragedy of the commons', *Science*, vol. 162, pp1243–1248
Hardoy, J. E., Mitlin, D. and Satterthwaite, D. (1992) *Environmental Problems in Third World Cities*, Earthscan Publications, London
Hardoy, J. E., Mitlin, D. and Satterthwaite, D. (2001) *Environmental Problems in an Urbanizing World: Finding Solutions for Cities in Africa, Asia and Latin America*, Earthscan Publications, London
IIED, ODI, MRAG and WCMC (1999) *The Present Position: The Challenge in Regard to Protection and Better Management of the Environment*, Background paper for the Department for International Development, IIED, London
Landell-Mills, N. and Ford, J. (1999), *Privatising Sustainable Forestry: A Global Review of Trends And Challenges*, IIED, London
Leach, M. and Mearns, R. (1996) 'Environmental change and policy; challenging received wisdom in Africa', in M. Leach and R. Mearns (eds) *The Lie of the Land*, International African Institute in association with James Currey and Heinemann, Oxford, pp1–33
McGranahan, G. (2002) *Demand-Side Water Strategies and the Urban Poor*, PIE Series No. 4, IIED, London
Moser, C. O. N. (1993) *Gender Planning and Development; Theory, Practice and Training, Routledge*, London and New York

Patel, S. (2004) 'Tools and methods for empowerment developed by slum dwellers federations in India', *Participatory Learning and Action 50*, IIED, London

Patel, S. and Mitlin, D. (2004) 'The work of SPARC, the National Slum Dwellers Federation and Mahila Milan', in D. Mitlin and D. Satterthwaite (eds) *Empowering Squatter Citizen: The Roles of Local Governments and Civil Society in Reducing Urban Poverty*, Earthscan Publications, London

Redclift, M. (1996) *Wasted: Counting the Costs of Global Consumption*, Earthscan Publications, London

Roe, E. (1995) 'Except Africa: Postscript to a special section on development narratives', *World Development*, vol. 23, no. 6, pp1065–1070

Satterthwaite, D. (1998) 'Cities and sustainable development: What progress since Our Common Future?', in G. B. Softing, G. B. Kjetil Hindar, L. Walloe and A. Wijkman (eds) *The Brundtland Commission's Report – 10 years*, Scandinavian University Press, Oslo, pp27–39

Tiffen, M. and Mortimore. M. (1992) 'Environment, population growth and productivity in Kenya: A case study of Machakos District', *Development Policy Review*, vol. 10, pp359–387

UN-Habitat (2003) *Water and Sanitation in the World's Cities: Local Action for Global Goals*, Earthscan Publications, London

WCED (World Commission on Environment and Development) (1987) *Our Common Future*, Oxford University Press, Oxford

WHO (World Health Organization) (1992) *Our Planet, Our Health*, Report of the WHO Commission on Health and Environment, WHO, Geneva

World Bank (1990) *World Development Report – 1990: Poverty*, Oxford University Press, Oxford

# Index